sigrid wortmann weltge

bauhaus textiles

women artists and the weaving workshop

with 220 illustrations, 122 in colour

thames and hudson

for karin and kirsten

© 1993 Thames and Hudson Ltd, London

First paperback edition 1998

British Library Cataloguing-in-Publication Data
A catalogue record for this book is available from the British Library

ISBN 0-500-28034-7

Printed and bound in Singapore by C.S. Graphics

Half-title Von den Stoffen (Of Fabrics), an ink drawing on paper of 1916, shows Johannes Itten's early interest in textile patterns.

Frontispiece This carpet by Martha Erps, a sophisticated abstract composition, was the centrepiece in the living room of the Haus am Horn, the experimental house of the 1923 Bauhaus Exhibition in Weimar.

contents

in order to become an artist
one must be an artist,
and in order to become one,
one comes to the bauhaus;
to make of that 'artist' a human being again
is the task of the bauhaus.

otti berger [1]

the bauhaus existed
for a short span of time
but the potentials
intrinsic in its principles
have only begun to be realized.
the sources of design remain forever
full of changing possibilities.
the bauhaus is dead.
long live the bauhaus.

herbert bayer [2]

Gunta Stölzl and Marcel Breuer collaborated
on the *African Chair* of 1921. She used its
frame as her loom. The warp is threaded
through holes and crisscrosses the centre slat;
the weft is inserted in tapestry weave.

introduction

Walter Gropius in 1920.

Opposite Texture studies were an integral aspect of Bauhaus education from the time of Johannes Itten's *Vorkurs*. These studies by Anni Albers show (*clockwise from top left*) the imaginative use of corn kernels, metal shavings, twisted paper and seeds and grasses.

Six decades have passed since the Bauhaus, the foremost design phenomenon of our century, was forced to close its doors and witness the dispersion of some of its most illustrious proponents. Not until the 1960s did serious inquiry into the history of the institution occur. Since then scholarship has been ongoing. Nearly everything has been examined: the role of the workshops, the masters, painters and students, the teaching of design and architecture and the political climate in Weimar, Dessau and Berlin. Yet the Weaving Workshop, the longest standing and most successful of all the Bauhaus workshops, has received little attention. It has had two strikes against it: in the hierarchy of art and design, textiles and women share equally low positions. Moreover, like women, textiles have traditionally been cast in the supportive role: one notices the chair, but not its cover.

Lucia Moholy, taking issue with what she perceived as 'Questions of Interpretation' (*Fragen der Interpretation*), wrote in 1985, 'We are far removed from a complete overall picture'. She differs with 'some colleagues who hold the opinion that the history of the Bauhaus can only begin to become the historical truth when none of the participants is any longer alive. I myself, by contrast, believe that those of us who are still around have a duty to share as much as possible from our knowledge, our experience, our memories. . . .'[3] Although it is doubtful that a complete overall picture can ever be achieved, this book is intended to fill a void. Fortunately, some members of the Weaving Workshop were still alive to share their experiences, and others, who were related to them or knew them as friends, were also able to help. In exile, Anni Albers and Marli Ehrman educated a new generation of students, who have since become teachers, designers or both, and who have been generous in recounting their years as students and later as professionals.

This book is neither a catalogue raisonné nor a compilation of weave data.[4] Instead, it pays tribute to members of the Bauhaus whose names are not known to a larger public. Female students, who were among the first wave of women after World War I to aspire to membership of the professional design community, arrived at the school with an astonishing diversity of talents, convinced that this avant-garde institution would accept them as equals. Many already had extensive training in the arts. High-spirited and anti-bourgeois, they participated on many levels in the life of the Bauhaus. They were the friends and confidantes of some of the masters, boosting the latter's morale in times of personal conflicts and crises. True to their upbringing they were supportive of others, vaguely sensing their own loss but unable to change or overcome adverse cultural values. They received scant encouragement in their pursuit of non-traditional roles, and often their professional lives suffered. Instead of being fully integrated into the Bauhaus, they were segregated and given their own workshop – the Weaving Workshop – regardless of talent or inclination.

It is not surprising then that a fair number of women, despite their proficiency in weaving, chose to leave the Bauhaus and work in fields unrelated to textiles. For them the Weaving Workshop was nothing more than a base, a necessity to be tolerated for the sake of contact with the painters who were their reason for coming to the Bauhaus in the first place. Instruction from Johannes Itten, Paul Klee, Wassily Kandinsky, László Moholy-Nagy and Josef Albers was fundamental in shaping their professional lives. This side of the Weaving Workshop has received little attention.

The Weaving Workshop was also a barometer of the general climate at the Bauhaus. During the Weimar years the emphasis was on artistic expression, on individual pieces, reflecting the instruction and the design philosophies of the painters. Most of the latter remained hostile to the change of direction that occurred after the Bauhaus Exhibition of 1923: 'Art and Technology – A New Unity'. The weavers, too, were reluctant to leave art behind. But they did, and in doing so they moved into the forefront of the development of prototypes for industry. Indeed, they invented the concept of contemporary textile design. In Dessau, where the Weaving Workshop became known as a Laboratory for Design, many weavers felt compelled to denounce their former 'romantic' phase. Nevertheless, it is interesting that two of the most prominent weavers, Gunta Stölzl and Anni Albers, both designers for industry, returned to art weaving late in their lives.

Stölzl and Albers are names familiar to anyone with a knowledge of the Bauhaus. They were not only outstanding designers and educators but were articulate and, in the case of Albers, critical writers. It will become obvious that others had equally illustrious, but less publicized careers. Among these were Benita Otte, an accomplished artist and gifted pedagogue who spent a lifetime giving to others what she had received at the Bauhaus: Klee's colour theory, which she crystallized into a coherent teaching method. Marli Ehrman, the seminal presence at the New Bauhaus in Chicago, was Marie Helene Heimann before her emigration, a weaver and teacher of unusual talent. There were also those whose lives and careers fell victim to the Nazi purge. Friedl Dicker, a versatile artist and designer, and Otti Berger, a brilliant weaver, experienced this tragic fate.

The War years imposed what has been termed 'inner exile' on many Bauhäusler (as those associated with the institution were known) who remained in Germany. For some, however, the exile was very real and ranged from refuge in the Netherlands, France, Switzerland, England and Russia to Mexico and the United States. In America, Anni Albers and Marli Ehrman embraced their new homeland and continued their professional lives without interruption. Black Mountain College, Pond Farm, Chicago and, by extension, Mills College in California became outposts of the Bauhaus. American colleges changed their teaching methods and incorporated aspects of the *Vorkurs* (the preliminary course) into their curricula. The real gain, however, was a rebirth of handweaving

Hans Przyrembel, who studied at the Bauhaus
Metal Workshop under László Moholy-Nagy,
designed lighting fixtures and utilitarian
objects. His tea set is strikingly displayed on
a tablecloth by Margarete Reichardt.

Margarete Reichardt's structural fabric
enhances the smooth, shiny surface of Hans
Przyrembel's sugar bowl and cream jug.

Above Henry van de Velde's building of 1904 housed the Bauhaus from 1919 to 1925.

Above right Weimar retains its charming character even today.

in the United States. A new awareness of textile design as an independent entity was fostered through an unprecedented number of exhibitions across the country. Paralleling the evolution of the original Weaving Workshop, handweaving led to designing for industry, so commonplace today that its absence can hardly be imagined.

The theory has been advanced that the Bauhaus would have been largely forgotten had it not been for the exile of its most prominent members. Walter Gropius, Ludwig Mies van der Rohe, László Moholy-Nagy, Josef Albers, Ludwig Hilberseimer, Walter Peterhans, Herbert Bayer and Marcel Breuer have become household names. As architects, designers and educators they have kept the Bauhaus before the public. Textile designers in general do not achieve such prominence, but those who have become known spent the better part of their career in exile also: Gunta Stölzl in Switzerland, Margaret Leischner in England and Anni Albers, Marli Ehrman and Trude Guermonprez in the United States.

Acting as a clearing house for the American émigré community were Ise and Walter Gropius. With Herbert Bayer they organized the first Bauhaus Exhibition in the United States at New York's Museum of Modern Art in 1938. After the War, they mounted a massive relief effort involving everyone with ties to the Bauhaus, which linked the American Bauhäusler to those who had stayed in Germany and survived.[5] Gropius, ever the pragmatist, was the first to consider the idea of an archive and began collecting Bauhaus memorabilia and products, urging others, among them many weavers, to document their work. The Busch-Reisinger Museum of Harvard University in Cambridge, Massachusetts, where Gropius taught, thus became the repository of an impressive Bauhaus collection which was later augmented by two additional gifts: The Walter Gropius and The Lyonel Feininger Archives. It was here that the German art historian Hans Maria Wingler, supported by a grant from the Rockefeller Foundation, started his monumental documentation of the Bauhaus.

Gropius had not only founded the Bauhaus but also, throughout his life, nurtured the survival of its idea. Without his efforts, the remaining evidence of Bauhaus textiles and the majority of Otti Berger's fabrics would have been lost, and with them the proof that the beginning of contemporary textile design was firmly rooted in the Weaving Workshop of the Bauhaus.

acknowledgments

Textiles are among my earliest memories. Two working parents discussed the intricacies of woven cloth at the dinner table and inadvertently trained my eyes and my hands in its appreciation. The thread that connects me to my past has also led me to the future and is most likely the reason that textiles have been an integral part of my professional life. Years of research on the Bauhaus weavers resulted in the exhibition 'The Bauhaus Weaving Workshop: Source and Influence for American Textiles', which I co-curated with Sonja Flavin at the Paley Design Center of the Philadelphia College of Textiles and Science in 1987 and 1988. The response to a paper delivered in 1990 at the International Design History Conference at the Victoria and Albert Museum, London, made it clear that textiles should take their proper place alongside the more familiar products of the Bauhaus. The greatest debt in documenting the Weaving Workshop I owe to the Bauhaus weavers themselves. The example of their courage and fortitude in the face of personal and political upheavals was the inspiration for this book.

Several weavers, linked like myself to two countries, shared many hours of hospitality, memories and mementos. Their generosity and enthusiam have been vital to this project. The day spent at Anni Albers's home in Orange, Connecticut, will always remain fresh in my mind. Repeated conversations with Claire Kosterlitz and Lore Lindenfeld provided insight into the Dessau Bauhaus and Black Mountain College. Else Regensteiner graciously offered her home to me while I conducted research in Chicago and introduced me to family and friends of Marli Ehrman.

Equally important has been the support of several institutions. First among these is the Bauhaus Study Collection at the Busch-Reisinger Museum, Harvard University Art Museums, Cambridge, Massachusetts, where Emilie Norris and Peter Nisbet assisted my research enthusiastically. Elizabeth Gombosi ably handled the requests for photographic material. The Josef Albers Foundation in Orange, Connecticut, and especially Kelly Feeney, have been generous in sharing archival material, answering many questions and providing important illustrations. Matilda McQuaid at the Museum of Modern Art, New York, provided access to the Bauhaus collection.

The Chicago Historical Society made the Ray Pearson collection available for study, even though it had not yet been catalogued. Two research trips to the Bauhaus-Archiv Museum für Gestaltung in Berlin yielded essential information. Since then, Magdalena Droste, Elke Eckert and Sabine Hartmann have responded to innumerable queries and requests for illustrations. Maria Fazekas-Schnepel and Walter Schnepel of the Tecnolumen Archives in Bremen shared important papers and valuable illustrations, as did Katherine B. Crum of the Mills College Art Gallery in Oakland, California, and Michael Fedele of the Barry Friedman Gallery, New York. Takashi Mori of the Misawa Homes' Bauhaus Collection in Japan was also of tremendous help. It is a special pleasure to express my gratitude to them all. Two travel grants were of enormous assistance: one generously given by the Consulate General of the Federal Republic of Germany, New York, the other by the Philadelphia College of Textiles and Science.

My debt of gratitude to Yael Aloni-Stadler and Monika Veenhoff-Stadler is overwhelming. Their unfailing support has been pivotal to my project, yet their greatest gift has been their friendship. I have gained insight from conversations with Ruth Asawa, Monica Bella-Broner, Frank Ehrman, Sylvia Elsesser, Anneliese Itten, Myron Kozman, Jack Lenor Larsen, Nathan Lerner, Kathleen Nugent Mangan, Nancy Spiegel, M.C. Richards, Kay Sekimachi, Joyce Storey, Lenore Tawney and Tim Steele. Joella Bayer gave permission to quote from Herbert Bayer's poetry. Many others who have requested anonymity know of my gratitude and I would like to acknowledge it here once again.

For the opportunity to discuss my work and for careful reading of chapters in progress I would like to thank above all Julina Gylfe. Wilfred Frisby of the Paul J. Gutman Library cheerfully accepted requests to search out even the most obscure publication. I relied heavily on Catherine Berretta's skill, patience and attention to detail. My family and my friends not only accepted my immersion into this project but supported me fully. The sensitivity and understanding with which my husband, James E. Hassell, encouraged me every step of the way assures him of my deep gratitude.

chapter 1

beginnings

History has proven Schlemmer wrong.

Lyonel Feininger in about 1920.

Opposite The Bauhaus manifesto of 1919.
Woodcut by Lyonel Feininger.

The twentieth century bears witness to the power of personal persuasion to inspire and construct or, conversely, to destroy and devastate. Turbulent times generate leader and demagogue alike. It was the vision of an individual that shaped the destiny of design. By founding the Bauhaus, Walter Gropius initiated the transformation of architecture, design and design education in the modern world. The Bauhaus, in its brief existence, stands as a symbol of our age. Buffeted by opposing forces – confidence in art's redeeming power, reactionary opposition from within and without – its existence and its demise are testimony to the potency of singular convictions.

The life span of the Bauhaus has been amply documented. It will, therefore, suffice to sketch it here very briefly. Its first home was in Weimar, the idyllic capital of Thuringia, where it succeeded Henry van de Velde's School of Arts and Crafts. A Belgian, and a star of the Jugendstil movement, van de Velde was also one of the founders of the Deutscher Werkbund, a group of artists, architects and manufacturers whose goal was to improve the design of machine-made products. His cosmopolitan, progressive views were a distinct disadvantage in 1914, a year in which the spectre of nationalism rose as an augury of future repression. Branded an enemy alien, van de Velde was forced to resign but recommended Walter Gropius as one of his successors before leaving Germany. The school closed in 1915 and remained so for the duration of the War, a period during which Gropius, although on active duty in the military, negotiated with the Grand Duke of Saxe-Weimar to be appointed director of the School of Arts and Crafts. He replaced van de Velde after the War.

In 1919 Weimar had become the centre of the conservative Republican National Constitutional Assembly. Despite the ravages of postwar deprivations the town retained its romantic character as a place dotted with parks and historic buildings and the ubiquitous reminders of Goethe's culture. This charming, provincial spot was a most unlikely birthplace for a progressive, future-oriented institution. Weimar citizens no doubt assumed Gropius's appointment to mean nothing more than a continuation of prewar educational practices. But after uniting the School of Arts and Crafts with the Academy of Fine Arts, the new institution took the name 'Staatliches Bauhaus, Weimar' and as such made a radical break with tradition. Years of tension with the host town led to the masters' decision on 26 December 1924 to dissolve the school.

But by then, the Bauhaus (only five years old) had already become a *cause célèbre*. A number of cities expressed interest in the school, but it chose Dessau, a growing industrial centre best known for the Junkers aircraft industry. Under the leadership of its progressive mayor, Fritz Hesse, but in opposition to right-wing

Walter Gropius's building for the Dessau Bauhaus is a monument of the modern movement.

1 *Opposite* As early as 1920 Margarete Bittkow-Köhler experimented with abstract designs. This hanging is very similar to her apprentice piece, which the Bauhaus published in its catalogue, *Staatliches Bauhaus Weimar: 1919–1923*.

politicians, Dessau offered not only a new home, but also land for building teaching facilities and faculty residences. In 1926 the Gropius-designed Dessau Bauhaus, a landmark of modern architecture, opened its doors. Yet peace here proved as elusive as it had been in Weimar. By its very visibility and otherness – a radical new building, an international faculty and student body, avant-garde teaching practices – the Bauhaus continued to be the target of hostilities. With great difficulty it remained in Dessau until 1932 and after that survived only one more year in Berlin. Nazi opposition caused its final closure in 1933.

The Bauhaus has become the pre-eminent cultural phenomenon in the history of twentieth-century design. Compared to the long and illustrious life of many a German art school, its achievement in a time span of only fourteen years is astonishing. And yet, as prominent as the Bauhaus itself has been the question: what was that achievement? Mies van der Rohe perhaps came closest to an answer when he said that 'the Bauhaus was not an institution with a clear programme – it was an idea.' This idea, the subject of hundreds of books, is so intangible that neither students, nor teachers, nor later historians have ever been able to explain it fully. The fact is that the Bauhaus offered renewed hope and inspiration in its struggle to contribute to a more humane future and a contemporary, rather than a historicist, physical environment.

The Bauhaus was the idea of Walter Gropius, who expressed it publicly in his manifesto of April 1919. Lyonel Feininger's woodcut, depicting a cathedral amidst soaring lines and the radiating shafts of light from three sparkling stars, possible symbols for architecture, painting and sculpture, adorned the title page. The programme of the Bauhaus followed, its goals, principles, scope of instruction and admissions policy were all set out. Notwithstanding its emotional rhetoric, Gropius's declaration was alone among the plethora of German manifestos written both before and after World War I in becoming the rallying cry for a new artistic order.

In it Gropius deplored the isolation of the arts whose renewal could come only from the co-operation of artists and craftsmen. By elevating the level of the crafts to the status of the fine arts he envisioned the artist as 'an exalted craftsman' and called for the creation of 'a new guild of craftsmen without the class distinctions that raise an arrogant barrier between craftsman and artist.' In outlining the principles of the Bauhaus he declared that art is created independently of specific methods and, in contrast to a craft, cannot be taught. Therefore, the workshops would be central to the new school, indeed 'The School is the servant of the workshop and will one day be absorbed by it.' The manifesto begins and ends with a hymn to the architecture of the future: 'The ultimate goal of all visual arts is the complete building.'[2]

The workshops were thus at the core of the Bauhaus programme and while some were short-lived, others evolved and changed along with the rest of the institution. But their importance remained central to Bauhaus philosophy and they caused art education to take a completely new direction. Of all the workshops only one extended across the life span of the school from its foundation in 1919 to its closure in 1933: the Bauhaus Weaving Workshop.

7 Gunta Stölzl's facility with watercolour and ink on paper is evident in
this small work executed in 1921.

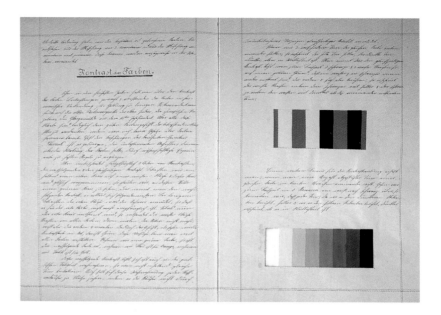

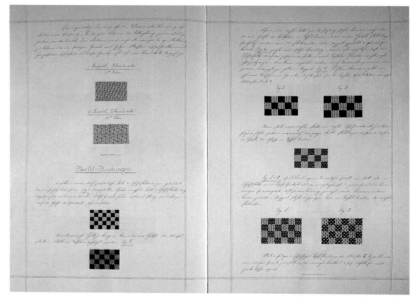

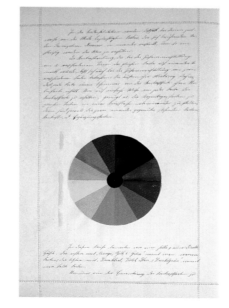

8–10 Pages from a student notebook dating from around the turn of the century attest to instruction in pattern drafts and colour theory, subjects that were commonly taught in German textile schools, but that were unavailable to the Bauhaus weavers in the early years.

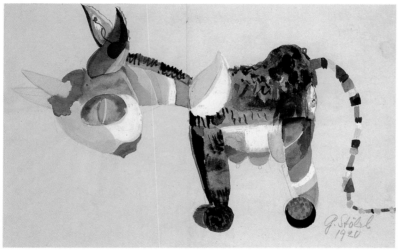

14 *Above* The Christmas or 'Dada' stall of
the Bauhaus at the Weimar Christmas market
was stocked with items handmade by the
students of the Women's Department using
donated material. Gunta Stölzl's colourful
design for a stuffed animal shows how even
the smallest scraps of fabric were used
creatively. Pencil, watercolour and gouache,
1920.

15 *Right* The Weaving and Carpentry
Workshops frequently collaborated on
projects. In 1921 Marcel Breuer produced this
side chair made from ebonized wood. Gunta
Stölzl wove the straps in a colour scheme
that shows the influence of De Stijl.

13 *Opposite* This exuberant little slit
tapestry of 1923 by Lore Leudesdorff shows
how freely she experimented with shapes and
colours without regard to consistency or
proper finishing.

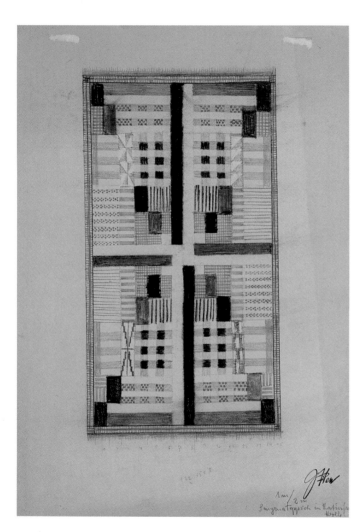 

16–18 Johannes Itten was keenly interested in textiles and designed many rugs. These date from the early twenties and are precisely executed on graph paper. After he left the Bauhaus in 1923, he set up — with Gunta Stölzl's assistance — the Ontos Weaving Workshops in Herrliberg, near Zurich.

19 *Above* Itten required his students to observe, feel and render the texture and appearance of objects. One such exercise is this collage, which dates from 1927.

20, 21 Here it is possible to compare Johannes Itten's design with the actual object (*opposite*). At the 1925 Paris 'Exposition Internationale des Arts Décoratifs et Industriels Modernes' he won a gold medal for one of his rugs.

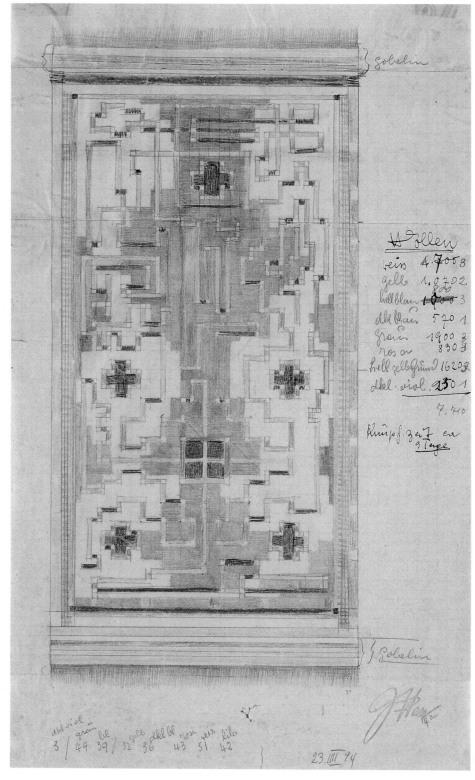

26 Paul Klee executed his watercolour *Red-Green Steps* in Weimar in 1923. Klee had a close relationship with the weavers: in Dessau he taught special design classes just for the textile students.

27 *Opposite* Georg Muche, who was form master of the Weaving Workshop from 1921 to 1927, painted his *Abstract Composition* in 1916, four years before he joined the Bauhaus.

28–30 The Weaving Workshop was prominently represented at the 1923 Bauhaus Exhibition. Its products were displayed in the experimental *Haus am Horn* and in the Bauhaus building. *Opposite above* A photograph of the display in the Oberlichtsaal reveals Dörte Helm's woven screen, Gunta Stölzl's rug with the Breuer/ Stölzl chair on top of it, as well as Ida Kerkovius's rug, which is also shown below. *Right* Benita Otte's wall hanging dates from the same year.

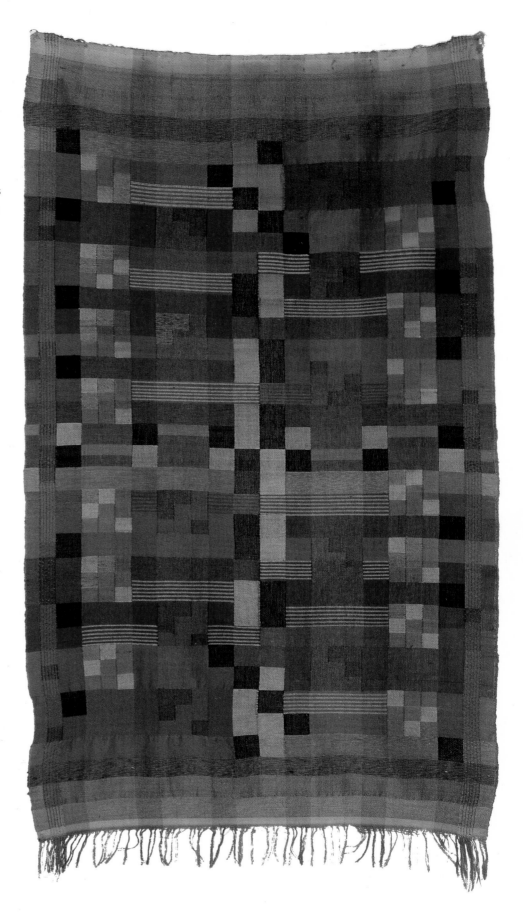

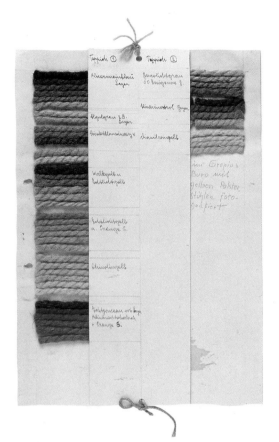

31–33 The director's office (*right*) was part of the 1923 Bauhaus Exhibition. Walter Gropius designed the furniture, Else Mögelin the wall hanging and Gertrud Arndt the rug, whose pattern and colour scheme can be seen more clearly in the yarn card and design shown above.

34 *Opposite* This silk tablecloth belonged to Walter and Ise Gropius, who gave it to the Busch-Reisinger Museum in 1951, indicating that it was made in 1923 by Benita Otte and 'still has its original label'. The aluminium tag, however, was only used after 1925 by the Dessau Workshop, by which time Otte had taken a position as teacher at Burg Giebichenstein.

chapter 2

the gender issue

Shelter and clothing are the products of complex technical attainments: the preparation and interlacing of fibres — spinning and weaving. Among the most ancient of human skills, they satisfy our innate desire for warmth and beauty. While their origin is shrouded in obscurity, archaeological evidence suggests that spinning and weaving were gender specific in many parts of the world, with one or the other performed by either men or women. In Europe, the highly respected masters of the medieval guilds were certainly male, as were the skilled silk weavers of Florence, Lucca, Lyon, Krefeld and other textile centres in the seventeenth and eighteenth centuries. It was illegal for women to belong to either the weavers' or tailors' guild.

> *Where there is wool*
> *there is a woman who weaves,*
> *if only to pass the time*
> OSKAR SCHLEMMER[1]

Gertrud Arndt, who was an excellent photographer herself, here poses with fellow-weaver Marianne Guck in a studied, elegiac composition with the warp of the upright loom suggestive of harp strings.

35 *Opposite* Designs for weavings were often executed in mixed media, like this collage by Gunta Stölzl from 1924.

With the rise of capitalism and the introduction of power looms in the nineteenth century, women joined the labour force in unprecedented numbers, replacing skilled male weavers not as professionals but as workers. As a consequence of the Industrial Revolution, the complex issue of design and craftsmanship was taken up by the Arts and Crafts Movement with its nostalgia for pre-industrial, even medieval, Utopia. Women, as Anthea Callen[2] has shown, played an important role in the movement, although few as autonomous, financially independent practitioners. Nevertheless, textiles evoke the image of centuries of needlewomen and rightly so. For it is not the craft itself but the designation of professional versus amateur that is at stake.

The Bauhaus envisaged the professional of the future as a designer with aesthetic and technical skills acquired from a master capable of teaching both. It was part and parcel of Gropius's concept of the *Gesamtkunstwerk* (total work of art), and Josef Albers, Marcel Breuer, Hinnerk Scheper, Joost Schmidt and Gunta Stölzl would prove him right. As the first fully trained Bauhaus students they later assumed the duties of *Jungmeister* (junior masters). In the meantime every workshop trained students under the dual tutelage of a 'form master', responsible for theory and creativity, and a 'workshop' or 'craft master' who taught the craft.

The admission policy of the Bauhaus stated that 'any person of good repute, without regard to age or sex, whose previous education is deemed adequate by the Council of Masters, will be admitted, as far as space permits.'[3] This egalitarian approach is evident in a variety of early documents, none more so than Gropius's note that there was to be 'no difference between the beautiful [sic] and the strong gender, absolute equality, but also absolute equal duties. No deference to ladies, as far as work is concerned, we are all craftsmen.'[4] Reality won out over Utopia. Gropius had severely underestimated the desire of women to study at the Bauhaus and was alarmed at the proportion of female applicants. Almost immediately the Council of Masters established a Women's Department, apparently in response to the wishes of its students. And only a year later, in 1920, Gropius suggested a 'tough separation, at the time of acceptance, most of all for the female sex, whose numbers are too strongly represented.'[5] Within six months, a circular to the Master Council re-emphasized that there should be 'no unnecessary experiments'[6] but rather that women should be directed into the Weaving, Bookbinding and Pottery Workshops after completion of the preliminary course. The Pottery Workshop, however, was less than keen to accept female students. Its form master, Gerhard Marcks, and Walter Gropius were of the same mind: 'if possible not to admit women into the Pottery Workshop, both for their sake and for the sake of the workshop.'[7] By 1922 the Bookbinding Workshop had been dissolved. This left only the Weaving Workshop open to women.

Unlike the other workshops at the Bauhaus the weaving studio was fully equipped. Helene Börner, the owner of the looms and weaving instructor under van de Velde, had signed a contract with the school which allowed her to use the facilities rent free but specified, as far as the students were concerned, that 'the ladies are students of the Bauhaus in terms of registration, rules and payment.'[8] Although Börner was retained as craft master until 1925, hardly anything is known about her background. A generation older than her charges, she would have been trained in a number of skills, such as embroidery, appliqué and the rudiments of weaving. Her education as *Handarbeitslehrerin* (the equivalent of a home economics teacher) was typical for women of her time and commanded little respect. The artist Fritz Mackensen's letter to Gropius dated 1915, the time Börner taught under van de Velde, confirms this commonly held view. Of the School of Arts and Crafts, Mackensen wrote, 'you have an incorrect impression of the school itself. Only trivial things were made in the workshops. . . . The students were for the most part ladies.'[9]

Mackensen, then director of the Weimar Academy, was at the height of his fame and writing from Worpswede, the art colony he had founded near Bremen. He had established his reputation thirty years earlier by winning the Gold Medal at the Crystal Palace exhibition in Munich for his brand of regional landscape painting. He would remain faithful to the same style for the rest of his life, unable to come to terms with Modernism or assess new directions in art. As a teacher he was only too familiar with female art students, who flocked in record numbers to Worpswede, as was later to be the case with the Bauhaus. One of them recorded in her journal how he commented on the painting of a classmate, questioning her 'with a penetrating stare, whether she had actually seen in nature what she was putting down. A strange answer: a quick "yes" and then a hesitating "no" as she was looking into the distance.'[10] The student whose work so bemused Mackensen was Paula Modersohn-Becker, the forerunner of German Expressionism, whose independently forged style of simplified forms Mackensen was unable to grasp.

At the Bauhaus the climate for female painters was not hospitable, and very few women were able to attend classes of their choice without enrolling in the Weaving Workshop. There were some exceptions to this, such as the American-born Florence Henri. A member of the Parisian avant-garde, she had embraced

Although several weavings were registered under Else Neustadt's name, it is unclear whether she continued as a weaver after she left the Bauhaus. This photograph dates from 1924.

Constructivism as a style rather than an ideology and had produced an impressive oeuvre of late Cubist paintings (pl. 25). Her introduction to the Bauhaus came through Margarete Willers, a member of the Weaving Workshop who had studied painting in Düsseldorf, Munich and Paris. Henri also met László Moholy-Nagy and Georg Muche and visited the Bauhaus in 1927. She attended classes taught by Moholy-Nagy, Wassily Kandinsky and Paul Klee and formed friendships with Irene and Herbert Bayer, Lou and Hinnerk Scheper and Anni and Josef Albers. Lucia Moholy, another close friend, supported her in changing from painting to photography,[11] a medium in which she was to become a pioneer. Her abstract mirrored compositions as well as her portrait studies reveal Henri not only as a brilliant artist but also as an extraordinary chronicler of her milieu. Henri's strong will and self-esteem enabled her to bypass the Weaving Workshop, in which other equally well established artists enrolled.

Students in the Weaving Workshop can be placed into roughly three categories. There are, first of all, those who were marginal and left without any trace of further professional involvement. To the second group belong women who completed most or all of their prescribed studies but because of other aspirations did not make weaving their artistic mode of expression. Many of these pursued distinguished careers outside the textile world. Ré Soupault is an example, who, then known by her maiden name of Erna Niemeyer, followed Itten from Vienna to the Bauhaus and, after her studies in the Weaving Workshop, turned her attention to film-making. In Germany she worked on abstract and Dadaist films. She later married the French Surrealist writer Philippe Soupault and became a prolific writer, translator and photographer. In 1938, living in Tunisia, she gained access to the *Quartier Réservé*, an area reserved for abandoned women whom she photographed in a starkly realistic, monumental and sympathetic manner. Published in 1988,[12] a year before the artist celebrated her ninetieth birthday in Paris, these photographs have lost none of their poignancy. Finally, there were those who embraced weaving as a lifelong career and not only excelled as designers but also as educators and disseminators of the Bauhaus idea.

To understand the history of the Weaving Workshop is to know that it was a niche for Bauhaus women, a place to channel female students with divergent educational aspirations. According to Stölzl, 'in the beginning, Bauhaus girls tried out every workshop: carpentry, wall-painting, the metal, pottery and book-binding workshops.'[13] It took courage to go against the prevailing sentiment which, as Marianne Brandt recorded, was that 'at first I was not exactly welcomed: a woman does not belong in the Metal Workshop was the opinion.'[14] Very few women – Brandt and Alma Buscher are exceptions – resisted the rationalization that 'the heavy plane, the hard metal, the painting of walls was not the right occupation.'[15] All others entered the one department generally found acceptable, where weaving was seen as 'primarily a woman's field of work'.[16]

During the early years the Weaving Workshop lacked any solid professional underpinning. The initial curriculum was hardly different from the hodgepodge approach of van de Velde's school. A contradiction also emerges: on the one hand, there was evident frustration over the lack of sophisticated instruction; on the other hand, students were at liberty to explore the properties of different materials, a distinct deviation from the prevailing attitudes in education. The early Weaving Workshop was almost an extension of Itten's *Vorkurs* (the preliminary course), which was a highly charged, meaningful experience for the students. Free experimentation, learning by trial and error unhampered by previous knowledge, was very much in the Bauhaus spirit. Yet, Stölzl conceded that students struggled to understand basic techniques, that the mechanics of weaving had to be studied thoroughly and could not be mastered by mere intuition.[17] Accounts of the Bauhaus women as autodidacts have led to the erroneous conclusion that professional instruction in general was simply not available at that time, but that, despite this privation, entirely new weave constructions were discovered in the workshop. Nothing could be further from the truth. European textile schools had a proud record of teaching textile technology as well as colour theory long before the Bauhaus existed. The Bauhaus weavers did not invent new structures but rather expanded their application. Once allied with industry, they realized that modern consumer goods, steel furniture, radios, automobiles and the interiors of contemporary buildings were poorly served by historicist fabrics. The present, of which they were so much a part, provided a challenge to which they responded with enthusiasm.

While these young women were not yet able to articulate their professional goals, their fervour and idealism were clearly directed toward a new future. With

Parties at the Bauhaus followed elaborate themes. Das Weisse Fest (the White Party) was held in 1926.

Below Marianne Brandt, dressed in a costume reminiscent of Schlemmer's ballet dancers, is ready for the White Party!

the right to vote came the privilege of enrolment in an institution that would have been beyond their reach a decade earlier. There was little complaining but rather great empathy for the struggles of the fledgling institution. If the school was poor, so were they. This was the grim reality caused by a war whose aftermath was still painfully evident. Yet, Gropius's visionary call had been heard. He had decried the 'unproductive artist' and, in proclaiming a new unity of artists and craftsmen, was looking for 'young people who take a joy in artistic creation and once more begin their life's work by learning a trade.'[18] His words spoke directly to them.

Moreover, they were in the company of artists whose passion for progress matched their own and further heightened their expectations. New theories and books were eagerly debated. There were frequent social contacts; the festivities themselves, written into the Bauhaus programme by Gropius, became creative enterprises. It was a giddy atmosphere of good will. The women, who usually expected little for themselves, knew that they were connected to a new venture of great importance. Only in retrospect does it become apparent that theoretical constructs at the Bauhaus dealt with all aspects of art and design except weaving. In the envisioned unity of art and craft serious discourse on textiles was missing.

The evolution of the Weaving Workshop from its designation as an insignificant base for playful exploration to a laboratory for industrial fabrics was slow. It was hindered by a *laissez-faire* attitude of lowered expectations. The greatest obstacle, as we will see, was the discrepancy between the objectives of the institution and those of its female students. When the emphasis of the Bauhaus shifted to art and technology, from individual textiles to industrial production, there was an understandable initial resistance. Once it was overcome the Weaving Workshop emerged as a professional entity in its own right. It set standards not only within the Bauhaus but also for textile production the world over. In 1919, however, this development could hardly be foreseen.

gunta stölzl

Gunta Stölzl was the dominant presence in the Weaving Workshop. In fact, its evolution paralleled her own development. The student who entered the Bauhaus in 1919 would leave it in 1931 as a consummate professional, the only female Bauhaus master.

> *It is because of her that one talks about Bauhaus fabrics*
> bauhaus, July 1931[1]

| Gunta Stölzl in a photograph taken in 1929.

Stölzl has been described as personally modest yet strong-willed and tenacious professionally, and as totally committed to her goals. From 1914 to 1916 she studied painting, ceramics and art history at the School of Applied Arts in Munich. During the following two years she served as a red cross nurse behind the front lines and in 1919 resumed her studies for an additional term. Actively involved in curriculum reform at her school, she encountered the Bauhaus manifesto which impressed her so much that she travelled to Weimar to meet Gropius. Stölzl vividly remembered her arrival: 'What did I find? A small group of students, more men than girls. A big building with studios which were partially occupied by the old academy, next to it large empty rooms, a workshop building, a cafeteria, a studio building for students, but only for men.'[2] She spent the summer of 1919 first in a glass workshop and then a mural-painting class before being accepted, on a trial basis, onto Johannes Itten's preliminary course. She was fully matriculated in the spring of 1920 and by the autumn had received a full scholarship.

Stölzl claimed that she co-founded the 'Women's Department' during her first year. It is certain that by 1920 she was active in the Weaving Workshop where she played a leading part from the outset. Her enthusiasm, vitality and the seriousness with which she pursued her quest for knowledge set an example to the other students and made her an undisputed role model. Anni Albers thought of her as the quintessential weaver, as 'having almost an animal feeling for textiles'.[3] She was passionate in her concern for the Weaving Workshop unlike any of the masters, and could thus make it hers almost from the beginning.

Stölzl, a student among other students in those days, immediately gave direction to the workshop by exploring the craft and passing on her findings. With admiration for Stölzl, Albers recalled those early days: 'There was no real teacher in textiles. We had no formal classes. Now people say to me: ''you learned it all at the Bauhaus''! We did not learn a thing in the beginning. I learned from Gunta, who was a great teacher. We sat down and tried to do it. Sometimes we sat together and tried to solve problems of construction.'[4] Stölzl's almost apologetic remark that students were autodidacts has often been repeated, but it should be clarified to mean 'technical autodidacts'. Nor should the much maligned early products of the workshop have to suffer from comparison with the later industrial textiles. It is true that some of them attest to the weavers' groping attempts to learn the craft without professional instruction; their execution is often amateurish. Selvages are wavy, the fabrics buckle, they are too tight. Yet many are remarkably well woven. The Weimar textiles have to be examined from a completely different point of view, not a technical but a visual one, for most of their creators already had a background in the arts.

Like Gunta Stölzl, almost all female students arrived at the Bauhaus with previous schooling. They were an exceptional group of pioneers at a time when educating women was not the norm. Barred from traditional art academies, they had studied at schools of applied arts and crafts, trade institutions and with individual professors. All of them were passionately interested in painting. Monica Bella-Broner simply said: 'We were all addicted to art.'[5] Georg Muche confirmed this statement in his autobiography. Itten's students, he said, did not fit the later perception of Bauhäusler as modern, pared down designers. Instead he said of them: 'They were and remained art enthusiasts.'[6] What attracted them to the Bauhaus in the first place was the lure of the painters – 'Klee and Kandinsky, those were the ones!'[7] – not instruction in weaving. A lifetime later Anni Albers remembered: 'Weaving? Weaving I thought was too sissy. I was looking for a real job: I went into weaving unenthusiastically, as merely the least objectionable choice.'[8]

Some women, such as Dörte Helm, Kitty Fischer, Else Mögelin, Margarete Willers and Ida Kerkovius, were accomplished artists by the time they arrived at the Bauhaus. In fact, Kerkovius, who was one of the older students, had been Johannes Itten's teacher when he was still a young art student in 1913 and 1914. She was a member of the 'Hölzel circle', a group of artists gathered around the painter Adolf Hölzel, who was best known for his contributions to colour theory. Itten formed a lifelong friendship with Kerkovius and recalled that at first he had found her paintings 'rather strange' – a verdict later to be repeated by the Nazis who included her in their roster of degenerate artists. However, Itten praised her as a teacher and kept his sketchbooks from those lessons. 'The most precious for me . . .', he wrote in his memoirs, was her 'analysis of compositions by Giotto and pictures by Cézanne in which the same principles occurred as in Giotto.'[9]

Far from being novices, then, most female students came with an impressive background of visual knowledge. Like Gunta Stölzl, who toured Italy in the summer of 1921 to see the painting and architecture that she had studied in Munich, they were acquainted with the masterpieces of the past. The Bauhaus attracted them precisely because they admired its painters and because they were longing to be a part of what they clearly perceived as the avant-garde. The fact that Gropius appointed painters and not craftsmen to head the workshops has been endlessly debated and either hailed as a stroke of genius or decried as out of touch with reality. It was a dichotomy akin to his initial aspiration to elevate crafts to the level of art, although art was perceived as independent and not teachable. As a method of attracting gifted students it worked. The allure of the painters proved irresistible to a bright, modern youth, and women were no exception. Contemporary art proclaimed its faith in the individual and, therefore, in them. On the heels of Germany's devastating defeat art seemed to be the only way left to affect society at large.

A view into the Weimar Weaving Workshop. The looms were the property of Helene Börner and had been there since van de Velde's days.

Notebooks, diaries and letters attest to the fecund atmosphere of the early years. Nowhere else had these young women been exposed to philosophies like those of their great Bauhaus teachers. Kandinsky's advice that they should discard old ways of looking went hand in hand with Gropius's dictum that the mind should be cleared of all previous knowledge, in order to approach every problem as if for the first time. Paul Klee's leitmotif, visual thinking, was absorbed like gospel by the students, who nicknamed him, after all, 'the dear Lord'. Johannes Itten opened up a whole new world of emotional and intellectual perceptions on the path to free exploration. Festivities were carefully planned according to themes. Evenings at the Feiningers' were filled with music. 'Even today', wrote Gunta Stölzl in 1968, 'I believe that most important of all was life itself. It was brimful with impressions, experiences, encounters and friendships which have lasted over decades.'[10]

Under Gunta Stölzl's unofficial direction – neither Helene Börner nor Georg Muche was able to advance the students technically – problems were overcome in a remarkably short time. Stölzl's quick grasp and understanding of the looms' possibilities, her natural affinity for the materials and her love of exploration rapidly transformed the workshop into a functioning entity. In March 1922 she took a dye course at a textile school in Krefeld with fellow-student Benita Otte and soon afterwards she activated the dye laboratory, which had been idle since van de Velde's days. In 1923 the Weaving Workshop participated in the first official Bauhaus Exhibition by furnishing the experimental Haus am Horn with textiles which were singled out for favourable mention by the critics. The textiles of the Weimar period, far from being failed industrial specimens, were the first to reject traditional tapestry-weaving in favour of a whole new design vocabulary. They were pioneering works in their own right and must be viewed as logical translations of the art education received by the students.

After all, the Bauhaus boasted two teachers who were also among the most prominent proponents of abstract art in the twenties, Wassily Kandinsky and Paul Klee. Another, the Dutch artist Theo van Doesburg, who had aspirations to join the school, made his headquarters in Weimar in 1921 and contributed to the intellectual ferment. All three men demonstrated extraordinary facility with the written word, which was articulated in profusion if not always with clarity. A torrent of theories was tested on students and staff alike. Many weavers have credited Paul Klee with their understanding of colour and form even though some of his ideas were digested only much later. 'One of his classes', Anni Albers remembered, 'was so far over my head that I didn't understand anything and had to leave. I was not yet ready for Klee and his thinking.'[11] Georg Muche, less of a theorist, kept to himself, working on his own development as an artist, while Johannes Itten had a profound effect on the students in these early years. Although vastly different in temperament, Kandinsky and Itten were both passionate about the artist's 'inner self' and communicated this message to their students. Itten's greatest gift to the weavers, however, was an awareness, a heightened sensitivity to the material itself – all material.

How could these artistic tenets, experienced on a daily basis, fail to be applied in the Weaving Workshop? Early works by Gunta Stölzl, Martha Erps and others show convincingly that the students had internalized the new visual language and were able to express themselves fluently. Many Weimar textiles display a sophistication of design unique in the history of weaving. A decade earlier Kandinsky had written in *Concerning the Spiritual in Art*: 'The more abstract is form, the more clear and direct is its appeal. . . . The more an artist uses these abstracted forms, the deeper and more confidently will he advance into the kingdom of the abstract.'[12] The weavers, in producing textiles of pure abstracted form, were heeding his advice. That neither weaving nor women could easily 'advance into the kingdom of the abstract' was yet another lesson to learn.

Gropius appointed painters to head the workshops. Paul Klee, here with Wassily Kandinsky in the latter's studio, was especially influential for the weavers.

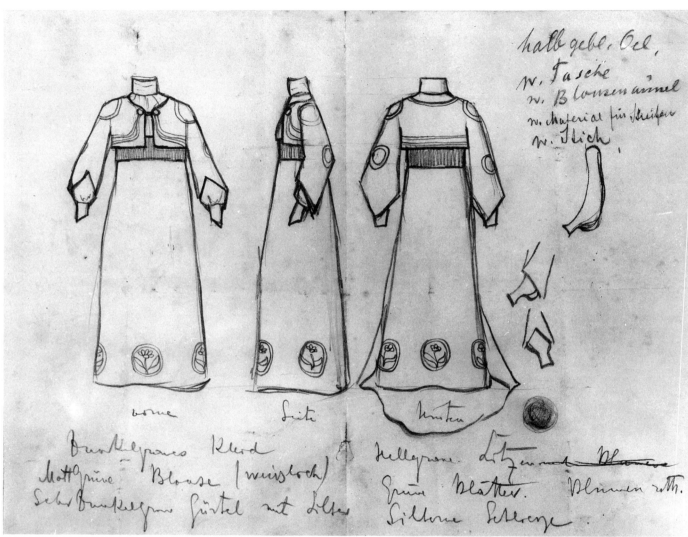

chapter 4

the question of identity

The Bauhaus manifesto was by no means the first to join the fray over the hierarchy of the arts. The debate regarding the relative values of fine and decorative arts, to which the English Arts and Crafts Movement had contributed in the late nineteenth century, was carried into the prewar years by the influential German magazine *Deutsche Kunst und Dekoration*. In issue after issue a veritable 'Who's Who' of the German and international Jugendstil avant-garde continued to wrestle with the unresolved conundrum. 'Mention a patron or friend of the arts today and immediately it conjures up the owners of paintings. Applied art, the decorative arts, they have sunk in the eyes of "the artists" to a low standing.'[2]

> *Today handweaving is a part of the creative impulse . . . correctly executed it emphasizes constructive form and abstract representation*
> WILL GROHMANN, 1931[1]

By the time Gropius issued his challenge for the removal of 'the class distinctions that raise an arrogant barrier between the craftsman and artist' the tension over what constitutes the decorative and what the fine arts had not diminished. Like a gauntlet it was picked up in defence of the sanctity of the fine arts. However, by the twenties, the front had broadened, the battle was no longer confined to the old adversaries. Now art itself, modern art with its multiplicity of leanings and formal proclamations, had to defend itself before an exasperated bourgeoisie. As clusters of European avant-garde painters jettisoned traditional styles in a euphoric, future-oriented optimism, they left in their wake a bewildered public. What had formerly been a direct experience now needed interpreters – critics who explained the new and infused it with meaning. It was no longer enough to trust one's eyes, the written word was required to elucidate the visual.

The compelling need, therefore, was to formulate explanatory theories. Once again the boundaries had to be redrawn, especially with regard to abstract art, which the general public linked to the two words artists most feared: ornament and decoration. Art-historical accounts tended to describe the evolution into Modernism as a linear sequence of Eurocentric events and values, dismissing entire branches of the arts by trivializing them as ethnographic artefacts or folk art. Yet abstract art, as has been readily conceded, was indebted to a whole range of sources, from mechanization to French symbolism, non-European art, and finally also to the decorative arts. Prominent and eloquent leaders of the English Arts and Crafts Movement, the Vienna Secession, Art Nouveau and Jugendstil advocated not only a total environment (the all-inclusive concept of a building *and* its contents), in other words a *Gesamtkunstwerk*, but also led the way toward abstraction. The statement that 'the first abstract work ever made was a painting'[3] is as misleading as crediting Picasso with the invention of collage. By the twenties, abstract art, fearful of being mistaken for decoration, disavowed part of its ancestry and asserted its superiority by expounding complex ideologies.

| Wassily Kandinsky.

Opposite These dress designs by Wassily Kandinsky date from 1911.

Basically, the fine arts denied the decorative arts any ability to communicate ideas or emotion.

At the Bauhaus, the concept of the *Gesamtkunstwerk*, the ideal that had attracted so many young people, was therefore not easily put into practice, despite the fact that some masters, such as Kandinsky, had firsthand experience in arts other than painting. In his Munich period, before 1911, he had worked on designs for dresses, jewelry, appliqué, furniture and pottery. And later, after Gabriele Münter, his companion of fifteen years, had purchased the house they shared in Murnau, he was largely responsible for the decorative scheme of its interior. He also spoke admiringly of the artistic integrity found in Russian peasant homes, just as he esteemed the ancient Bavarian peasant art of glass painting which he learned and practised. Kandinsky was well acquainted with artists like Otto Eckmann, Peter Behrens, August Endell, Henry van de Velde, Richard Riemerschmied and Hermann Obrist, who, before World War I, had ardently championed the decorative arts. Nevertheless, he felt that 'if we begin . . . and devote ourselves purely to a combination of pure colour and abstract form, we shall produce works which are mere decoration, which are suited to neckties and carpets.'[4] But he also noted that 'It must not be thought that pure decoration is lifeless. It has its inner being, but one which is either incomprehensible to us, as in the case of old decorative art, or which seems mere illogical confusion, as a world in which full-grown men and embryos play equal roles, in which beings deprived of limbs are on a level with noses and toes which live isolated of their own vitality.'[5] In choosing to equate full-grown men and embryos, and thereby art and 'mere' decoration, Kandinsky makes a compelling point, one which was to be echoed not only by other prominent contemporary writers, notably Hans Hildebrandt, but also by the Bauhaus weavers themselves.

For Bauhaus students the conflicting theories of their masters, often in contrast to the aims of the institution, proved perplexing. How should they interpret Gropius's belief that art cannot be taught or learned, a belief shared by Kandinsky? Could this be reconciled with the latter's conviction that the theories he conveyed in his teaching were not only applicable to painting but to other media as well? Did Itten's faith in the development of the individual's creative personality embrace all or only certain students? For women, who were attempting to become integrated as professionals into the art world, the ambiguities were profoundly disturbing. They were at the Bauhaus because it had promised equality in the choice of a profession. In reality they found that their role within the institution was defined and formulated by their teachers. Only then did it become apparent that they were assigned talents and capacities viewed as innately female, of which a special predilection for textiles was only one.

Uttered in total confidence, the masters' opinions, such as Kandinsky's rhetorical statement above, were based as much on their fear as on time-honoured supremacy and authority. One fear was of a change in the criteria for art, another that the crafts might get the upper hand. The most important fear dealt with the image of the Bauhaus itself. The institution, which had not yet realized its promise to make architecture its ultimate goal, was loath to be perceived as

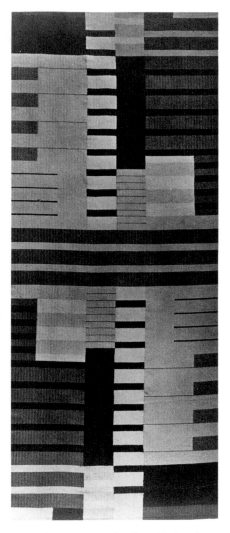

This silk tapestry in red, yellow, black and grey by Anni Albers was woven in 1925. Its location is unknown.

another school for applied arts, or, as Oskar Schlemmer noted in 1922, 'somewhat better than an arts and crafts school'.[6] It did not elude Schlemmer, the inveterate observer and journal keeper, that the spectre of such an image loomed even larger as the success of the Weaving Workshop grew. After witnessing a confrontation with a group of students who repeated their demand for the formation of an architecture department, Schlemmer mused: 'I do not know whether the call for this workshop came in response to the threat posed to the Bauhaus by certain successful undertakings. For the ceramics and weaving workshops are well on their way to becoming the hallmark of the Bauhaus, if they are not that already. The label of a good arts and crafts school should thus come as no surprise.'[7] The painters perceived function and production as threats to art and the 'inner need' of the artist. For this reason, Kandinsky would oppose the direction toward 'Art and Technology – A New Unity', the credo of the Bauhaus after 1923.

The unity Gropius had hoped for proved to be an elusive goal. Much later, when both had found new careers in America, Anni Albers would continue to ponder this dilemma: 'If we believe that the visual influences us, we must conclude that we are continually adding to disunity instead of to wholeness, that we are passing on the disunity which brought our objects about.'[8] Gunta Stölzl's question as to whether weaving belongs at all with the other arts and whether a weaver struggles with the same creative impulse as any other artist is therefore not a rhetorical one. Under discussion, after all, was the legitimacy of her own profession. She was well aware that what she created on paper was measured by a different standard from what she created on the loom. The Bauhaus painters' prejudice against the functional object was too well articulated not to be fully understood by the weavers. Indeed, most early textiles, if isolated from function, conformed to the criterion of art. It is here that one must look for the weavers' resistance to changing direction and leaving art behind. In their reluctance to embrace industry they merely reflected the opinion of the painters, yet, unlike the work of the painters, that of the weavers was deemed to be lower in rank.

Art, in its search for form, expresses itself in more than one voice. If the position of weaving within the arts was unclear, its exigencies on the weaver were not. Here Gunta Stölzl could take an unequivocal stand. She believed that the search for form, the relationship of shapes, lines and colours were merely enriched by structure and texture, the hallmarks of her craft. From her own accounts it is clear that she subscribed to the criteria by which art was measured: its formal, theoretical constructs paired with intellect and inner compulsion. She could only agree with Kandinsky's words that 'That is beautiful which is produced by the inner need, which springs from the soul.'[9] The spiritual aspect of creating art, essential to the Bauhaus painters, was also her own and would remain so for as long as she worked. She did not lose it despite the enforced restructuring of her initial goals and could thus answer her own question regarding the nature of her craft with a resounding 'Yes! Weaving is an aesthetic whole, a unity of composition, form, colour and substance.'[10]

chapter 5

the weaving workshop and johannes itten

B y 1922, only three years after the institution's formation, the Weaving Workshop could claim more students than any other at the Bauhaus. This is the more surprising since its development was incidental rather than planned. The Women's Department, its predecessor, had no defined programme of studies and from 1919 to 1920 occupied its students with a variety of textile-related activities, including the crafting of stuffed animals and dolls. These items, the most popular on the Bauhaus stall at the 1919 Weimar Christmas market, sold quickly, most likely to the people who had donated the scraps of fabric solicited by Gropius. The lack of materials and funds during the postwar years remained a serious drawback, but it did not prevent students from learning to apply their talents in an increasingly meaningful way. It was, in fact, the will, energy and enthusiasm of the young women, combined with the calibre of their previous training, that gave direction to the Weaving Workshop and ensured its swift rise to importance within the institution.

> *More audaciousness than planning*
> GUNTA STÖLZL, 1968[1]

| Johannes Itten in 1923.

Outwardly, too, a definite structure emerged. The Weaving Workshop now conformed to a daily schedule of six hours work: four in the morning and two in the afternoon. Regular attendance was mandatory, although visiting other workshops was not only possible but encouraged. Students were responsible for all equipment, and their projects became the property of the Bauhaus. The Council of Masters monitored every workshop as well as the ability and performance of individual students. As early as 1920, the masters expelled a young woman from the Weaving Workshop on grounds of irregular attendance and laziness. The Bauhaus also practised a strict selection process and admittance to the institution thus became a personal victory.

In July 1921 the school released a detailed curriculum for Workshop VIII, the official designation for the Weaving Workshop. Students were expected to acquire a thorough knowledge of looms and weaving techniques and a familiarity with diverse materials. Embroidery, reeling, knotting, knitting, crochet and sewing were also listed along with book-keeping, cost accounting and a comprehension of professional weaving literature. The Bauhaus followed the traditional guild model of workshop education, the apprenticeship. A final project was part of the journeyman's examination and qualification. Since Weimar had no Handelskammer (the formal examining board of the guild) the weavers could not be given an outside diploma. Nevertheless, a number of extant projects testify to the adherence to journeyman practices. Students could only begin their apprenticeship after completing the *Vorkurs*. This preliminary, or 'basic course', as it was called by its creator, Johannes Itten, became mandatory in 1921.

Johannes Itten joined Lyonel Feininger and Gerhard Marcks on Gropius's staff in the founding year of the Weimar Bauhaus. Of the three, he was the only educator and brought with him a contingent of fifteen students from his teaching days in Vienna. A charismatic man, Johannes Itten believed in the intrinsic creativity of each individual and showed a genuine concern for young people, a fact that has been overshadowed by the theatricality of his demeanour. As a follower of Mazdaznan, a religious leaning loosely based on Zoroastrianism, he not only dressed the part, with his severe, monk-like outfit and shaven head, but also adopted a diet of vegetarian fare seasoned with large quantities of garlic. Itten shared with many of his contemporaries a deep despondency over the War and its aftermath, a failure he regarded as an indictment of Christianity. In turning to Eastern thought and practices he hoped to 'find a new foundation for a true, humanitarian way of life'.[2] He made it his mission to teach the whole person, to awaken students to their own potentialities, not only intellectually and artistically but physically as well. Eventually Itten would discard his youthful eccentricity – he abandoned Mazdaznan in 1936 – but his strong belief in the creative powers of each student never wavered.

A centring process of meditation and breathing exercises preceded Itten's formal class sessions. To further relax and loosen the body he asked students to draw with both hands, which often resulted in surprising calligraphic, almost oriental designs. He also tried to extend the self-awareness of each young person beyond personal consciousness to a heightened sensitivity for the properties of materials. Later he recalled that 'we tried to experience the essence of all forms'.[3] A collage of 1927 (pl. 19) by one of his students at the Itten School in Berlin documents Itten's demands for experiential identification with the characteristics of any given texture. That he had a keen responsiveness to textiles is already evident in his own drawing from 1916 entitled *Von den Stoffen* (Of Fabrics). Itten, who owned an impressive library of books on rugs and textiles, studied these from a historical and a design perspective. His drawings are precisely executed on graph paper (pls 16, 17, 18, 20). Several finished works from the twenties and thirties were purchased by museums and have survived the War years. At the 1925 'Exposition Internationale des Arts Décoratifs et Industriels Modernes' in Paris, where he exhibited as a member of the Swiss section, he won a gold medal not for his paintings, although these were represented as well, but for one of two rugs (pl. 21). *La Revue Moderne* published a laudatory review: 'Squares and rectangles of a perfect symmetry, dark colours knowingly balanced; a design to make one dream of Chaldean or Egyptian art applied to modern taste, such are the characteristics of these two works.'[4] Itten's role during the founding years of the Bauhaus and his commitment to workshop education have been played down. There is no doubt that his influence on the weavers was considerable. Gunta Stölzl confided in her journal 'Itten – great things begin to crystallize, secrets, great connections become clear, what I vaguely feel becomes conscious and can therefore be developed.'[5]

As important as the experiments with materials was Itten's teaching in colour theory. His own indebtedness went beyond Johann Wolfgang von Goethe, Wilhelm von Bezold and Eugène Chevreul to his mentor Adolf Hölzel, and he shared fully the latter's conviction that colour, although a science, conveys deep spiritual and emotional qualities. Itten, like Kandinsky later, promoted colour as an essential aspect of workshop instruction, which was applicable to all media. Both men also used the language of music to describe colour – harmonic sounds, chord variations, tones. Itten believed that his students would arrive at a full understanding of art, the unity of sound, colour and form, through subjective experience and objective perception. To this end he persuaded Gropius to hire Gertrud Grunow, who supported Itten's teaching by coaching students in theories of harmonization. These theories were based on the belief that true spiritual and physical equilibrium, a necessity for the subconscious urge to create, could be obtained through the experience of colour and sound, that the stimulation of one sense would activate another. Like the twelve tones of the chromatic scale, twelve specific colours were assigned to particular parts of the body. In 1920 Hildegard Heitmeyer published an article in *Die Tat – A Monthly for the Future of German Culture* and referred to Grunow's theories as 'physical-spiritual education', the creation of ordered harmony through colour and sound. The importance of Grunow's influence, not only on the Bauhaus students but on Gropius as well, has been largely overlooked and is only now receiving renewed attention.

Itten's theory of colour contrast can be seen in a wide variety of student projects. One of them, a silk appliqué executed around 1920 (pl. 22), is a rare example of work from the early years of the Weaving Workshop. In its exuberant spontaneity it runs counter to the scarcity and drabness of the times and affirms Itten's own dictum: 'Colour is life, for a world without colour appears dead.'[6] The reflective quality of the silk and the staccato rhythm of its overlapping shapes contrast sharply with the measured organization of an appliqué by Ida Kerkovius (pl. 23) dated around 1921 or 1922. Here, the muted effect is due to the absorptive nature of the material, felt. Fading has further dulled the colours[7] but not their sophisticated placement. Although the eye focuses on the central circle, it is forced to follow the rhythmic rotation of the entire composition, which remains deliberately open-ended.

Another striking example of appliqué work is the curtain executed by Dörte Helm around 1920 or 1921 for the Sommerfeld House. Adolf Sommerfeld, a building contractor and owner of a saw mill, commissioned Walter Gropius and Adolf Meyer to build a residence from the salvaged lumber of a battleship. Although Sommerfeld dealt with the architects' private practice, Gropius seized the opportunity to involve the Bauhaus workshops. Today it is almost inconceivable that second year students would have the opportunity to take charge of an interior design scheme, yet Gropius hardly interfered, and the result pleased his patron as much as himself. Although the chevron pattern of the back wall seems to demand a simple entrance, Joost Schmidt's elaborately carved door, flanked by two metal radiator covers, stands out in bold independence. The rectangular entrance is dominated by a large diamond shape on sturdy supports which in turn holds a variety of abstract patterns based on triangular shapes. Helm's appliquéd curtain echoes not only Schmidt's design but also the triangular parquetry of the floor. Her work, restrained and elegant, is sensitive to the inherent quality of the material, taking full account of the softly gathered draping to provide additional

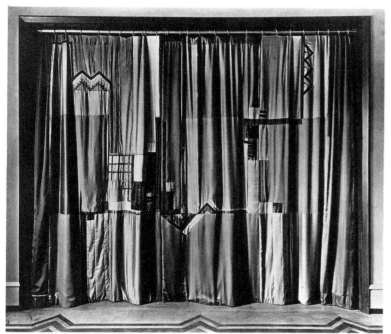

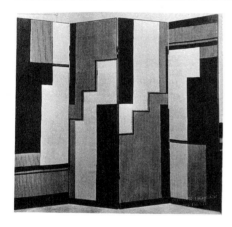

When Gropius's firm received the commission for the Sommerfeld House he involved the workshops in the interior scheme. The entrance (*top right*) was designed by Joost Schmidt in 1921 or 1922. Dörte Helm's appliquéd curtain (*top left*) echoes Schmidt's design. In 1923 Helm formally entered the Weaving Workshop. This woven screen (*above*) dates from the same year.

linear chiaroscuro. The curtain for the Sommerfeld House is not, however, strictly speaking, a product of the Weaving Workshop since, at the time, Dörte Helm, although a student at the Bauhaus, was not yet a weaver.

Before the twenty-two-year-old Helm arrived at the Bauhaus she had studied at the Art Academies of Kassel and Weimar and the School of Applied Art in Rostock, where she had been given a solo exhibition of her work in 1920. With her background in painting and sculpture, it was natural that she would enrol in the Mural Workshop. After participating in the interior design for the Sommerfeld House she passed her journeyman's examination before the painter's and lacquerer's guild in Weimar. When Gropius completed the Fritz Otte House in 1922, he again involved Bauhaus students in the execution of the interior scheme. This time Helm participated in painting murals. In the summer of 1923 she entered the Weaving Workshop and became a member of the committee for the Bauhaus Exhibition. A woven screen dating from the same year shows her bold approach to abstract design and her ease in working with large surfaces. She only stayed in the Weaving Workshop for a year before moving back to Rostock, yet in that time she executed a number of textiles. Two of them, a tapestry and a bedspread, are listed in the 1925 property inventory of the Bauhaus. Her career as a free-lance artist, interior designer, illustrator of children's books and writer came to an end when the Nazis forbade her to work.

During the early years in Weimar the weavers could not have envisioned the industrial textiles that would be created in the Dessau Workshop. Marcel Breuer's tubular chairs date from 1926.

The spirit of exuberance and experimentation of the founding years is particularly evident in a co-operative effort between Gunta Stölzl and Marcel Breuer. The Weaving and Carpentry Workshops were natural allies and would co-operate in the future but never again with as idiosyncratic a product as the *African Chair*, which dates from 1921 and may have been Breuer's first attempt at making furniture. The *African Chair* has been hailed as the epitome of the early romantic and expressionistic period of the Bauhaus, with influences ranging from African and Hungarian folk art to Itten's teaching. A five-legged throne, the roughly planed and brightly painted chair frame served as Stölzl's loom. She threaded the warp through pierced holes from one side to the other, crisscrossing over a central slat. The weft was then inserted with a needle in tapestry weave. One can only imagine the position of the weaver and the chair during the process! The pattern of the exposed warp on both sides and in the middle section complements the stripes of Breuer's painting. The chair has an almost anthropomorphic presence, its raised arms bidding the spectator to stand and gaze rather than sit upon it.

In the same year Breuer built a more conventional chair for which Stölzl wove straps in red, white, blue and black (pl. 15). The colour scheme alone acknowledges the De Stijl artists who would assert their influence on the Weimar Bauhäusler quite noticeably. Apparently, van Doesburg later approved of Breuer's creation although not of its curved back. Whether he had any opinion of the cover is not known. Stölzl's weaving dominates the chair, not only with its bold colour scheme but also with the visible texture of the material which contrasts sharply with the polished wood. Later collaborations between the two workshops in Dessau would result in the cohesive unity of fabric and chair and would be advertised with technical specifications including the elasticity of the material. Giving the taut appearance of trampolines, chairs by Breuer and Mies van der Rohe would be covered with smooth, strong fabrics made either from horsehair or from so-called iron yarn, a high-twist waxed and polished cotton. The Dessau chairs, which are icons of modernity and symbols of the era of industrial design, have nothing in common with the furniture of the early years, with its exploration and bold exuberance, except to stand as barometers of the school's development.

In the early Weimar years Stölzl did not envision industrial fabrics, but she had begun to realize that it was impossible to develop professionally without proper technical instruction. The Bauhaus must have come to the same conclusion for, despite its desperate financial situation, it sent both Stölzl and Benita Otte to Krefeld, once in 1921, to take a month-long course in dyeing, and the following year to study weaving and fibre technology. While it has been argued that the style of Bauhaus textiles altered due to increased standardization, the real change occurred because of newly acquired technical abilities. Even the freedom to experiment has its limits. True liberation from restraints relies on professional expertise. The Bauhaus weavers developed their early textiles under felicitous circumstances: an atmosphere that encouraged personal exploration, the commitment and leadership of Gunta Stölzl and artistic instruction by a group of teachers never again assembled under the same roof.

The exhibition 'Staatliches Bauhaus' in 1923 was held in a variety of locations, including van de Velde's building, for which Herbert Bayer designed the entrance.

measure in the pursuit of our art.'[10] Stölzl missed her friend and noted that 'Otte is now very favourably employed in Halle and loves it. They treat her royally because of her Bauhaus stamp. We visit one another every Sunday.'[11]

Unfortunately, it was Otte's connection to the Bauhaus that proved to be disastrous in 1933. Not even relatively small craft schools were immune to the Nazi wrath, and she and her fellow Bauhäusler were summarily dismissed. From her exile in Switzerland, Stölzl wrote 'Now everyone connected with the Bauhaus who was at the school in Halle is gone – my friend Otte as well, a situation which gives me reason to find my own situation bearable.'[12] In 1929 Otte had married Heinrich Koch, an interior designer and photographer who directed the photography department at Burg Giebichenstein. In 1933 they moved to Prague, where their artistic collaboration was cut short by Koch's death the following year, the result of a tragic accident. Also in 1934 Otte was offered a position in Bethel, near Bielefeld, as director of the Weaving Department at the von Bodelschwinghsche-Anstalten, a therapeutic institution, where she continued to weave and teach until her official retirement in 1957; unofficially she was involved with the organization until her death in 1976. During her years in Bethel she developed Klee's colour theories into a coherent, well-organized teaching method. Otte was a consummate artist, a gifted pedagogue and a generous friend. Of all the Bauhäusler, she came closest to being a disciple of Paul Klee, whose ideas she passed on to a new generation of young people.

Otte's versatility was put to the test in 1922, when the Bauhaus began work on its first public exhibition. Mounting hostility from the craft guilds, the Academy of art, the nationalistic Thuringian government and Weimar citizens, who were suspicious of the unconventional young Bauhäusler, had forced the issue. An ultimatum made continued financial support dependent on a demonstration of the school's productivity. Gropius, who regarded an exhibition as premature, was extremely reluctant to present the Bauhaus to the public. Yet he immediately directed his considerable organizational and administrative talents toward making the event possible and appointed a planning committee of masters and students. In addition, the Council of Masters decided to hold an open competition for the design of a sample house. It was to be a fully-furnished residence intended to prove to the outside world the close collaboration between the Bauhaus workshops. Georg Muche, who chaired the exhibition committee, submitted the winning plan, for which Benita Otte had rendered the elevation and isometric drawings. The house was built under the technical supervision of Gropius's partner, Adolf Meyer.

The Haus am Horn, named after the street – *am Horn* – in Weimar in which it was situated and referred to as either a model or an experimental house, was Cubist in design. Prefabricated industrial material and the maligned flat roof heightened its sparse, pared-down appearance. Its nucleus was the family room, a large central square with clerestory windows surrounded by the rest of the living space. Predictably, the stark modernity of its exterior met with largely negative reactions and invited comparison with the *Gemütlichkeit* (cosiness) of Goethe's garden pavilion, which was in close geographical proximity. The interior of the house, although no less avant-garde, generally fared better. Benita Otte, in collaboration with Ernst Gebhardt, designed a kitchen so functional that it has become a prototype for the contemporary kitchen concept. László Moholy-Nagy's ultra-modern lighting fixtures were the product of the Metal Workshop. The Carpentry Workshop made furniture designed by Marcel Breuer, Erich Dieckmann, Erich Brendel and Alma Buscher. The same critics who expressed bewilderment that the house was designed by a painter and not by an architect were quick to notice the absence of paintings on its bare walls. This might explain why the textiles, which softened the severity and angularity of the rooms and its furniture, were for the most part favourably received.

The living room, at least as judged from the angle of the camera, looks bottom-heavy. Marcel Breuer's couch, squat and solid, does not seem to belong with his skeletal chairs and table. The unifying element is Martha Erps's rug. Like an island it anchors the ensemble. Squares, rectangles and stripes echo the shapes of the furniture, but are placed in an intricate, visually stimulating abstract composition. Boldly balanced curved and stepped designs beckon the visitor to enter and then direct the eye onward to the adjoining room. Even a well-disposed observer like Fritz Wichert, who wrote in the *Frankfurter Zeitung*, was unprepared for the sophistication of Erps's concept. He described the technical aspects of the house's interiors as 'perfect. They are the best of their kind at this

Georg Muche's experimental Haus am Horn was part of the 1923 exhibition. *Above* The modern kitchen designed by Benita Otte and Ernst Gebhardt. *Right* The living room with furniture by Marcel Breuer and a rug by Martha Erps.

Products of the Pottery and Weaving Workshops were displayed in the 1923 exhibition, as seen here in room 40.

time,' especially the chairs and beds. 'In the main room there is a rug. It is colourful but without a distinct pattern. The Bauhaus people do not know about pattern, only about geometric lines and shapes. But order, the decorative expression one is used to, they try to avoid.'[13]

It is regrettable that the extent of the Weaving Workshop's participation in the interior scheme of the Haus am Horn has been so poorly documented. Although it is certain that Agnes Roghé designed the rug in the lady's bedroom and Lies Deinhardt the bedspread, individual weavers were often not credited for their works – who designed or wove the cover for the couch in the living room? – or, if they were, as in the case of an area rug by Gunta Stölzl, no photographic record has survived.

The Haus am Horn was, of course, only one aspect of the 1923 exhibition. Special displays were also set up in the workshop buildings. Vestibules, halls and stairways were transformed by murals and wall paintings. Even the director's office was open to the public (pl. 33). Here Gropius could present his idea of a modern executive space through furniture he had designed himself. The geometric clarity of the room is accentuated by the overhead Constructivist lighting, also by Gropius, which is echoed in Gertrud Arndt's area rug. Twelve yarn samples (pl. 31) and Arndt's watercolour design (pl. 32) have survived and make it possible to visualize the colour scheme. Unlike the Haus am Horn, Gropius's office eschewed bare walls. An abstract silk hanging by Else

Mögelin,[14] mounted between wooden boards, is in harmony with both the interior architecture and the shape of the furniture.

It is estimated that between 15 August and 30 September 1923 fifteen thousand visitors travelled to Weimar to see the exhibition, which was inaugurated with the famous 'Bauhaus Week', five dizzying days of avant-garde events. One could hear music, even premiere performances, by Paul Hindemith, Ferruccio Busoni, Ernst Křenek and Igor Stravinsky. Schlemmer staged his *Triadic Ballet*, first seen in Stuttgart a year earlier, and his *Mechanical Ballet*. Films with the latest slow-motion effects attracted rapt audiences. J.J.P. Oud spoke on modern Dutch architecture and Wassily Kandinsky on Synthetic Art. But the high point was Gropius's opening lecture 'Art and Technology – A New Unity', which announced the direction the Bauhaus was to take from that point onwards.

It is clear from the critical reaction in the press that the contribution of the Weaving Workshop to the exhibition of 1923 helped advance the overall image of the Bauhaus. Yet even before the event the weavers' products had sold relatively well, as had those of the Pottery Workshop. In a small way these two workshops helped alleviate the dire financial situation in which the Bauhaus found itself during the worst period of inflation. Unlike the Pottery Workshop, the Weaving Workshop was hampered by the scarcity of material, a result of Germany's dependency on foreign markets and severe postwar restrictions. Weaving as a craft is also far slower than pottery. Describing a wall hanging of 1922, now in the Busch-Reisinger Museum in Cambridge, Massachusetts, Gunta Stölzl wrote that its execution took nearly three months.[15] The lack of time and resources, however, often spurs the best designers to achieve the almost impossible. The sheer number of pieces in the exhibition, many of them very large, attests to the industriousness of the weavers, the quality to their complete understanding of the overall Bauhaus goals. A stylistic comparison between a tapestry of 1921 by Hedwig Jungnik and Else Mögelin's hanging in Gropius's office, shows how far the weavers had moved beyond their early concepts. Although Jungnik's design was abstract, it was still dimensional since she made heavy use of hatching, a traditional tapestry method employed to achieve shading. By contrast, Mögelin's hanging, also abstract, is entirely flat, thereby accentuating not only the inherent property of the textile itself but also that of the wall it adorns.

During its years in Weimar, the Weaving Workshop attracted women of unusual talent and determination. Many of these found weaving unsuited to their temperament and personal goals and, although often accomplished weavers, channelled their artistic energy into unrelated fields. Martha Erps, Ida Kerkovius, Dörte Helm and Ré Soupault are among them. Others, such as Gunta Stölzl, Benita Otte, Margarete Willers, Gertrud Arndt, Anni Albers and Marli Ehrman, would become pioneer textile designers, transform traditional expectations of the medium and excel as educators. All of them had contributed to the success of the Weaving Workshop at the Bauhaus Exhibition and at trade fairs in Frankfurt and Leipzig. The Weimar Weaving Workshop, despite its tentative beginning, had proved itself an asset to the school. In Dessau, where the emphasis shifted to industrial design, an influx of new talent was ready for the challenge.

36 *Opposite* This cotton rug for a child's room by an unidentified weaver is an example of the crisp geometric design of many Dessau textiles. It is marked with the Dessau aluminium grommet and dates from 1929.

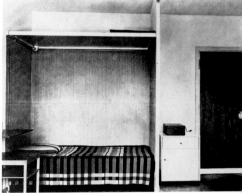

43 The student apartments at the Dessau Bauhaus were, like the building itself, designed by Walter Gropius. The sleeping alcove (*above*) was a compact, functional unit.

42 Stölzl's maturity as a designer is evident in the blanket (*left*) for the sleeping alcove of the Dessau student apartments, which takes the interior scheme of the room into full consideration. The blanket was woven in the Production Workshop and affixed with the aluminium grommet.

44 An overwhelming workload did not prevent Gunta Stölzl from working on individual pieces, such as this gouache on paper, a design for a rug which dates from 1926.

45 *Above* Despite the emphasis on industrial fabrics, students continued to execute a variety of textile designs like this gouache on paper by Hilde Reindl dating from 1928.

46 *Right* Geometric designs by some weavers, such as this watercolour on paper by Gunta Stölzl, gave rise to the term 'Bauhaus style', a designation Walter Gropius rejected.

47 Critics have commented on the similarity between Josef and Anni Albers's work. While Anni Albers explored the technical possibilities of multi-layered weave constructions, Josef Albers experimented with sandblasted, flashed glass, as in *Upward* of 1926.

48 *Opposite* This intricate triple-weave of 1926 exemplifies Anni Albers's skills as a designer and weaver and very much bears her own individual stamp.

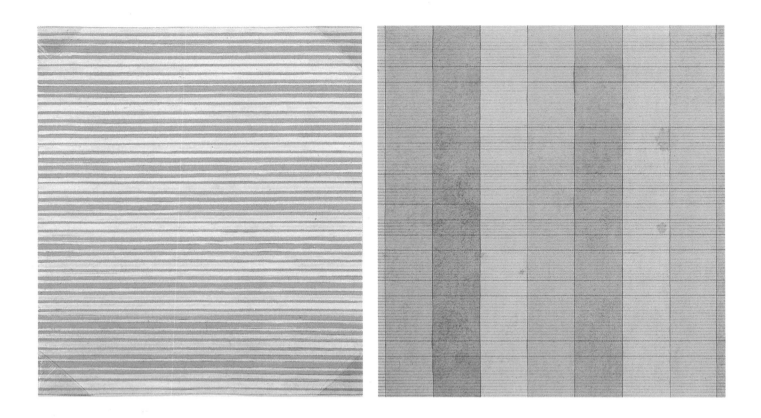

52–54 Three student projects from 1928. *Above* A design by Hilde Reindl. *Above right* A watercolour on paper by Léna Bergner. *Below* A design in ink on graph paper by Grete Preiswerk.

55, 56 *Opposite* Margaret Leischner's curtain material from 1927 (*inset* and *background detail*) in wool, cotton and chenille addresses itself to the demands of the modern interior. It has acoustic properties and is reversible.

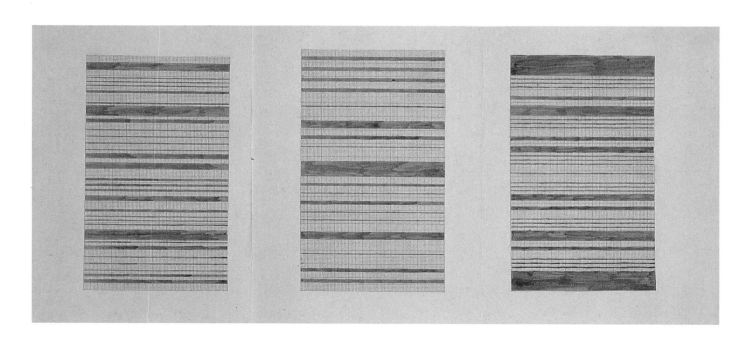

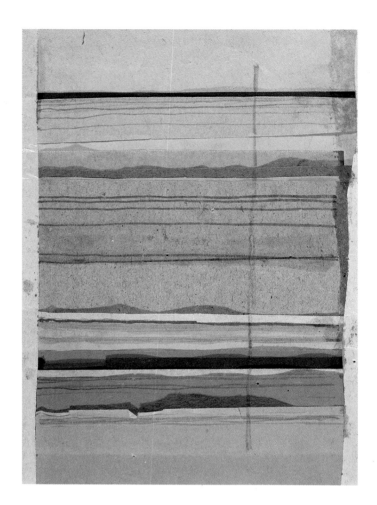

57, 58 Shown here are designs executed *c.* 1927 in a variety of techniques. Margarete Willers used watercolour and strips of coloured paper for a rug design (*left*), for which she indicated measurements in the margin. Léna Bergner used watercolour and gouache on paper for her rug design (*below*).

Opposite

59, 61 Léna Bergner's watercolour (*above left*) and Gertrud Preiswerk's collage with coloured paper (*below left*) are designs for rugs executed in 1928.

60 *Right* Otti Berger's *Tasttafel* (texture board), also of 1928, demonstrated not only the textures of yarn but also, by inserting small squares of paper, the relationship between colours.

64 *Right* All Bauhaus parties were creative enterprises. The *Metallisches Fest* (Metallic Party), however, was among the most elaborate stagings held in Dessau. This invitation dates from 1929.

65, 66 In 1930 the Czech Magazine *RED*, with the cover designed by Karel Teige, devoted an entire issue to the Bauhaus. It carried Otti Berger's seminal article 'Stoffe im Raum', in which she examined the role of textiles in interiors.

67 *Opposite* The visual interest of Gunta Stölzl's upholstery fabric lies in the quality of the yarns and the construction of the weave.

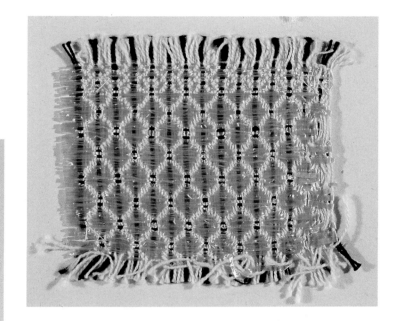

68, 69 *Above* and *above right* are two examples of stretch fabrics developed by Gunta Stölzl. Fabrics such as these were supposed to integrate themselves into interiors without drawing undue attention to themselves.

70 At her Studio Flora in Zurich Stölzl added fabrics for apparel to her range. These small samples (*right*) unfortunately cannot convey the luxurious feel or drapability of the material.

71–73 By varying the colour combinations of these prototypes for industry, Otti Berger was able to change the appearance of the weave construction. She was the only designer of the de Ploeg Company whose initials appeared on samples and thus became a marketing asset.

74 *Opposite* This rug by Otti Berger belonged to her friend Ludwig Hilberseimer and was exhibited at the Museum of Modern Art in New York in 1938. She wove it *c.* 1930 in smyrna wool and hemp.

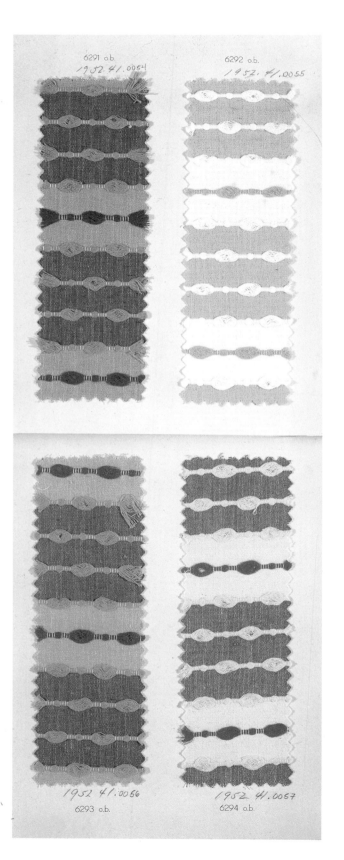

6291 o.b.
1952.41.0054

6292 o.b.
1952. 41.0055

1952 41.0056
6293 o.b.

1952 41.0057
6294 o.b.

chapter 7

dessau — a new direction

This double-exposed portrait of Otti Berger by Lotte Beese includes the beloved balconies of the studio building in Dessau.

77 *Opposite* Kitty van der Mijll Dekker wove this hanging in 1935, after she had emigrated to the Netherlands.

In September 1926, exactly one year after construction had begun, the studio building of the Dessau Bauhaus was ready for occupancy. The official inauguration of the new headquarters took place three months later, on 4 and 5 December 1926, and was attended by fifteen hundred national and international guests. It was a celebratory end to the gloom caused by the expulsion from Weimar and the uncertainty of the interim period. Yet this apparent success, especially that of the extraordinary new architecture which received extensive press coverage, was but a momentary respite from the continued financial hardship and political opposition that lay ahead. Would Mayor Fritz Hesse have invited the Bauhaus to Dessau had he foreseen the endless struggles, the repeated personal interventions necessary to shield it from attacks, the pleading with city officials for budget allocations? During the festivities not even he could have guessed that by 1932 the National Socialists would be in power, have placed him under 'protective custody', and be about to close the school for which he had been a tireless and ardent champion.

For the Weaving Workshop, described by Hans Maria Wingler as 'a decisively important factor in the development of the Bauhaus',[2] the opening ceremonies were a victory. Following a brief temporary stay in a warehouse, it was now located in a light-filled space on the second floor of the workshop building with its own dye shop in the basement. Yet it had barely escaped closure. 'There was a time when the very existence of the Workshop was in danger because the budget was so limited that the mayor of the city of Dessau pleaded with Gropius to shut down one of the workshops and he proposed the Weaving Department.'[3] Gropius 'was loath' to give in to this demand and fought hard for the survival of the textile department. For one thing it would have meant the 'exodus of almost all of the female student body' since 'few [women] were in other workshops.'[4] And the potential of the Weaving Workshop — so evident at the Bauhaus Exhibition and at fairs in Frankfurt, Leipzig and Stuttgart in 1923 and 1924 — was confirmed by representatives of the Dessau Trade Union who travelled to Weimar in 1925 to inspect personally the Bauhaus, about which they clearly felt ambivalent. They reported that 'after a short lecture by Professor Gropius, the director of the institution, we were shown to a room with Bauhaus textiles. These were unique. . . . The Weaving Workshop seems to be better than others. Its products clearly demand recognition, which cannot be said of the Carpentry Work-shop. . . .'[5]

The pressure to reduce the number of workshops made Gropius even more determined to gain financial independence from the city budget, a desire he shared with the weavers.[6] In 1924 he had noted with satisfaction that companies already had 'an active interest in the products of the Weaving Workshop . . . [it]

can be characterized as the best equipped in Germany.'[7] But two years later he issued a report entitled the *Failings of the Workshops* which was highly critical of overall performance. The Weaving Workshop, he complained, was still producing individual pieces which could easily have been woven as yard goods. It was imperative to develop designs, samples and swatch books for distribution among architects, the way 'any textile mill' does. He rejected all excuses and called for systematic production until commercial mills could be found to take over industrial manufacture of the workshop's designs.[8]

The workshop was certainly capable of commercial production. Its physical relocation from Weimar to Dessau had prompted its complete reorganization. Since few looms had been taken along it was possible to acquire a much greater variety of equipment. Apart from warping reels there were carpet frames, shaft, dobby and countermarch looms, some with as many as twenty-four harnesses, as well as Jacquard looms. The acquisition of the last of these in June 1925 caused a serious disagreement between the weavers and Georg Muche which reverberated throughout the Bauhaus. Diaries and letters of other Bauhäusler testify that this was more than an internal workshop matter. Oskar Schlemmer reported to his wife that 'Muche returned Saturday evening from Berlin in a truck with seven looms which he had bought there for an outrageous price, to the horror of poor Gunda.'[9] Muche's purchase consisted of Jacquard looms, which the weavers considered unsuitable, but which, it turned out later, were exactly right. Lack of communication and mutual distrust seem to have been the root of the misunderstandings between Muche and the weavers, with Stölzl and Muche blaming each other. She resented the fact that he left all practical matters, including the hiring of staff, to her. She had, for example, found a weaver familiar with all types of looms, Kurt Wanke, who became technical assistant and general trouble shooter. Muche let it be known that he was 'tired of being a businessman' and he complained 'bitterly about his job'.[10] It appears that Muche approached Gropius about a possible appointment to the proposed architecture department, but was politely declined.[11] The fracas, which lasted well over a month and was so serious that some thought Stölzl would have to leave, actually led to her appointment as technical director of the workshop, a solution which satisfied the weavers' demand for recognition of her abilities.

The most far-reaching change in the reorganization of the Weaving Workshop was its division into two separate units, one, the Experimental and Production Workshop, for experimental work and the development and production of industrial prototypes, and the other, the Teaching Workshop, for instruction. Ironically, Georg Muche had advocated a similar plan three years earlier when he submitted his 'Proposal for the Economic Organization of the Weaving Workshop'. Moreover, he had argued that the Bauhaus should fairly remunerate its weaving students by purchasing all suitable products instead of paying hourly wages. To his recommendations he had appended a table with precise amounts: payment for individual weaving methods, deductions for technical and formal mistakes and income derived from prototypes and licensing agreements. He was adamant that prices of products sold to the public be strictly calculated according

to general business practices. They should reflect all operating expenses, including the upkeep of the facilities.[12] During the Dessau years a very similar plan became standard practice. In 1927 Gertrud Arndt submitted exact calculations for her *Teppich Toost Nr. 4* (carpet No. 4 'Toost'). She recorded 645 working hours at 30 Pfennige and 45 hours at 50 Pfennige, the weight and price of all materials as well as a 30 per cent workshop fee and 50 per cent for general expenses. She then worked out two separate prices, one for the sale of the actual carpet, the other for the sale of the design.[13]

The Weaving Workshop was open to all students who had successfully completed the *Vorkurs*. Itten's preliminary course had been restructured after his departure in 1923 and was now taught by Josef Albers and László Moholy-Nagy. It was mandatory for everyone and remained a prerequisite for matriculation. Aspiring weavers were admitted to the Teaching Workshop on a six-month trial basis after which they had to agree to stay for another full year. The education was thorough and demanding. It comprised theoretical and practical training in all aspects of textiles, including designing, familiarity with the property of materials and a variety of equipment, and dyeing and finishing techniques. A full roster of other mandatory courses supplemented this rigorous eighteen-month apprenticeship. The informality of the Weimar years and the ease with which students had moved between workshops and become involved in a variety of projects was no longer possible. Students who had passed the examination in handweaving and dyeing could transfer into the Experimental and Production Workshop, which accepted only weavers who had certificates, either from the Bauhaus or from other weaving schools. The emphasis in Dessau was on advanced instruction in geometry, weaving technology, analysis, dyeing techniques and the use of mechanical equipment, as well as on experimentation on new designs for interior fabrics and industrial production. Furthermore, students participated in administrative tasks, such as book-keeping and calculation of wages. Field trips to spinning mills, dye workshops and wool, silk and cotton factories familiarized them with the requirements of industry, in which they were encouraged to seek internships or summer jobs. Since the weavers continued to take other required courses, the daily schedule was gruelling. Classes started at seven o'clock in the morning and ended at nine o'clock at night with a two-hour midday break. Saturdays were reserved for sport activities, outings and leisure. Traute Wagner, who came to the Bauhaus with a diploma from the Sorau Textile School, remembered that instruction and homework, especially from Paul Klee's class, kept her so busy that she was up from six in the morning till midnight with rarely enough energy left to participate in parties.[14]

Since the Teaching and Experimental and Production Workshops shared the same space, the weavers experienced the entire range of the craft, inspiring them toward greater achievement in a shorter time span. They were directly and concretely confronted with art and design concepts, something that 'was completely lacking in other schools'.[15] They were expected to develop 'from the beginning the right attitude to the responsibilities of work — mainly their responsibility to the materials and the tools. Any slackness or any mistakes affected their fellow workers and led therefore in a simple way to self-education and a feeling of responsibility to the job.'[16] Stölzl's use of the expression 'self-education' is important, for, despite the distinct new rational and technological focus, the programme 'was not fixed' but was 'a living thing that was always changing.' It was only natural that she sought in prospective students the 'essential for this profession', qualities she herself embodied: 'love for the material, which includes a sensitive awareness of the unlimited qualities of the raw material, imagination, a good feeling for colour, patience, perseverance, originality and a flexibility of the mind as well as the hand.'[17] Students who had completed three years of instruction took their journeyman's examination before the Weavers' Guild in Glauchau, after which they were issued a Bauhaus diploma. They entered industry or the teaching profession equipped with technical and artistic expertise unique at the time. Moreover, they had been subjected to constant challenges, encountered both freedom and discipline, and acquired strengths of character that remained with them throughout their personal and professional lives.

Ruth Hollós is a good example of such a graduate. Her Bauhaus diploma 'number 12', dated 2 June 1930, is in effect a detailed description, term by term, of the curriculum, as well as a commentary on the hierarchy of instruction. She entered the Weaving Workshop in 1924 after taking the *Vorkurs* and signed her apprenticeship contract in 1925. Two years later she passed her journeyman's examination before the guild in Glauchau but remained with the workshop until March 1928. The diploma is specific about her practical and theoretical training in textiles as well as her independent achievements: design and execution of samples for yard goods and individual pieces, development of prototypes for curtains and upholstery sold to industry, handknotted rugs and woven tapestries and participation in large commissions, such as the Theater Café in Dessau and the Piscator apartment in Berlin. Among her teachers – in Dessau the designation 'master' was abandoned and the academic term 'professor' reinstated – the diploma lists, among others, László Moholy-Nagy, Wassily Kandinsky and Paul Klee. Although Gunta Stölzl's signature as head of the department appears next to that of Hannes Meyer, the director of the school, neither her name as Hollós's teacher, nor indeed, that of any other weaving instructor, has been recorded. Yet, the successful completion of Hollós's career as a student was very much a testimony to Stölzl, her mentor. The young woman's achievements, as described on the diploma, echo Stölzl's often expressed goals as an educator: 'Ruth Hollós is endowed with superior talent for creative work. Her expertise is supported by energy, discipline, diligence and great perseverance. Her marked sensitivity for the material and its potential, combined with her strong sense for colour leads her to excel in design. One can expect her to achieve a great deal in the pedagogical realm due to her calmness and self-assurance. *She is capable of meeting all the demands of a leading position.*'[18] Between 1930 and 1933, the school issued eighteen official diplomas to weavers,[19] all but three to Dessau students. The three Weimarians were Ruth Hollós, Helene Nonné-Schmidt and Anni Albers.

A weaver engaged in carpet knotting on an upright loom in the Dessau Workshop.

Despite the improved studio space, the lack of adequate funds and materials, so prevalent during the Weimar years, continued in Dessau. Anni Albers remembered that this privation directly affected the style of the textiles, particularly their colours. The Dye Workshop, supervised by Lis Beyer, dyed yarns in large batches so that many weavers had to use the same colours. Albers found it difficult to work with 'what was there, without a personal choice. I wanted sometimes just a skein or two but that was not possible, and often the available colours were not very subtle.'[20] Gropius, who felt that the products of the workshops were of the utmost importance to the economic well-being of the school, was only too aware of these problems. Nevertheless, there was hardly a time when he did not urge masters to press for greater productivity and the completion of all projects, 'for only then will it be possible to support the students economically.' Furthermore he felt that students must 'be educated to believe that they are acting in their own best interest when they offer all their good work to the Bauhaus, for only then can the Bauhaus be strengthened financially and acquire artistic recognition. . . . Works that are not deemed good enough may be offered to the students against repayment of the cost of materials.'[21]

Although the Bauhaus was the official owner of all student work, ambiguities arose from time to time which had to be resolved. In 1921 the Master Council was confronted with Friedl Dicker's request for permission to sell one of her rugs outside the Bauhaus at a better price. Gropius reminded the masters of the ownership rule, but the real debate centred around two conflicting problems: that the Bauhaus would not be able to accumulate a first-rate collection of objects if the best student work went elsewhere, and that the most talented students would simply leave because of financial hardship. Even though Gropius called Dicker's request 'a dangerous precedent', the matter was settled when the Master Council voted to pay her an adequate sum.[22] By 1925 the Bauhaus had bought and catalogued approximately nine hundred textiles. Four of these became the subject of a dispute between Gropius and the Weimarer Kunstsammlungen (the Weimar Art Museum), each laying claim to the weavings. In the end both sides emerged victorious since it was agreed that Helene Börner, who was retiring from teaching, would weave exact copies of the pieces in question.[23] Sometimes students purchased their weavings, or, as in the case of Anni Albers, their parents did.[24] Sometimes, after having left the Bauhaus, they applied for permission to borrow their work for exhibitions. In 1932 Otti Berger was invited to participate in the show 'The Creative Work of Women' and asked the school for the loan of her piano cover woven 'for professor klee, as well as the rug for a child's room . . . i shall label the works "apprenticeship projects otti berger, bauhaus dessau".'[25] Berger's request, written in Herbert Bayer's lower-case alphabet adopted by everyone at the Bauhaus, was precise in crediting her pieces. Evidently this had not always been practised. In 1924 a group of weavers led by Mila Lederer and Gertrud Arndt protested that the school marked exhibit pieces simply 'Bauhaus' without attributing them to each individual by name.[26] Legally, however, the Bauhaus was permitted to do so since the reproduction rights came with the purchase of the work. Another issue that arose every so often was the use of studio space. In Weimar several students, among them Kerkovius, Otte, Stölzl and Mögelin, had petitioned the Master Council to permit work in the studio during the Easter vacation. It had been 'categorically rejected'.[27] Mies van der Rohe replied to a request from Otti Berger in 1932, writing that 'as an exception and in recognition of your work, we shall allow you the use of a studio, free of charge, until the end of the summer vacation.'[28]

For Stölzl the move from Weimar was bittersweet. Some of her friends had left the Bauhaus altogether. Dessau, unabashedly industrial, lacked Weimar's charm – it 'is an ugly town and I shall never feel at home here'[29] – but her administrative, pedagogical, technical and creative talents were at last officially, if not equitably, acknowledged. Her first appointment in April 1925 as technical director was subject to a three-month notice of termination. On 1 April 1927, after Muche's resignation, she assumed the direction of the entire workshop. As *Jungmeister* she had become the embodiment of Gropius's vision, not a specialist, but a truly competent, fully integrated professional. The scope of her responsibilities was staggering. She was in charge of the development of the new curriculum, the hiring of support personnel, the purchase of equipment and

The aluminium tag with the logo 'BAUHAUS DESSAU' was affixed to all fabrics leaving the Dessau Weaving Workshop.

material, formal teaching, overseeing the Experimental Workshop, designing textiles for industry and trade fairs and the execution of commissions. To her brother she admitted that 'the work at the Bauhaus devours me, literally'.[30] When she found out that she was the only faculty member passed over for a rise, she resolved not to renew her contract, a tactic that had positive results.[31] Most of all, she regretted 'that the work is really too much . . . there is not enough time left for personal creativity. After eight hours in the workshop the reserves for serious work at night are gone.'[32]

One of the first major projects in Dessau was the workshop's participation in furnishing the new facilities. Twenty-eight apartments were designated as student dormitories. They were located on four floors of the studio building, each with a balcony, the perfect spot for sunbathing and people watching. As backdrops for innumerable photographs the balconies have become the quintessential emblem of the Bauhaus. The students, in memory of their years in Weimar, named the new building after the old: the Prellerhaus. In the period photographs the rooms appear pared down and modern, arranged with strict geometric angularity (pl. 43). This architectural quality is also evident in Gunta Stölzl's blanket (pl. 42), which makes a strong statement in an otherwise bland interior. It is interesting to compare Stölzl's design to Margarete Bittkow-Köhler's hanging from 1920 (pl. 41). Horizontal and vertical lines are, of course, the basic design elements in any weaving. The triangle follows as a close second. Bittkow-Köhler interrupts the regularity of her stripes with pyramidal shapes reminiscent of folk art, especially Navajo rugs. It is an admirable piece for a first-year student and shows great promise, yet the design is predictable. The Stölzl blanket, by contrast, is complex in the interaction of horizontal-vertical and positive-negative elements. The asymmetry alleviates any boredom, and the blanket's slim vertical stripe provides the needed horizontal accent for the back wall of the sleeping alcove. Stölzl s work reveals the maturity of an artist-designer who has integrated formal and aesthetic concepts and applied both to the end use. These two pieces, separated by six years, exemplify the development from weaving per se to the hotly debated, so-called 'Bauhaus style' – a designation Gropius fought against all his life. The dormitory blankets were woven in the workshop and each was given the Dessau aluminium tag that was to be affixed to all production pieces from then on.

Despite the growing emphasis on fabrics for commercial application, many weavers continued to work on individual designs. In this they were no different from their colleagues in other workshops. Ise Gropius recalled that 'in the Bauhaus most of those who worked on industrial products often sought new stimulation and release by doing paintings and sculptures. So did the weavers, and, therefore, it is not surprising that one sees very individual pieces produced while, at the same time, work patterns were going out to industry to produce yard goods.'[33] Although the actual number of female students declined sharply during the remaining years of the institution, the Weaving Workshop moved into a phase of great productivity. It had attracted and trained designers of unusual and diverse talents who were now ready to leave their imprint on textile design and define it for the future.

chapter 8

from craft to industry

The tenet of the Dessau Weaving Workshop was to develop affordable, durable, contemporary textiles for a broad market.

> *The craftsman is today outside of the great process of industrial production; the designer belongs to it.*
> ANNI ALBERS, 1961[1]

Lotte Beese gathered her fellow-weavers for this group photograph of 1927. Bottom row, left to right: Ruth Hollós, Grete Reichardt and Anni Albers. Middle row, left to right: unknown, unknown, unknown, Léna Bergner, Lis Beyer, unknown. Top row: unknown, Margarete Heymann, Gertrud Arndt, Kurt Wanke, Gunta Stölzl and Gertrud Dirks.

For the weaver it was no longer enough playfully to discover personal inclinations by chance. Instead she began systematically to investigate a whole range of design problems in an environment that resembled a laboratory more than a studio. In such a setting, the key to success must be co-operation and a common strategy. It has been pointed out that the workshop practised teamwork more than any other department at the Bauhaus, despite the fact that interpersonal conflicts and school politics were as common there as elsewhere in the school. But the physical proximity and the overlapping of its teaching, production and experimental functions fostered discussion on all levels. While an individual piece may grow organically on the loom, an industrial textile needs a plan that can be repeated or altered. Construction, weave drafts, composition and choice of colour for warp and weft are important considerations. In the design process, the end product dictates the starting point.

Few weavers who had joined the Bauhaus before 1925 moved to Dessau. But those who did – among them Gertrud Arndt, Gunta Stölzl, Marie Helene Heimann (who would become Marli Ehrman), Lis Beyer, Anni Albers, Ruth Hollós and Helene Nonné-Schmidt – made significant contributions. Other, new talents would also play decisive roles, especially Lisbeth Oestreicher, Gertrud Preiswerk, Otti Berger, Margaret Leischner and Grete Reichardt. Unencumbered by nostalgia for the founding years, the newcomers dubbed the old-timers 'Weimarians'. The Bauhaus was known to attract forceful personalities and the Weaving Workshop was no exception. The students held distinct, often opposing, points of view regarding the future of weaving, the philosophy of design and their own role, and these became the subject of heated discussions. One of the recurring debates centred around handweaving versus industry.

Although Gunta Stölzl had prepared the initial Dessau curriculum and would revise it again in 1931, placing a solid emphasis on industry involvement, she was perceived as anti-technical. She clearly championed the hand loom as a tool for industry, aiming 'to educate young people through the discipline of handwork, to the development of a flexible artistic and technical expression.'[2] In 1926 she wrote that 'today the mechanical weaving process is not yet far enough developed to provide the possibilities existing in handweaving, and, since these are essential for the growing creativity of a person, we deal mainly with handweaving; for only the work on the hand loom provides enough latitude to develop an idea from one experiment to another. . . .'[3] This view is still held by many educators today who deplore an essentially theoretical textile design education without direct experience on the hand loom. There is no doubt that Stölzl loved the

from craft to industry 97

process and the intimacy with the loom and the material. Anni Albers believed that she was 'much more of a textile person than I ever was',[4] her intuitive approach in sharp contrast to Albers's rational intellectualism. Léna Bergner and Otti Berger were critical of Stölzl, although when Berger was in charge of the Weaving Workshops several years later, she came to understand Stölzl's pedagogical commitment and the validity of her point of view.

Strong opinions were voiced but they were not necessarily logical. The arguments were often unfocused, not only because the issues were unclear, but also because the weavers lacked a broader perspective. The root of the conflict between handweaving and industry lay, at least in part, in their own uncertainty about their professional identity and also in the mixed messages they received from the masters, who saw weaving as women's work, and not part of a serious 'male discipline'. Industrial design, wedded to the 'machine aesthetic', was just emerging in the mid-twenties and was, rightly or wrongly, often identified with the Bauhaus. Textile design, which shared equally in technological advances, consistently received, as it still does, little critical attention. The weavers had emerged from the strictly craft-oriented Weimar workshop, where they had been left largely to their own devices. They were, in fact, quite provincial and one wonders how much, if anything, they knew about international trends in design. At the Wiener Werkstätte, Maria Likarz and her colleagues had already designed bold abstract textiles before World War I. Most were printed, a medium the Bauhaus did not attempt until shortly before it closed, but some were woven. Liubov Popova, who exhibited in Berlin at the 'Erste Russische Kunstausstellung' (First Russian Art Exhibition) in 1922, thought easel painting too exclusive and applied her art to Constructivist textiles and fashions. By the time the Dessau workshop was operational, the 1925 'Exposition Internationale des Arts Décoratifs et Industriels Modernes' (International Exhibition of Modern Decorative and Industrial Art) in Paris, to which Germany was not invited, was history. Sonia Delaunay and Sophie Täuber-Arp had received rapturous acclaim for their designs. Eileen Gray, self-taught like the Bauhaus weavers, was working in Paris, designing not only furniture but also very modern, geometric rugs. These women had embraced careers, regarded themselves as professionals and belonged to a circle of like-minded artists.

The Bauhaus weavers were in a very different position. They knew that several professors were openly disdainful of textiles. Instead of working independently in a large metropolitan area they belonged to a tight-knit unit, a 'family', and as such they were highly visible. Non-bourgeois sexual mores were confused with personal freedom. Everyone's life at the Bauhaus was exposed, personally and professionally. Few women around them were models of independence, rather they were pillars of support to the men in their lives.

Lily Uhlmann Hildebrandt, whose love affair with Gropius was common knowledge, is an example. Like Kerkovius, Hildebrandt had been a student of Adolf Hölzel and she specialized in glass painting. But she was also a muralist and even designed fabrics. During the founding years of the Bauhaus she was Gropius's bedrock, physically, intellectually and spiritually. She helped prepare and install his architectural exhibitions. She solicited new members for the Circle of Friends of the Bauhaus, a fund-raising group which functioned as a salon with evenings of music and readings. When her four-year relationship with Gropius ended, she remained friends with him and other Bauhäusler until the end of her life.[5] Her place was taken by Ise Frank, whom Gropius married in 1923, and who embraced the Bauhaus with great enthusiasm. As a fundraiser, diplomatic emissary and supporter of her husband's idea, Ise Gropius worked tirelessly, first in Germany and later in exile in England and the United States. Mayor Fritz Hesse recalled in his autobiography that 'what was true for all wives of the Bauhaus masters, also became apparent during conversation with Frau Gropius: she *lived* in the work of her husband.'[6] The devotion of each of these women was to the career of her partner rather than to her own. Many weavers regarded their work not as a lifelong pursuit but as a stopgap until marriage. Of those who married other Bauhäusler only Anni Albers maintained a separate identity from her husband.[7]

Another source of discontent among the weavers was the widening polarization between industry and craft that had replaced the earlier conflict between art and craft. In each case, women were identified with the latter. As mechanization and industrialization increased, the role of the designer gained in status and attracted males. Women lost ground. They had no more precedent for functioning in the world of design than in the world of architecture. This fact might account for the steadily decreasing number of students in the Weaving Workshop.[8] They simply could not yet see themselves in a technologically oriented world. On a handicraft level, however, women could be quite successful. The Bauhaus-trained Benita Otte was a valued teacher at Burg Giebichenstein, a craft-oriented institution, and many energetic women headed their own studios.

The parallel career of Alen Müller-Hellwig, a weaver not connected with the Bauhaus, might serve as an illustration. Five years younger than Stölzl, she was of the same generation as the Bauhaus weavers. At first she worked in all areas of textile design, passing her journeyman's examination as an embroiderer in 1923, followed by her master's examination in weaving in 1928. However, her

Below Alen Müller-Hellwig's stand at the Grassi Museum, part of the Leipzig Spring Fair in 1930.

Below right Müller-Hellwig's monochrome, light-coloured rug was a novelty in the thirties because it was devoid of pattern. It was commissioned by Mies van der Rohe and Lilly Reich for the 1931 Building Exhibition in Berlin. The bed is by Lilly Reich.

education at the Arts and Crafts School in Munich was the antithesis of the Bauhaus training and was a disappointment. It was a traditional, one-sided, passive acquisition of excellent mechanical skills. Designs were executed from already existing cartoons or were obtained from the library. In 1926, aged twenty-four, Müller-Hellwig opened a studio as an independent weaver in Lübeck, joining a number of other successful small workshops in northern Germany. Over the years she employed a steady number of weavers and trained many apprentices. In 1930 she was represented at the Grassi Museum, part of the Leipzig Fair, with predominantly geometric hangings, rugs and cushions, an indication that Bauhaus designs were well known by that time. Müller-Hellwig was able to make valuable contacts and received commissions from architects, among them Hugo Häring and Mies van der Rohe. Between 1929 and 1933 her textiles were to be found in Mies's Tugendhat House, his German Pavilion in Barcelona and at the Building Exhibition in Berlin.[9] She never crossed the line from craft to industry but executed her weavings in response to clients' requests. Her geometric designs were largely derivative and lack an understanding of abstraction. Yet, her career was in many ways more successful than those of most Bauhaus weavers.

The ambivalence of the weavers is nowhere better expressed than in their own writing. In 1926 both Nonné-Schmidt and Stölzl published articles about the Weaving Workshop. They reveal little about the process of design but speak volumes about the weavers' self-perception and internalization of gender stereotypes. While Stölzl concludes her article in *OFFSET* magazine by simply stating that 'weaving is primarily a woman's field of work',[10] Nonné-Schmidt is specific about the differences between male and female artists. The reason that the artistic woman works mostly two-dimensionally, Nonné-Schmidt explains, is that she lacks 'the spatial imagination characteristic in men', therefore weaving is the 'field of work appropriate to a woman and her talents. In addition', she argues, 'the way the woman sees is, so to speak, childlike, because like a child she sees the details, instead of the over-all picture.' She hastens to assure the reader that 'the woman's way of seeing things is not to be taken as a deficiency, rather it is simply the way she is constituted, and it enables her to pick up the richness of nuances which are lost to the more comprehensive view.' Woman's love of detail is complemented by her feeling for colour in which she finds 'free rein of expression in the multitude of possible nuances.' Despite the 'accomplishments of the Women's Movement', Nonné-Schmidt does not believe that woman's nature will change but instead argues that there are 'indications that woman is counting on her limitations, considering them a great advantage.' As if responding to criticism, she writes that 'The fact that in the Weaving Workshop we are developing *standard types* for certain purposes, with regard to material, texture and color, by no means represents a lack of imagination.' Afraid that this lack of imagination might be taken as a female characteristic, she explains that 'it is the result of the work which the Bauhaus as a whole attempts to accomplish. For to exercise voluntary restraint in using the means of expression requires discipline.'[11]

An interesting corollary to these views is the book *Die Frau als Künstlerin* (Woman as Artist) by Lily Uhlmann Hildebrandt's husband, the art historian Hans Hildebrandt. Published in 1928, several years after his wife's affair with Gropius had ended, it is full of conflicting notions, often to the point of parody. Both Hildebrandts had close ties to the Bauhaus and, since he wrote about some of the Bauhäusler, one can assume that the weavers knew the book. With supreme assurance it affirmed every popular preconception, especially that of the dabbling female: 'Important alone is the fact that the multitude of dilettantish women and those who remain dilettantes even while practising a profession is considerably larger than the number of men who remain on that level.'[12] Some of his statements seem to paraphrase Nonné-Schmidt; on the other hand they may simply reflect the thinking of the time: 'The fundamental characteristic of female creativity is already evident in childhood: the delight in colour . . . the striving for pleasing effect, the sense for surface decoration, ornamental liveliness, orderliness in smallness, the inferior talent for spatial representation, . . . playfulness, instead of overall planning . . . the tendency for the superfluous.'[13] Where Nonné-Schmidt describes woman's way of seeing cautiously as 'so to speak childlike', Hildebrandt is certain that the mature male artist is incapable of producing art with 'that certain charm that emanates from the work of primitive peoples and children' and asks 'is it not the case that so very many women, even some of the best, most organized, intelligent and refined, are nothing but big, big children?'[14] At a time when the weavers were wrestling with a new definition for textile design, they read that 'even though in ornament the language of form itself is the invention of man – the female understands to chatter in it charmingly.'[15] Almost thirty years later Anni Albers wrote that 'it is interesting in this connection to observe that in ancient myths from many parts of the world it was a goddess, a female deity, who brought the invention of weaving to mankind. When we realize that weaving is primarily a process of structural organization this thought is startling, for today thinking in terms of structure seems closer to the inclination of men than women.'[16]

Yet, 'thinking in terms of structure' was precisely what the Bauhaus weavers were doing. The new architectural structures also demanded new structures in weaving. It has been noted that Gropius made a brilliant decision when he chose the name Bauhaus. While the literal reference is to *bauen* (to construct) and to the dwellings of medieval craftsmen surrounding cathedrals under construction, symbolically it pays tribute to monuments as expressions of their own time and to the unity of all the arts. Although the architecture department was not established until 1927, architecture was regarded as the supreme art form at the Bauhaus. The conflation of *bauen* as construction and *bauen* as structure became the underlying philosophical concept of the Dessau Weaving Workshop.[17] Both these senses of *bauen*, as Anni Albers observed in her eloquent essay, 'The Pliable Plane: Textiles in Architecture', 'construct a whole from separate parts that retain their identity, a manner of proceeding, fundamentally different from that of working metal, for instance, or clay, where parts are absorbed into an entity.'[18] How far the weavers had come was acknowledged by Stölzl, who wrote that 'our idea about the home in 1922 to 1923 was very different from that which we have today. Our textiles were still permitted then to be poems laden with ideas, flowery embellishment and individual experience! They quickly drew approval from a broad public, even outside the Bauhaus walls – they were the most easily understandable and, by virtue of their subject matter, the most ingratiating articles of those wildly revolutionary Bauhaus products.' But then, she continued, 'gradually there was a shift. We noticed how pretentious these independent single pieces were: cloth, curtain, wall hanging. The richness of colour and form began to look much too autocratic to us, it did not integrate, it did not subordinate itself to the home.'[19]

Stölzl's article appeared in the July 1931 issue of the *bauhaus* magazine, which featured a fabric by Margaret Leischner on the cover. The weavers were experimenting with structure as the main element, using the characteristics of the material itself, skilfully juxtaposing its properties. The contrasts in the weft of Leischner's fabric are manifold: the yarn is both thick and thin, a result of the spinning technique, but also soft and tactile, qualities that are further heightened by the shiny, strong orderliness of its companion thread, a uniform braid. The warp, manipulated into a single leno weave – a twisting of the warp to prevent the weft from sliding – assures the stability of the construction. This emphasis on material is also evident in Marli Ehrman's fabric. The yarn is allowed to demonstrate its own characteristics and, although the grid pattern is carefully planned, it is offset by a slight, almost accidental shift in the weave. Predictably, Anni Albers's leno fabric of 1929 betrays her strong sense for rhythm and order. The black thread adds a decidedly graphic quality, evident in so much of her work. With these and similar open-weave textiles the Bauhäusler advanced a completely new concept in curtains, which, while shielding a person from view, nevertheless admitted light, at the same time mitigating the psychological coldness inherent in rooms with vast expanses of glass.

Functional textiles presented an unexpected challenge to the weavers. If fabrics were to become an 'integral', even 'subordinate' part of the modern building, the role of the designer had to change as well. Criteria other than personal, artistic expression had to be taken into consideration: research into the end use of the fabric, rethinking of traditional applications and the production of samples from which the most suitable textile could be chosen. The weavers embraced novel materials, such as the newest man-made fibres, raffia, bast and Cellophane. Other factors were of importance also. Households had fewer, if any, servants, so that easy maintenance, wearability and even reversibility became a part of the equation. 'Textiles for everyday use', Stölzl wrote, 'are necessarily subject to accurate technical, and limited, but nevertheless variable, design requirements. The technical specifications: resistance to wear and tear, flexibility, permeability or impermeability to light, elasticity, light- and colour-fastness, etc., were dealt with systematically according to the end use of the material.'[20] And finally, the weavers aimed their products not at the individual connoisseur but, through affordability, at a cross-section of contemporary society. In all of this they broke new ground.

Opposite (clockwise from top left) Margaret Leischner's leno fabric was placed on the cover of the July 1931 issue of *bauhaus* magazine.

The date of the fabric is not known. Marli (Heimann) Ehrman's sister, Adelheid Heimann, photographed it as an assignment in her photography course at the Reimann School, Berlin, in 1936 or 1937.

Anni Albers's ribbed, silvery material is an excellent example of a structural fabric. Woven on a cotton warp with a Cellophane front for increased light reflection and a chenille back for sound absorption, it was tested and photographed by the Zeiss Ikon Company in October 1929.

Anni Albers, leno weave, 1929.

bauhaus zeitschrift für gestaltung 2,1931

herausgeber: bauhaus dessau ● schriftleitung: josef albers dessau bauhaus

juli

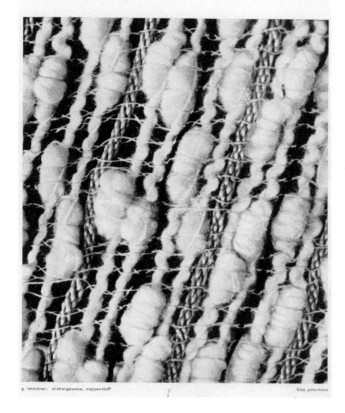

g. leischner. drehergewebe, noppenstoff   foto peterhans

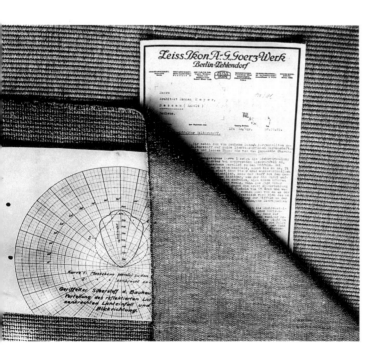

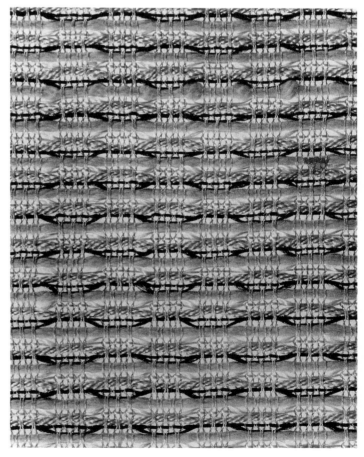

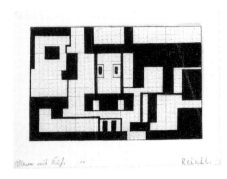

Hilde Reindl did her best to make a cow conform to graph paper.

One of the most widely acclaimed Bauhaus fabrics was Anni Albers's curtain and wall-covering material for the auditorium of the Bundesschule des Allgemeinen Deutschen Gewerkschaftsbundes (the Educational Centre of the Trade Union) in Bernau. Working independently, not as part of a team, she had developed an entirely new solution to the problems of light and acoustics. The ribbed, silvery material was woven on a cotton warp with a Cellophane front for increased light reflection and a chenille back for sound absorption. The Zeiss Ikon Goertz Company tested the fabric scientifically and wrote a formal evaluation confirming the effectiveness of her creation. Albers, well into her eighties and always modest about her achievements, spoke of it with genuine pride as 'something I am really happy to sign with my name, for that was a completely new approach.'[21] It also earned her the Bauhaus diploma. The Trade Union Headquarters were designed by Hannes Meyer, who became director of the Bauhaus in 1928. Like Gropius earlier, he involved the workshops in furnishing the interior of his building. The weavers supplied curtains, area rugs, bedspreads and cushions.[22]

Anni Albers was intrigued by the possibilities of the more sophisticated equipment in the Dessau Weaving Workshop, especially the Jacquard loom. This loom, introduced by its inventor, Joseph Marie Jacquard, at the 1801 Paris Industrial Exposition, was developed from the earlier, hand-manipulated draw loom and ever since has been of the greatest importance in producing figured textiles. It employs punched cards for the automatic selection and pulling of cords which lift the warp in a pre-planned pattern. In essence it is the forerunner of the computer. Indeed, the computer is now used instead of cards, which, during the Bauhaus days and until recently, had to be punched by hand, a time-consuming and exacting chore that does not permit any errors. All kinds of interior fabrics are associated with the Jacquard loom, from cheap, run-of-the-mill patterns to the most exquisite designs and sumptuous recreations of seventeenth- and eighteenth-century silks. It was used for the reproduction of tapestries which had fallen into a long decline, the poor aesthetic quality of these copies in no way affecting their popularity in bourgeois homes. The Bauhaus weavers demonstrated, however, that the Jacquard loom could also acquit itself as the perfect instrument for the contemporary weaver. For Anni Albers it was ideal. It translated her geometric designs into crisp, flat textiles with precisely articulated lines, something the hand loom would have been unable to do.

The affinity between the designs of Josef and Anni Albers – they were married in 1925 – has often been pointed out. Paul Klee, who continued to teach design concepts to the weavers in Dessau, was certainly a seminal influence. Did Gunta Stölzl know his whimsical *Pastoral* (pl. 50) of 1927? In 1928 she completed what is, without a doubt, the most sophisticated Jacquard weaving produced at the Bauhaus, *5 Chöre* (5 Choirs, pl. 51). It shows her supreme mastery of this demanding medium. Although the piece is entirely flat, the central panel seems to be a visual pun. It floats like a separate, superimposed hanging, held in place by four black bars. Yet, instead of interrupting the symmetry of the piece, it is very much a part of it, drawing attention not only to itself but also to the adjoining

sides. Stölzl's understanding of colour and light and her careful placement of abstract shapes makes *5 Chöre* a never-ending source of visual pleasure. It is a Jacquard design of the highest sophistication.

Far from being a sterile laboratory, the Weaving Workshop fostered and nurtured diverse talents. The technological development of prototypes for industrial fabrics in no way precluded creative work or downright fun. If the weavers had entered the Weimar workshop by default, they knew the parameters in Dessau. Slowly, the role and responsibility of the designer vis-à-vis society crystallized. And when the Bauhaus finally added its department of architecture in 1927, the weavers were called upon to make their contribution to the modern environment as equal partners.

chapter 9

bauhaus fabrics

On 4 February 1928, Walter Gropius petitioned the Dessau magistrate to release him from his contract two years before it expired. The constant crossfire from various outside groups – conservatives, unions and political agitators – and the internecine feuds, endless financial struggles and overwhelming workload had taken its toll. Diplomacy, negotiations and wrangling for funds had consumed his time and energy and seriously curtailed his professional activity. On more than one occasion he had supplemented the Bauhaus accounts with his personal money. To trade all of this for a return to private architectural practice – he wanted to leave by 31 March – held great appeal. Moreover, Gropius believed that the school was well enough established to function without him and that the man he proposed as his successor, Hannes Meyer, was qualified to carry on his work.

Since the newspapers published the story without delay, Gropius had no choice but to announce his resignation at a student party the same evening. The festive atmosphere gave way to shock and disbelief. A student representative, Fritz Kuhr, took the floor and made an impassioned speech reminding Gropius that 'for the sake of an idea we have starved here in Dessau' and pleaded with him not to 'leave now. . . . Hannes Meyer as the Director of the Bauhaus is a catastrophe.' Kuhr's impromptu address contained profound insights. It acknowledged what Mies van der Rohe would say decades later, that the Bauhaus was an idea, specifically Gropius's idea, and that his vision had inspired students not only to 'starve' but also to discover their full potential and become that special breed, Bauhäusler. Without him, would they be able to sustain their distinctiveness? While Kuhr did not want to malign Meyer personally, he was afraid that 'the door will be opened for the reactionaries.'[2] Instead, it was Meyer's radical nature that changed the Bauhaus.

Hannes Meyer was actually Gropius's second choice. Mies van der Rohe, who had been approached first, declined the offer. Meyer was a newcomer to the Bauhaus, having been appointed to the architecture department only a year earlier. He had quickly proven himself to be a hard worker, a welcome addition to the school, which, despite its troubles, was just then receiving the highest number of applications from students. Meyer had studied in his native Switzerland as well as in Berlin and was widely travelled. His interest in architecture lay in an absolute break with the past and his reduction of 'all things in this world [as] a product of the formula: [function times economy]'.[3] Meyer had kept a low profile during his first year at the school, which Gropius later interpreted as a deliberate concealment of his personal views and intentions.[4] Only too aware that, in Dessau as well as in Weimar, the Bauhaus's liberal attitudes were interpreted as being too left wing, Gropius had been determined to

All of us regret that the Bauhaus we loved has simply ended.
GUNTA STÖLZL, 1928[1]

Otti Berger photographed in the Dessau Workshop.

The masters assembled for a group photograph in 1926 for an article on the Dessau Bauhaus in *Das Illustrierte Blatt*. Evidence of the recent construction is still visible.

Nr. 50 Seite 1131

(Rechts) Die Laboratoriumswerkstätten und Lehrräume. Im Souterrain die Bühnenwerkstatt, Druckerei, Färberei, Bildhauerei, Heizkeller. Im Hochparterre die Tischlerei und die Ausstellungsräume. Im ersten Obergeschoß die Weberei, im zweiten Obergeschoß die Wandmalereiwerkstatt, Metallwerkstatt, sowie zwei Vortragssäle, die durch

Klappwand zu einem großen Ausstellungsraum vereinigt werden können. — Vom ersten und zweiten Stockwerk führt eine Brücke zu dem Atelierhaus links (siehe Abbildung 2 auf Seite 1154).

Der Maler Paul Klee, Meister des Bauhauses, in seinem Atelier.

Flur in der Verwaltungsetage des Brückenbaues.

Beleuchtungskörper. Metallwerkstatt.

isonbereit. Der Magistrat stellte die Summen zur Verfügung, die dazu nötig waren, dem Bauhaus ein würdiges Heim zu schaffen. Der bauleitende Architekt war Direktor Gropius selbst. So entstand der imposante Baukomplex (der gesamte Bau bedeckt rund 2600 Quadratmeter Grundfläche und enthält 32 000 Kubikmeter umbauten Raums) und in der Nähe, inmitten grüner Tannen, eine kleine Siedlung für die Professoren, hier „Meister" genannt. Ein internationaler Lehrkörper, jung in der Gesinnung, wie es der Geist des Instituts verlangt. P. Z.

abgehalten wurde, war bereits ein recht erfreulicher Gesinnungswechsel festzustellen. Das Bauhaus und seine Produktion wurden jetzt ernst genommen. Ein Jahr später begannen die Quertreibereien der thüringischen Regierung. Das Bauhaus drohte zu verschwinden. Die fortschrittlichen Zeitungen brachten spaltenlange Berichte, die fast wie Schwanengesänge klangen. Die Stadt Dessau jedoch war der Retter. Diese mittlere Industriestadt in der Nähe der Elbe, zwei D-Zugstunden von Berlin entfernt, übernahm den gesamten Betrieb und tat nach ein Be-

Die Meister des Bauhauses: (von links nach rechts) Josef Albers, Hinerk Scheper, Georg Muche, Ladislaus Maholy-Nagy, Herbert Bayer, Joost Schmidt, Wa'ter Gropius (Leiter des Bauhauses), Marcel Breuer, Wassily Kandinsky, Paul Klee, Lyonel Feininger, Gunta Stölzl, Oskar Schlemmer.

avoid politics and maintain absolute neutrality. He had, therefore, asked Meyer about his 'leanings and he answered that he was politically entirely disinterested. . . . No indications of his leftish inclinations became apparent.'[5] Gropius's tolerant nature and his appreciation of a colleague's professional competence, regardless of personal beliefs, was respected even by those who disagreed with him. He saw no reason to distrust Meyer's words, although others experienced clear misgivings. Schlemmer, for one, noted, like Stölzl, that 'everyone seems to think that the old Bauhaus has breathed its last.'[6]

For the moment the most visible change was in the make-up of the staff. When *Das Illustrierte Blatt* published its laudatory article on the Dessau Bauhaus in 1926, it featured the now well-known photograph of the Bauhaus masters, with Gunta Stölzl as the only woman. Two years later, the configuration of the faculty had changed drastically. Herbert Bayer, Marcel Breuer and Lucia and László

| This is Otti Berger's fabric *Preciosa*.

Moholy-Nagy had resigned. Oskar Schlemmer's departure in 1929 also meant the end of the theatre department. Any sense of community was lost almost immediately, at least among the old-timers. The growing estrangement between Feininger, Klee and Kandinsky – the latter had assumed the title of deputy director – only made matters worse. Among the new appointments were the city planner Ludwig Hilberseimer and the photographer Walter Peterhans. The Dutch architect Mart Stam, who had earlier declined Gropius's offer to join the faculty, became a frequent guest lecturer.

On taking charge in 1928 Meyer immediately de-emphasized the unity of art and technology, upholding only the latter, which set him on a collision course with Moholy-Nagy. Moholy's commitment to formal and aesthetic goals conflicted with Meyer's socially oriented pragmatism and his advocacy of an entirely functional, practical programme. 'Let us compare the Bauhaus with a factory,' Meyer said to the students in his first address as the new director. 'Do we want to be guided by the requirements of the world around us, do we want to help in the shaping of new forms of life, or do we want to be an island?'[7] he asked. Meyer favoured collective work and redesigned the courses and the workshops to relate to architecture. He maintained that the masses, not the luxury trade, should shape the nature of designs. Meyer's domineering attitude alienated many but also made the Bauhaus genuinely productive for the first time.

In its steady evolution toward designing industrial prototypes the Weaving Workshop had reached a stage that was in line with Meyer's aspirations. Yet Meyer, by no means a champion of textiles, was more critical of the weavers than supportive. The dissension between the Weimarians and the newcomers also exacerbated this situation, as the discussions among the weavers centred around the condemnation of earlier workshop products and the adoption of structural fabrics. Structural can be defined as a surface that derives its visual interest from the construction of the weave as well as the property of the yarns. Texture supersedes the pre-eminence of colour, although colour can also be a factor. Fabric designs based on the theories of Klee or on the use of visual elements, such as triangles and stripes, were associated with an earlier phase of the workshop and were even denounced by some. As it turned out, both structural and colour-oriented designs persisted side by side. Such friction regarding new stylistic directions is, of course, the staple of art and design communities as well as of critics, who are dependent on changing attitudes and ideologies. That the Bauhaus now considered textiles to be a subject of serious discourse at all was a tribute to the weavers. By advocating or dismissing styles, by debating the role of weaving in society, they had finally joined the dialogue that is so essential in defining theory. And just as the viewpoints of their colleagues in art or architecture differed, so did theirs.

The multiplicity of outlooks within one career is best exemplified by Léna Bergner, who entered the Dessau Bauhaus in 1926 at the age of nineteen. An exceptionally gifted student, she was also, like so many Bauhäusler, idealistic and impressionable. She studied with Albers, Kandinsky, Moholy-Nagy, Schlemmer and Joost Schmidt, but it was Paul Klee who impressed her the most. In 1926 the weavers had requested a course in formal design for which Gropius suggested Muche. The response was unequivocally negative. As Schlemmer reported to his wife, the students declared that '"Muche is not needed in the workshop." Apparently the written declaration was sharply worded: Gunda is not involved; it all comes from the weavers, who are now prepared for the worst; the student body is backing them and considers this a test of whether it still has any say or not.'[8] The students prevailed, and from 1927 until his resignation in 1931 Klee gave classes in design concepts geared to weaving. Léna Bergner often found it hard to understand Klee's short explanations but, like Anni Albers, experienced 'the full impact of his thoughts much later when we were practising our career. . . . In his critique, Paul Klee always tried to understand our intentions, gave us brief suggestions and encouraged us to continue to develop our ideas.'[9] Klee was especially close to the weavers since he had tailored his teaching of formal composition to their requirements. 'In his course', Bergner wrote, 'he dealt with the law of the surface itself, as well as the relationships between forms and colours. . . . In addition to formal instruction, the weavers gathered for occasional meetings at which, under Klee's leadership, the fabrics were critically analysed.'[10]

When Hannes Meyer became director, he met with all the workshops to get to know them. Bergner recalled that it was at such a meeting that the issue of structural fabrics was raised for the first time. Previous Bauhaus weavings were immediately labelled 'decorative', unsuitable for the new functionalism Meyer advocated. A 'heated discussion' followed, which split the Weimarians and the newcomers into two camps, but Meyer's goal to orient all design activity toward mass production 'convinced the young students'.[11] Bergner participated in two internships as a student. One was at a dye school in Sorau, which gave her enough expertise to oversee the Bauhaus Dye Shop when she returned, and the other was in the Ostpreussische Handweberei (East Prussian Handweaving Mill) in Königsberg, where she was hired as director after her graduation in 1930. In 1931 she followed several Bauhäusler, among them Hannes Meyer, to Moscow. Later she became his second wife. Although Bergner thought of her approach to material, construction and colour as 'biological' – satisfying all aspects of human needs – her outlook and style adapted themselves to each specific situation. She claimed, for instance, that although students had admired its potential, the Jacquard loom had been despised in Dessau. When she found a position as a textile designer in a large Russian mill, she rediscovered the Jacquard loom and loved it. The Soviet government, in the course of its first five-year plan (1928–32), had denounced abstract and Constructivist theories and was pressing everyone into propaganda work. Bergner responded by designing pictorial fabrics that featured such themes as the Socialist city, the radio and the new metro system. The second Soviet five-year plan (1933–37) de-emphasized propagandistic themes and advocated 'the beautification of Socialist life', a *Kulturpolitik* (cultural policy) that now demanded decoration 'such as flowers and folkloric motifs'. For someone who had been so vehemently involved in the advocacy of structural fabrics this shift to agitprop raises questions about the integrity of the designer. But, Bergner explained: 'At that time it was: Shall we create what is needed, or shall we insist on our own ideas and renounce collaboration? The decision was not a difficult one.'[12]

Léna Bergner and Hannes Meyer left Russia in 1936 when foreigners were no longer welcome. They were hoping to work in Spain but the Civil War interfered. Germany was not an option. They returned to Meyer's native Switzerland where his activities in Russia were held against him. He received few commissions. Bergner, however, took up carpet-weaving. In her designs she considered 'all psychological means which enrich human life'.[13] In essence, though, she returned to Klee's theories and the careful placement of colours, creating once again abstract designs. In 1939 the couple emigrated to Mexico. A government-sponsored plan to set up centres for weaving among the Otomi Indians, which Bergner was to head and for which she had planned the facilities, the curriculum and the textbook, was abandoned. She was forced to work in a variety of jobs, utilizing the graphic skills she had acquired in the Bauhaus Advertising Workshop. In 1949 Bergner and Meyer returned to Switzerland where she continued to design and weave carpets, until Meyer's death in 1954 forced her to seek more profitable employment. Personal decisions and political circumstances thus prevented Bergner from pursuing a career commensurate with her talents and her extraordinary training at the Bauhaus.

1928 and 1929 were extremely productive years for the Weaving Workshop. The wall coverings and curtains for the Café Altes Theater in Dessau had been delivered on time and were favourably received. Anni Albers broke new technological ground with her sound-proof and light-reflective fabric for Hannes Meyer's Trade Union School in Bernau. There was a steady and increasing demand for sample fabrics and prototypes which were purchased by mills and mass produced under the label Bauhausstoffe (Bauhaus fabrics). Just in time for Christmas 1928, the Weaving Workshop organized a commercial exhibition which was held at the Bauhaus. The 1929 Spring Fair in Leipzig turned out to be an unqualified financial success. Stölzl received a letter from the Vereinigte Seidenwebereien (the United Silk Mills) in Krefeld, asking to visit the workshop in anticipation of placing Bauhaus students as interns in their mill.[14]

In addition, the weavers participated in several exhibitions. In June 1929 they showed their work in Stockholm. The exhibition 'Ten Years Bauhaus', which travelled through Germany and Switzerland, included a completely new range of fabrics. Anni Albers and Gunta Stölzl assisted the art historian Ludwig Grote in preparing a travelling exhibition of modern wall hangings. It included works by Anni Albers, Rosa Berger, Margarete Bittkow-Köhler, Martha Erps, Emil Hartwig, Ruth Hollós, Ida Kerkovius, Else Mögelin, Benita Otte, Hilde Rantsch, Gunta Stölzl, Ruth Vallentin and Margarete Willers and represented both the Weimar and Dessau workshops. But far from being solely a Bauhaus undertaking – the Circle of Friends of the Bauhaus supported this venture – the exhibition was sponsored by a number of private collectors and museums in Chemnitz, Lübeck, Essen, Magdeburg and Hamburg. The Bauhäusler were in good company. Among the thirty international exhibitors were Sophie Täuber-Arp, Fernand Léger, Jean

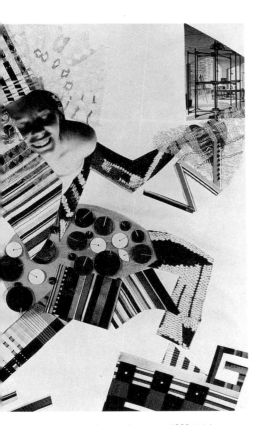

During his farewell party in 1928 Walter Gropius was presented with a portfolio entitled 'Nine Years Bauhaus. A Chronicle'. It contained Stölzl's collage.

Lurçat, Louis Marcoussis, Alen Müller-Hellwig, Johanna Schütz-Wolff, Christian Rohlfs and Karl Schmidt-Rottluff. It opened to great acclaim at the J.B. Neumann Gallery in Munich in October 1930.[15]

The increased activity in the workshops did not, however, preclude a vigorous social life. Outings, picnics and sports events were extremely popular. The proximity of Berlin – the capital was a two-hour train ride away – also put cultural events within reach. 'Berlin', Stölzl wrote to her brother, 'is simply fabulous, our trips are never made in vain, and we can enjoy it to the full.'[16] She liked Bertolt Brecht's *Threepenny Opera* so much that she saw it twice and wrote that she was looking forward to a party at the Gropiuses' to which she had been invited. She also took groups of students to Berlin, not only to visit textile collections, but also to introduce them to museums and galleries. The Bauhaus parties, which had been spontaneous or improvised events in Weimar, continued in Dessau as elaborate productions. In the past, Gropius's birthdays had been much anticipated annual celebrations; his farewell party became the grand finale. To honour the founder of the Bauhaus, Schlemmer staged the production *Neun Jahre Bauhaus* (Nine Years Bauhaus), in which Stölzl had a part and which was accompanied by a portfolio chronicling the events of the past nine years. A collage, featuring several familiar fabrics, was Stölzl's contribution. It shows a smiling but downcast figure, who is stopped by the 'G' for Gunta at the bottom, and who either offers a veiled heart to 'W', representing Walter, or points to the 'W' of the Weaving Studio in the upper corner. The Bauhaus parties were forerunners of sixties 'happenings', carefully planned and eagerly awaited. Themes, costumes, masks, staging and décor took weeks of preparation. Open to outsiders, the festivities increasingly attracted visitors from other cities as well. Much acclaimed was the Bauhaus Jazz Band, which even went on tour. One of the most elaborate parties, Das Metallische Fest (the Metallic Party), was attended by Mayor Hesse and various government officials. Informal dance parties were standard fare on Sunday evenings. Poetry readings, musical offerings – Paul and Lily Klee sometimes gave violin and piano recitals – and modern dance performances attracted an astonishing roster of avant-garde artists to provincial Dessau. Although these were unquestionably cultural events of the highest calibre, they also fostered a community spirit that mitigated individual antagonism and united, at least for the moment, all Bauhäusler.

The intensity of Bauhaus life made occasional absences almost a necessity. Most Bauhäusler had a penchant for travel. 'I am beginning to learn Russian and would like to go to Moscow next spring or summer', wrote Gunta Stölzl to her brother in December 1927,[17] and by the following May she was there to attend the International Congress for Architecture. Two Bauhaus students, Arieh Sharon and Peer Bücking, also made the trip. Stölzl probably did not know Sharon well before they met in Moscow, but there they became friends and fell in love. A year later, they were married and had a daughter. Before coming to the Bauhaus in 1926 – Sharon studied there until 1928 – he had lived and worked for six years in Palestine, where he had already distinguished himself as an architect and builder of the first kibbutz structures. Hannes Meyer was, therefore, not appointing a novice when he made Sharon supervising architect for the Educational Centre of the Trade Union in Bernau. Later he put him in charge of his Berlin architecture office. Sharon returned to Palestine in 1931 and became one of the leading avant-garde architects and town planners whose urban design, public buildings and reconstruction projects have become an integral part of present-day Israel. Even before their divorce in 1936, Stölzl and Sharon barely lived together. For Stölzl, the marriage turned out to be a hurtful, unfulfilled union with grave political consequences. However, her indomitable spirit, and the delight with which she observed the development of her daughter, helped her through the difficult years ahead.

If one looks at Stölzl's accomplishments during these busy years, one realizes how little time she took for herself. On the other hand, she was now able to draw on the support and assistance of talented and professionally qualified weavers. The hiring policy for the Weaving Workshop, however, was erratic and confusing; positions were short-term, underpaid or even unsalaried. Anni Albers and Otti Berger became assistants in 1928, Albers in April on a full-time basis and Berger in November working part-time. In January 1929 the Master Council directed Albers to teach design theory as an unpaid part-time employee. A salary based on the contractual hourly wage was promised commencing in the summer term. Instead, she became acting director of the workshop from 1 September until 1 November.[18] In March the city of Dessau renewed Stölzl's contract, granting her a studio space and a child subsidy, but no pension.

The preparation of samples for industry had now become routine and continued at a steady pace. Mills bought prototypes for fabric manufacture on a large scale. In July 1930 the Weaving Workshop signed a contract with Polytextil, a large incorporated textile company, which was to produce and market workshop fabrics under the label 'bauhaus-dessau'. The agreement between Polytextil and the Bauhaus was spelled out in detail and is a good indicator of the kinds of fabric the workshop was now able to supply. 'The purpose of the Bauhaus collection', the contract stated, 'is to supply a broad market with reasonably priced, artistically and technically exceptional upholstery and curtain fabrics.' The initial line of twenty fabrics was to match the original Bauhaus prototypes as closely as possible. Polytextil requested first refusal on new samples if they fell into the normal production category for interior textiles. In any event, a panel of prominent Bauhaus members was to assess all samples before they were offered to Polytextil. The company agreed to advertise only unified collections clearly marked as 'bauhaus-dessau'. All materials had to be colourfast, and the development of new colourways was the responsibility of the workshop. The company agreed to grant the weavers access to the production process at all times. All financial matters, from individual licensing fees to expenses incurred on travel, were carefully spelled out.[19] For the students, the agreement with Polytextil presented a unique opportunity to be involved in every phase of the enterprise, from concept and design, to technical specifications, cost accounting and shipping. Stölzl, who always considered the work of the Weaving Workshop as primarily pedagogical, was justly proud that industry increasingly recognized

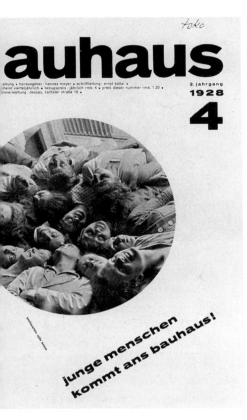

toko

auhaus

altung • herausgeber: hannes meyer • schriftleitung: ernst kállai •
heint vierteljährlich • bezugspreis: jährlich rmk. 4 • preis dieser nummer rmk. 1.20 •
mverwaltung: dessau, zerbster straße 16 •

2. jahrgang
1928
4

junge menschen
kommt ans bauhaus!

The slogan 'young people, come and join the bauhaus!' and Lotte Beese's photograph of the weavers appeared on the cover of *bauhaus* magazine No. 4. Student enrolment rose under Hannes Meyer's directorship.

forces and a steady move to the right in the country as a whole. Its high political profile was clearly hurting the institution and, since Mayor Hesse came under personal attack as well, he decided to make a clean sweep. Meyer was summarily dismissed. Before he and a group of Bauhaus students moved to the Soviet Union, he penned a biting, at times hysterical sounding, open letter to Mayor Hesse.

When he had arrived, Meyer wrote, he had found that 'inbred theories closed every approach to a form for right living; the cube was king, and its sides were yellow, red, blue, white, gray, black. . . . The square was red. The circle was blue. The triangle was yellow. One sat and slept on the colored geometry which was the furniture. One lived in the colored plastic forms which were the houses. On their floors lay, like carpets, the psychological complexes of young girls. Art stifled life everywhere. Thus', Meyer continued, 'a tragicomic situation arose: As Director of the Bauhaus I fought against the Bauhaus style.' Meyer's lengthy epistle proudly acknowledges that in only two years 'industry became greatly interested, engaged trained Bauhaus students and concluded license agreements for the manufacture of Bauhaus textiles, lamps, standard furniture and wallpaper.'[26] Five years later, writing from Moscow to weaver Lisbeth Oestreicher, a considerably mellowed Meyer was capable of self-mockery: 'Léna is working on a tapestry . . . imagine I bought a rug for ourselves, a Caucasian one. Thank goodness, the Bauhaus does not have to witness this outrage. The rug is full of figures and ornaments, a real psychological complex. This woven picture lies at the foot of the bed and pleases me every morning – now you know that my affection for weaving is greater than my conviction. That should really comfort you, for if an adversary like myself has become so reactionary, things should soon look up.'[27]

1930 was a turbulent year not only for the Bauhaus as a whole but for the Weaving Workshop as well. After Meyer's departure in August, the school closed until October when it reopened with Mies van der Rohe at the helm. Margaret Leischner became head of the Dye Workshop, and Anni Albers and Otti Berger stepped in as instructors or acting directors of the workshop when needed. An incident with far-reaching consequences, however, came unexpectedly in the guise of a personal attack on Gunta Stölzl. Three students, Grete Reichardt, Ilse Voigt and Herbert von Arend, were critical of Stölzl's private life and accused her of improprieties. The specifics were not spelled out, but it was evident that the dismissal of Meyer had encouraged reactionary forces to come to the fore. Both Stölzl and Klee had supported Meyer, both had been with the Bauhaus from the beginning. Now Klee had finally decided to leave and Stölzl mourned his parting as 'a very great loss'.[28] Otti Berger immediately dispatched a letter to the three students asking for '1) proof of the accusation of impropriety on the part of the workshop director, 2) an explanation of the behaviour of the student representative Grete Reichardt, 3) how are you envisioning future co-operative work within the workshop and with the director given your attitude?' The letter accused Ilse Voigt of neglecting her duties and asked for 'a precise written reply' so that a general workshop meeting could be promptly scheduled. Margret Dambeck, Bella Ullmann, Gertrud Preiswerk, Gerhard Kadow, Margaret Leischner, Tonja

T. Lux Feininger's photograph is the basis for this collage with pull-out tabs. Top row, left to right: Lisbeth Oestreicher, Gertrud Preiswerk, Léna Bergner, Grete Reichardt. Bottom row, left to right: Lotte Beese, Anni Albers, Ljuba Monastirsky, Rosa Berger, Gunta Stölzl, Otti Berger, Kurt Wanke.

Rapoport, Otti Berger, Anni Albers, Elisabeth Henneberger and Elisabeth Ahrens signed the letter.[29]

Despite the support of a clear majority of workshop members, Stölzl realized that 'everything is being destroyed by jealousies and a hunger for personal power. I am in a difficult position 1) because of Sharon – H. Meyer, 2) because I am on too friendly terms with my workshop, 3) because six old-timers have left and the new ones are being incited by certain people, who, on top of everything, are supported by masters.'[30] The masters Stölzl was referring to were Walter Peterhans, who was friendly with Grete Reichardt, and Kandinsky, who had actively lobbied against Hannes Meyer and also opposed Stölzl's liberal views. As she saw it, they 'will be able to finish me off because I make them uncomfortable.'[31] Stölzl perceived correctly that 'the Bauhaus now rests on a very weak foundation, both internally and externally.'[32] The city government and the Mayor were worried that too much publicity would again focus on the already shaky institution, and Klee and Mies warned Stölzl against taking a stand. Gropius, in whom she had confided, was troubled by the events and sympathized fully, 'since I have experienced similar camarillas against myself',[33] but he, too, thought that she had been correctly advised to give notice for the sake of finding future employment. After a prolonged period of tension, during which the accusers had been expelled by the student council and then reinstated by the masters, Stölzl handed in her resignation which was to be effective from 30 September 1931.

During the next year the Bauhaus records occasionally referred to Ilse Voigt and Herbert von Arend as troublemakers who claimed compensation for designs. In each case their petition was denied. No trace remained of Ilse Voigt after 1931. Herbert von Arend passed his journeyman's examination as a weaver in Glauchau in 1932. He enlisted as a 'professional soldier',[34] fought in the War and was captured and held in Russia as a prisoner. In 1949 he returned to Germany where he pursued a career as a civil servant in the revenue department. After his retirement in 1973 he rediscovered weaving and executed wall hangings in a variety of techniques. Grete Reichardt was an exceptionally gifted and versatile student at the Bauhaus. Although her journeyman's examination and Bauhaus diploma were in textiles, she was also active in Schlemmer's theatre department, the Carpentry Workshop and Paul Klee's painting class. She designed individual projects and prototypes for industry and participated in commissions. From 1930 to 1931 she worked as an independent assistant in the Weaving Workshop followed by a two-year sojourn in the Netherlands. She returned to Germany in 1933 and established her own handweaving studio. She was active throughout the War years. In 1939 she received a gold medal at the Milan Triennale and in 1942 she passed her master's examination with the Handelskammer in Erfurt, enabling her to train young weavers. After 1945 Reichardt became a prominent presence in the former East Germany where she received a number of honours and commissions. She also advised the East German government on the restoration of the Haus am Horn and the Dessau Bauhaus. Her late work had little in common with her early textiles for industry – Reichardt claimed that she was the only Bauhaus weaver to experiment with Cellophane – and comprised a range of approaches from free-standing sculptural steles, woven in the round, to traditional pictorial hangings, such as still lifes, birds and flowers.[35]

1931 was an extremely busy year for the Weaving Workshop: Anni Albers and Margaret Leischner each directed the workshop for periods of time. The weavers participated in a 'Modern Wall Hangings and Leather-Work' exhibition as well as the important 'Building Exhibition' in Berlin. The Bauhaus honoured Gunta Stölzl by dedicating the 1931–32 issue of *bauhaus* magazine to her accomplishments. Otti Berger, who had worked for industry, returned in October to teach a four-week course on the organization of labour in an industrial mill. Although an anonymous newspaper article predicted Berger's appointment to succeed Stölzl as a foregone conclusion, Mies van der Rohe instead appointed Lilly Reich. The new director, an accomplished designer, had no formal background in weaving and was not popular with the students. After prolonged negotiations, especially with regard to working hours and salary, Berger took on the technical and artistic direction of the workshop. Reich remained as titular head and Berger consented to view her position as an assistantship. The workshop expanded its programme to include textile printing and, for a short time, the van Delden Company manufactured printed curtains and table-cloths. As before, the workshop continued to supply woven prototypes for industry. Berger worked closely with several companies in developing new fabrics, including material for aeroplane seats. All this activity is astonishing considering the precipitous decline in the number of students. As the enemies of the institution, buoyed up by the support of the National Socialist Party, gathered enough strength for the final assault, the Dessau City Council overruled Mayor Hesse's objection and, on 22 August 1932, voted to dissolve the Bauhaus. At that point the Weaving Workshop had three full-time students, two visiting students and one guest student left.[36]

the purge

For the Weaving Workshop 1932 was a year of uncertainty and transition, of hope and despair. In the space of a decade

Michiko Yamawaki was a student in the Weaving Workshop from 1930 to 1933. After her return to Japan, she actively disseminated Bauhaus teaching methods in publications and as an instructor in Japanese art schools. Hajo Rose took this photograph around 1932.

the most populated Bauhaus workshop had been reduced to a handful of students. Ruth Cohn, Kitty van der Mijll Dekker, Greten Neter-Kähler and Tonja Rapoport had graduated. Kurt Wanke's contract was not renewed. Otti Berger, who had combined teaching with free-lance work, resigned in September and opened an independent design studio in Berlin. The real crisis, however, was the dissolution of the Dessau Bauhaus and its relocation, as Mies van der Rohe's private school, to an empty telephone factory in Berlin. Mies had been able to negotiate a number of concessions, most importantly the rights to the name Bauhaus and ownership and retention of patents and licences. Some furnishings, including looms, made the move to Berlin before Gropius's building was vandalized, a sad portent of the impending cataclysm. Classes in Berlin resumed in October, a testimony to the tenacity, determination and commitment of both staff and students. It was also gratifying that the work of the preceding years had borne fruit, for companies continued to purchase woven prototypes. In addition, Lilly Reich and Josef Albers selected a range of printed designs by Hajo Rose and Gerhard Weber which the van Delden Company produced as curtains and table-cloths until 1933. The market and the consciousness of the consumer had been penetrated by Bauhaus fabrics. They were not only well known but also, as an advertisement declared, 'hallmarks of good taste. . . . They fit into every home'.[2]

1932, from 5 January until her dismissal by the Berlin magistrate on 31 December, was also Lilly Reich's year as director of the Weaving Workshop. She was forty-seven and well established, an independent, professional woman who had earned a reputation in the fields of fashion, furniture design and interiors. Reich's inclusion of fashion as an integral aspect of design – an extension of the *Gesamtkunstwerk* as it were – was a novelty; it had never been a part of the Bauhaus philosophy. At the Wiener Werkstätte, however, where she had gone in 1908 to work with Josef Hoffmann, there had been no compartmentalization, but instead an affirmation of textiles as an integral part of life: from dress to Paris *haute couture*, from upholstery fabrics to curtains, from wall coverings to rugs and wall-to-wall carpets. Returning to Berlin in 1911, she befriended Anna and Hermann Muthesius who had studied *in situ* the reforms made by the English Arts and Crafts Movement in architecture, interiors and dress. Anna Muthesius's book on dress reform[3] contributed to the passionate discourse on healthier and more individualistic clothing that was at its height between 1900 and 1910. Even Henry van de Velde published articles on reform of 'artistic' dress. He also organized exhibitions, which included the extraordinary designs of Else Oppler with whom Reich later collaborated.[4] Anni Albers's reference to clothing in an article on 'Economic Living' sounded like a faint echo of the earlier debate: 'we must design . . . unencumbered by the weight of history. It is not enough to improve old forms. . . . Compare our dress: it meets the demands of modern travel, hygiene and economics (you cannot travel by rail in a crinoline). . . .'[5] Reich's championship of good design was broad-based and inclusive and had received early recognition from the Deutscher Werkbund, which elected her, the first woman ever, to its Board of Directors in 1920.

Lilly Reich's background fully qualified her to direct the Weaving Workshop, and while students from other departments respected her, she was faced, as Muche had been before her, with opposition from the textile students. Like Muche, she was not a weaver, a fact that seems to have been held against her; unlike him, she was fully conversant with the vocabulary of textile design. It must have been obvious even to her detractors that to lead a department one need not understand weaving technology. Like any other discipline, it can be taught by a qualified professional, which Otti Berger did expertly at the workshop. But there were philosophical and personal conflicts between Reich and Berger, and apparently also between Reich and the students who boycotted her classes. Moreover, Berger, the consummate technician, was also an exceptional teacher, admired and loved by her classes. She firmly believed that it was necessary to treat 'people as individuals and not as students . . . to develop the workshop in a direction which can be justified to the outside world, for each age demands its own spiritual and intellectual principle.'[6] One can further speculate that the weavers were accustomed to viewing the design process in terms of the characteristics of individual woven fabrics, whereas Reich most likely subscribed to a broader approach. Had the closure of the Bauhaus not been imminent, the Weaving Workshop might well have taken an entirely new direction under her leadership. Little is known about Jutta von Schlieffen's role as Reich's assistant during the few months before the Bauhaus's final closure, except that she had been a student at the Weimar workshop from 1922 to 1924.

Reich met Mies van der Rohe in the mid-twenties. Their relationship was both personal – Mies lived apart from his wife and three children – and professional. Although they shared a flat, throughout her career Reich maintained her own office. All her work was directed toward clearly assessing the function of design. She understood the effect of textiles in interiors and exhibition spaces. Her carefully placed rugs, curtains and partitions were never afterthoughts but were fully integrated partners in an overall scheme. For the 1927 'Exposition de la Mode' in Berlin she and Mies van der Rohe designed the Silk and Velvet Café, 'a single passage of space within the larger show where visitors could relax over coffee, seated in Mies's MR chairs . . . surrounded by lengths of tall draperies suspended with elegant simplicity from slender metal rods . . . hangings done in black, orange and red velvet and black and lemon yellow silk reflected Reich's exceptional way with textiles as well as her vivid, opulent sense of color.'[7] Reich and Mies collaborated on designs for furniture, exhibitions and architectural projects. Among these were the celebrated German Pavilion and the exhibition halls – realized by Reich – at the Barcelona International Exposition in 1929 and the Tugendhat House in 1930. Her influence on him and his reliance on her talents as a creative force were profound. 'Many ideas [and] plans can be traced to her: for instance, I know for certain that the chair for the Tugendhat House, registered under Mies's name, was her design.'[8] Mies disliked the administrative duties associated with his projects and the directorship of the Bauhaus and was glad to leave these matters to Reich's organizational skills. The career of Mies van der Rohe was strengthened by the ideas and actual projects of Lilly Reich. Yet while he experienced a meteoric rise to fame in the United States, she remained in war-torn Germany, denounced by the government, barely able to survive, but faithfully tending to the legal matters of his business. After 1945 she reopened a studio for architecture, design, textiles and fashion and assisted in planning the curriculum for the interiors and architecture course at the Institute of Fine Arts in Berlin. She died in 1947. The exceptional breadth of Reich's career deserves wider recognition than it has thus far received.

In a last burst of optimism the Weaving Workshop introduced a revised curriculum, continued negotiations with textile companies and enjoyed representation on the van Delden stand at the Leipzig Spring Fair in 1933. But in April the police closed and sealed the building, and three months later, on 20 July 1933, the staff united behind Mies van der Rohe's decision to dissolve the Bauhaus for good. It was not enough for its enemies. With very few exceptions, anyone, whether artist, designer, educator or student, who had ever been associated with the institution in Weimar, Dessau or Berlin became the target of an unprecedented campaign of attacks. The vociferous vendetta against the Bauhaus was aimed at obliterating all vestiges of the institution, and the destruction of Oskar Schlemmer's murals in Weimar was only the beginning. The instigator for this was Paul Schultze-Naumburg, director of the Weimar school since 1930, and member of the inspection team that had doomed the Bauhaus in Dessau. The author of *Art and Race*, Schultze-Naumburg distinguished himself as among the most active of the early hate-mongers. The Bauhaus was no stranger to animosity, but with Hitler's rise to power, terror and intimidation became all-pervasive. Although many years in the making, the rapidity, ferocity and thoroughness of the assault caught many by surprise. There was no collective uproar. 'An ominous silence has fallen over art and cultural circles', wrote Schlemmer to Gunta Stölzl in 1933. 'It is all up!'[9]

Stölzl's forced resignation from the Bauhaus preceded its closure by less than two years and may have helped her in securing a refuge before the deluge of uprooted Germans poured into the rest of Europe. With her marriage to Arieh Sharon in 1929 she had automatically lost her German citizenship and become a Palestinian subject. Moreover, Sharon was Jewish. All this had irritated the right-wing posse which had ousted her in Dessau and had contributed to their charge of 'impropriety'. It had been counted against her then, now it added once more to the precariousness of her existence. Stölzl encountered the fate of every displaced person: the struggle for legal papers. The need for authorization to work, residence permits, a valid passport and a host of official forms kept her in a perpetual state of insecurity. 'I do not have the faintest idea where I could go if

Switzerland is no longer an option – France, Paris – every place is saturated with émigrés, none of whom know how they can make a living.'[10] Not until 1935, when she feared she might become stateless, did she receive a British passport. In 1925 Stölzl had commented that Benita Otte was treated 'royally because of her Bauhaus stamp'; in 1933 the craft school Burg Giebichenstein was forced to terminate the contracts of Otte and other Bauhäusler because of it. 'All my friends in Germany', wrote Stölzl from Switzerland, 'have to start life all over again . . . just as I had to here.'[11] But her position in Zurich was by no means secure. The handweaving studio she had started in 1931 with two other Bauhäusler, Gertrud Preiswerk and Heinrich-Otto Hürlimann, experienced financial difficulties and had to close a year and a half later. Commissions were sporadic and barely paid the bills for herself and her young daughter.

Despite these frustrations, Stölzl integrated into Swiss society and never lost her gratitude to her host country. She joined several professional organizations, including the Swiss Werkbund, which enabled her to participate in exhibitions. Over time, she collaborated with a number of textile companies. Her willingness to accept all kinds of commissions and the technical expertise that she used to execute them, enabled her to endure these years of hardship. She designed and produced an astounding variety of textiles, from prototypes for machine-woven curtains, wall coverings, table-cloths, rugs, upholstery and apparel fabrics to individual projects like theatre curtains and interior schemes. Her business, which she opened in 1937, went by the name of Studio Flora. Contacts with other Bauhäusler were curtailed by the War, but somehow messages got through. The past was a strong bond. 'New friends', wrote Schlemmer to Stölzl in 1942, '– ah, they are few and far between, and you are very right that one gets the greatest pleasure from seeing the old ones, who have already become part of history.'[12] To her new friends, Stölzl added a new family. In 1942 she married Willy Stadler with whom she had another daughter. She was now a Swiss citizen.

Largely through Gropius's initiative, American interest in the Bauhaus began as soon as communication with Europe was restored after the War. Stölzl sold a hanging to the Busch-Reisinger Museum in Cambridge, Massachusetts, in the late forties, and another one to the Museum of Modern Art in New York in the fifties. Subsequent purchases and gifts of weave samples have augmented both collections. Germany did not pay tribute to the Bauhaus until the sixties, due in part to the division of the country and the location of both Weimar and Dessau in the Eastern zone. Hans Maria Wingler, who undertook the monumental documentation of the Bauhaus with the support of a Rockefeller grant, staged the first exhibition of the Weaving Workshop in Darmstadt in 1964. Stölzl was prominently represented. From the moment Gunta Stölzl first encountered a loom, she recognized her innate talent to transform yarns into complex, limitless varieties of woven entities. When the joyous experimentation of the Weimar years gave way to Dessau functionalism, she not only adapted but also pioneered new materials and fabrics. As an educator she was modest, free from jealousies, consistently encouraging and eager to recognize exceptional talent. Weaving was her life. She had experienced first-hand the challenges of the medium and now, in her later years, returned to the starting point, delighting once again in weaving as art. Gunta Stölzl died in Switzerland in 1983.

In 1930 Gunta Stölzl wrote a glowing letter of recommendation for Otti Berger. It extolled Berger's 'artistic talents' and her 'work, executed with great intensity and perseverance as the best that has been produced in the workshop.' She mentioned Berger's pedagogical gifts, her capability as a leader in Stölzl's absence, and again returned to her work 'which will speak as the most eloquent testimony for her abilities.'[13] Berger was a prolific letter writer herself, keeping in touch with the Alberses and other friends after she left the Bauhaus. Yet her correspondence took a very different turn in 1933 when she experienced far worse difficulties in Germany than Stölzl had in Switzerland. Berger was suddenly forced to seek a residence permit, even though she had lived in Germany since 1926.[14] In December, a month after its establishment by Joseph Goebbels, she petitioned the Reichskammer der Bildenden Künste (the Reichs Chamber for the Fine Arts) for membership and included photographs of her work.[15] The Reichskammer was the authority charged with enforcing a newly enacted law that exerted control over all branches of art and design by the granting of membership, or, conversely, the prohibition to work. Berger's request was denied on the grounds that 'you are a foreign non-Aryan.'[16] Although a subsequent residence permit was approved in 1935, in 1936 she was notified that 'you do not have the required abilities and trustworthiness ... and since you do not meet the requirements of the Reichskammer I herewith deny your application and forbid you to practise your profession. . . .'[17] The extent of the harassment becomes apparent when the Revenue Department advised Berger, a Jew, that exemption from church taxes hinged on proof of legal withdrawal from a religious community.[18]

Unlike that of any other weaver at the Bauhaus, Berger's reputation as a designer was international. While in Stockholm in 1929, she was asked to give lectures about the Weaving Workshop, which pleased Hannes Meyer, 'for you will know how to say the right things.'[19] A year later the Czech magazine *RED* carried her article on Bauhaus weaving. Hardly a year went by without some publication by or about Berger. In 1931 she wrote about 'The Special Role of Handweaving' in *Der Konfektionär* (The Clothing Manufacturer), and *International Textiles*, a multi-lingual Swiss journal, featured her work repeatedly. Under the heading 'Fabrics by Otti Berger' the magazine wrote in 1934: 'It is seldom that one designer deserves special mention from among the great collection of anonymous products in the textile industry. We are making an exception in this case. . . .'[20] *Domus*, the Italian design magazine, illustrated five examples of Berger's fabrics in its November 1935 issue.[21]

In her Berlin studio, which was partially furnished with looms bought from the defunct Dessau Bauhaus, Berger pursued her quest for the ideal industrial fabric. She developed prototypes for car, train and plane upholstery material and in 1932 registered a patent for a double-weave fabric with layers of artificial horsehair and artificial silk. It was one of several new fabrics she patented, some of them chemically treated, some containing new materials like plant fibres or Cello-

Opposite

Above This fabric with acoustic properties was registered by Otti Berger as a patent. It was intended to be mounted about thirty-five centimetres (fourteen inches) from the wall and lit from behind to create a luminous surface.

Below This sample, marked '5488 o.b.', is one of hundreds which Otti Berger designed for the de Ploeg Company in the Netherlands.

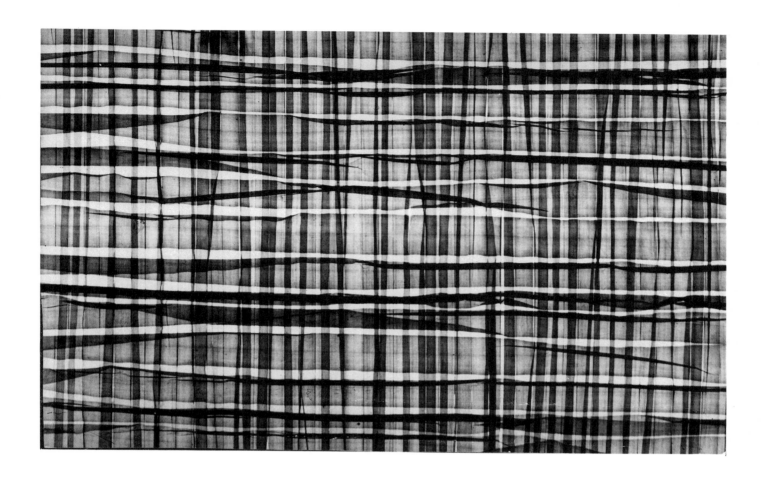

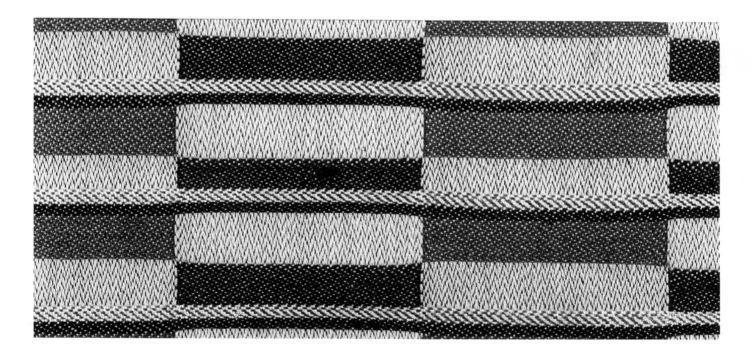

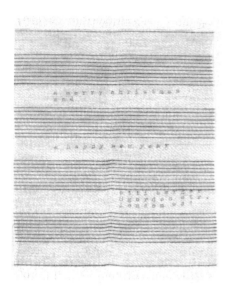

During one of the loneliest times in her life, December 1937, Otti Berger sent Alexander Dorner greetings typed onto a diaphanous plain weave fabric of Bombyx silk. It read: 'merry christmas and a happy new year. otti berger 8 gordon street london WC1'.

phane. From 1933 to 1937 Berger developed an unparalleled range of designs for the de Ploeg Company in Bergeyk, the Netherlands. Although it was de Ploeg's policy to keep its designers anonymous, an exception was made on Berger's insistence, and her initials were prominently displayed along with the names of her designs. When the Nazi edict forced Berger to close her studio, she left for London, taking the de Ploeg collection and other samples with her. The rest was put in storage in Berlin.

In the mid-thirties England was a haven for refugees from Germany. For Otti Berger, 1937 and 1938 were the beginning of sad and lonely times. In the past she had been able to compensate for her disability, almost total deafness,[22] but now, combined with her inability to speak or understand the language, it became an insurmountable obstacle. 'The English', she wrote to a friend, 'are very reserved. I believe it takes ten years before one has a circle of friends. I am always alone and find it difficult because I do not know English and cannot hear. . . . on the other hand, I am really enthusiastic about the mentality of the English people.'[23] She kept in touch with her Bauhaus friends, so many of them displaced like herself. The Gropiuses, Marcel Breuer, László Moholy-Nagy and Lucia Moholy – the Moholys had separated in the late twenties – were also in London, and for a while Berger stayed with Lucia Moholy. Possible leads for employment were exchanged among the exiled, but as Berger wrote to her friend Alexander Dorner, until 1933 director of the Hanover Art Museum, 'I dare not look up the people whose addresses you gave me since I do not speak English',[24] and in this she was not alone. Yet Berger was able to design a collection of fabrics for Helios, a division of Barlow & Jones, and in 1938 it looked as if her situation might change for the better. To a friend she wrote optimistically that, 'I have two offers at the same time and do not know how to decide since I am going to America at the beginning of next year, to Moholy's New Bauhaus. H. is going too, but with Mies.'[25]

Berger was referring to Ludwig Hilberseimer. Their relationship had continued after she left the Bauhaus, and apparently, although there was no legal proof, she transferred to him the rights to her estate and her patents. In 1938 Hilberseimer came to England. Berger must not have recognized the gravity of the political situation on the Continent, for, despite his warnings, she went via Prague to Yugoslavia to visit her ailing mother. The denial of a visa to the United States sealed Otti Berger's fate. Many of her friends, among them Hilberseimer and the Gropiuses, emigrated to America before 1939, and it is surprising that, despite the War, their letters, a great solace to Berger, continued to reach her in Zmajavac. In July 1941 Hermann Göring gave orders to prepare for the 'final solution of the Jewish question'. Three years later, Otti Berger and her family were deported to a concentration camp in Hungary. From there she took her final journey to Auschwitz. In 1951 Ise Gropius initiated the transfer of Otti Berger's fabrics, samples, pattern books, weave drafts, manuscripts and teaching notes to the Busch-Reisinger Museum. In lengthy and complicated negotiations she was able to obtain Hilberseimer's consent, use her contacts in London to release Berger's work from storage there, get customs permissions for shipment and the

Busch-Reisinger's willingness to pay for transport.[26] 'What became of her things in Berlin,' Hilberseimer wrote, 'I do not know.'[27]

It is estimated that between twenty and thirty Bauhäusler were killed in concentration camps or perished otherwise during the War.[28] Like Otti Berger, whose tragic fate she shared, Friedl Dicker had studied at the Weaving Workshop, but during its earlier phase. She was a member of the group of students, among them Gyula Pap, Franz Probst, Naum Slutzky, Anni Wotiz, Margit Tery-Adler and Franz Singer, who followed Johannes Itten from Vienna to Weimar in 1919. All of them later distinguished themselves as outstanding artists and designers. In 1920, however, they were embroiled in political and philosophical controversies at the Bauhaus which prompted Gropius to refer to them as 'the gifted-Jewish Singer-Adler group . . . understandably opposed by the Aryans.'[29] Dicker left the Bauhaus in 1923 and formed a partnership with Franz Singer. Their first collaboration was in Berlin, but when the 'Singer-Dicker Studio' moved to Vienna it joined the ranks of the most sought-after architects and designers. Dicker and Singer designed houses, shops, interiors, child centres, furniture and textiles. From 1931 to 1934, the year she was taken into custody and forced to emigrate to Czechoslovakia, Dicker worked independently. Despite her detention, she continued to design and to teach drawing but also joined a group of politically active German and Austrian émigrés. In 1936 she married Pavel Brandeis, and together they decided to decline a visa to Palestine. Personal hardship but unrelenting professional activity marked the years between 1938 and 1942. Dicker continued to teach, pursue free-lance projects and design textiles for the Spiegler company, which recognized her achievement with a gold medal. Unable to travel herself, her work was exhibited in 1940 at the Royal Arcade Gallery in London.

Friedl Dicker's career as an artist and designer was remarkably varied. Her interiors were so functional that they are avant-garde even by today's standards.

Lily Hildebrandt took this portrait study of Friedl Dicker in 1920.

Her furniture and textile designs suited their purpose precisely and, more often than not, reflected her strong social convictions. For the stage she created costumes and sets of high originality. Dicker's paintings, whether portraits, landscapes or still lifes, elicit a strong emotional response from the viewer; her images of interrogations are frighteningly evocative. Yet her distinguished career and her multifaceted talents are but one measure of a woman whose spirit was stronger than the depravity it encountered. During the last two years of her life, after she had been deported to the Terezin ghetto in 1942, she taught drawing and design to the camp children clandestinely.[30] The surviving drawings and paintings by these children fall into two categories: realistic depictions of camp life and its grim living conditions and abstractions which soar in explosions of colour. They are at once chilling documents of inconceivable barbarity and evidence of the indomitable spirit that knows beauty even in the face of destruction. Most of the children shared their teacher's fate and were gassed in Auschwitz. Their art remains as testimony to their own courage and to the heroism of Friedl Dicker.

It was the tragedy of the Bauhäusler to belong to the generation between the two Wars and to represent a sensibility at odds with society at large. The effects of the years 1914 to 1918 were deeply felt. The men who were alive carried the precarious burden of the survivor; women, in unprecedented numbers, were deprived of partners. Inflation, poverty and hunger had become the norm. Yet these conditions also fuelled their idealism and youthful fervour. The Bauhäusler believed in the possibility of change and saw themselves as pivotal to the reconciliation of art and life and the betterment of society. What they faced instead was the rise of the police state in the thirties and the negation of the very values on which they had based their professional and personal futures. Their cosmopolitan outlook was under attack as non-German, their personal lives scrutinized from a racial perspective, since relationships or marriages between Jews and non-Jews were forbidden by law. When anti-Semitism became the policy of the Hitler government, and non-Aryans were prevented from practising their profession, the passing of the Nuremberg Laws in 1935 deprived German Jews of their one fundamental protection, their German citizenship.

The diploma that Edeltraut Wagner received from the Weaving School in Sorau is thus an inadvertent chronicle of the time. She graduated at the height of Germany's runaway inflation in 1923 when the price for duplicating her diploma was three million marks, including stamp tax. She may well have tendered the emergency money designed by another Bauhäusler, Herbert Bayer. Wagner attended the Bauhaus from 1925 to 1926, and enrolled in the Weaving Workshop, although she studied exclusively under Albers, Klee and Kandinsky. Both she and her husband, Dr Hans Kosterlitz, came from upper-middle-class Jewish families that did not think the events in Germany would affect them. As it turned out, they escaped in the nick of time and emigrated to the United States in 1938. Wagner had the foresight to get all of her papers in order and, once again, had her Sorau diploma copied. This time it bore Hitler's swastika. In America, Edeltraud Wagner Kosterlitz became Claire Kosterlitz, adding to her married

Margaret Leischner not only developed novelty yarns for R. Greg & Co., South Reddish, Stockport, but also designed fabrics which maximized the textural and structural quality of these yarns. The above fabric is reversible. She also designed this curtain fabric (*below*) for R. Greg & Co.

name the first name of her grandmother, since soon after their arrival 'the War broke out and everyone here was very anti-German.'[31] While helping her husband re-establish a medical practice in the United States, Kosterlitz pursued an active career as a painter and exhibited widely in New York and New Jersey galleries.

In 1938, the year Otti Berger left, Margaret Leischner emigrated to England. Would Berger's future have been different if Leischner had arrived earlier? They had worked closely in Dessau and shared the same orientation toward industrial textiles. Leischner received her Bauhaus diploma in 1931. From 1932 to 1936 she headed the Berlin Textile and Fashion School but also worked as a consultant and free-lance designer for a number of companies. She took her master's examination in 1936. In England, Leischner immediately integrated into the textile world around Manchester, where an unusual group of forward-looking personalities held leading positions. Sir Raymond Streat, chairman of the Cotton Board, founded the Colour, Design and Style Centre in 1942 at the height of the War. It was the first design centre in the world dedicated to an industry and became famous for its innovative approach, including international market research, scholarships for students and exhibitions. Sir Raymond had the foresight to know that the industry would have to redirect itself after the War, and in this spirit, many companies encouraged design experimentation despite the difficult political and economic situation. European émigrés thus found new opportunities in and around Manchester. Felix Loewenstein, the former director of the Pausa Company in Stuttgart, which had maintained close ties to the Bauhaus, now worked for Helios, where Marianne Straub, the eminent Swiss designer, headed both the woven- and printed-textile divisions. Kurt Lowit, now a refugee, had worked with the English industry since the 1920s and became an important figure in textile circles. He would later be in charge of production at Wardle's of Leek and be responsible for the screen printing of many of the Edinburgh Weavers's prestigious printed cottons. These prints included one based on the *Shelter Sketchbooks* of Henry Moore and one on Graham Sutherland's *Green Rose*.[32] Margaret Leischner's unique background predestined her to play an important role in such an environment. At the Bauhaus she had been trained in every facet of the design process. She was now able to apply it on a broad level. As a consultant and designer she developed new yarns and fabrics for a number of companies. As an educator she disseminated the Bauhaus idea to another generation of students. From 1948 until 1963 she was senior lecturer and head of the Weaving Department at the Royal College of Art in London and in 1952 became a fellow of the Society of Industrial Artists. She also acted as an assessor for the Ministry of Education's art examination for the national diploma in design. 'There can be no doubt', wrote Donald Tomlinson, 'that she was a great teacher, whose standards gained the respect . . . of the textile industry. . . . Her students' . . . fabrics frequently had a subtle graphic imagery and fashionable sense of colour, as well as sound architectural and technical competence.'[33] Margaret Leischner was among the fortunate few who were able to establish a flourishing career abroad.

Bauhäusler also found refuge in the Netherlands, either permanently or on their way to other destinations. Paul Citroen, a Dutchman who studied at the Bauhaus from 1922 to 1925 and then worked in Berlin as a painter, returned to his native country in 1933 and founded the Nieuwe Kunstschool (New Art School). Although the curriculum included weaving, few students enrolled in the weaving course. For a brief time, Katja Rose, a former Bauhaus student, taught at the Nieuwe Kunstschool, but it never played a major role in educating textile designers. By contrast, the Gerrit Rietveld Academy in Amsterdam, under the leadership of Mart Stam, could almost be considered an outpost of the Bauhaus. There, two weavers left their imprint: Greten Neter-Kähler and Kitty van der Mijll Dekker. They had been students at the Bauhaus during its last phase from 1929 to 1932. Each brought specific strengths to her teaching: van der Mijll Dekker an emphasis on technology and structures, Neter-Kähler stressed colour and materials. Both women also collaborated with Hermann Fischer, but personal crises and the unfavourable economic conditions in the Netherlands presented a constant struggle for their handweaving studio. The same economic hardships were encountered by Lisbeth Oestreicher, who studied at the Bauhaus from 1926 to 1930. As a member of the Weaving Workshop she had participated in designing prototypes for Polytextil and Pausa. Like Berger, she was prohibited from working in Germany. She never found a position in the Dutch textile industry commensurate with her background. By designing patterns for knitted and crocheted sweaters she managed to make a living until 1940, when she was deported to the Westerbork concentration camp. The liberation of the camp in 1945 by Canadian troops saved Lisbeth Oestreicher's life.

The persecution of Jewish workshop members followed the pattern of Hitler's racist policy in general. The deaths of Otti Berger and Friedl Dicker were part of the planned extinction of Eastern European Jews, and Jews in the Netherlands and other occupied countries soon also became targets. What remains unclear is why some Aryan weavers were singled out and forbidden to work while others continued to practise their profession throughout the Nazi era. Prominence was not the criterion. The weavers, unlike the rest of the Bauhäusler, were not well known beyond textile circles. Not one weaver had the stature of a Mies van der Rohe, a Kandinsky or a Klee. Textiles, moreover, do not readily subvert the masses from official ideology. None were included in the 1937 'Degenerate Art' exhibition in Munich. For every weaver free to work in peace, another became the target of harassment. At least eighteen left Germany, although this figure can only be approximate. Some, such as Margaret Leischner, emigrated on their own, most followed their husbands into exile. A small minority was forced into 'inner emigration' – the silencing of a person – which was accompanied by the prohibition to work or government-enforced labour elsewhere. Dörte Helm, Else Mögelin and Ida Kerkovius fell into this group. They were officially designated as degenerate artists. Tellingly, all three were also painters. Extant statistics about the weavers' lives are fragmentary and inconclusive. The seeming randomness with which the otherwise efficient Nazi bureaucracy victimized certain weavers and exempted others raises questions which have not yet been answered.

78 *Opposite* Don Page wove this untitled pictorial hanging while he was a student at Black Mountain College, North Carolina.

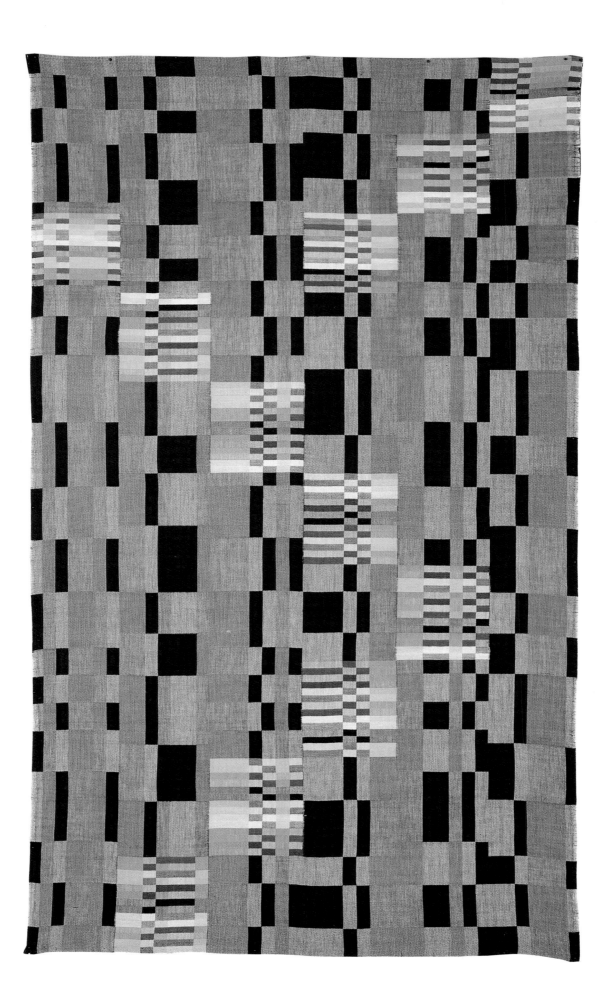

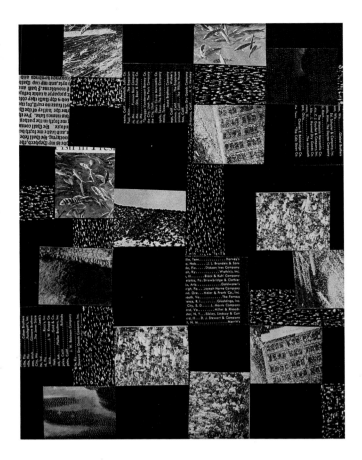

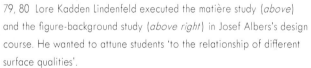

79, 80 Lore Kadden Lindenfeld executed the matière study (*above*) and the figure-background study (*above right*) in Josef Albers's design course. He wanted to attune students 'to the relationship of different surface qualities'.

81 *Right* Students at Black Mountain College were always on the look-out for interesting scraps of material to use for texture studies. This one, made of metal shavings by Kadden Lindenfeld, was an assignment for Anni Albers's class.

82 *Below* After her graduation Kadden Lindenfeld worked as a designer for industry. Lurex gives this apparel fabric, developed on the hand loom for the Forstmann Company in 1949, its elegant touch.

84 *Above* One of the top-of-the-line fabrics Kadden Lindenfeld designed for the Herbert Meyer Company. Although the material appears textural, the look is achieved through construction, not by the use of textural yarns.

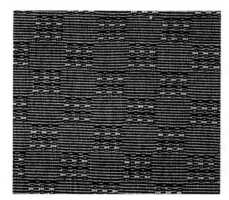

83 *Right* Double-woven fabric by Kadden Lindenfeld, part of her student portfolio at Black Mountain College.

85 *Above* Anni Albers abandoned weaving in 1970 and turned to graphic work. Many viewers feel that her graphic work, like her screen print *GR I*, is strongly evocative of weave drafts.

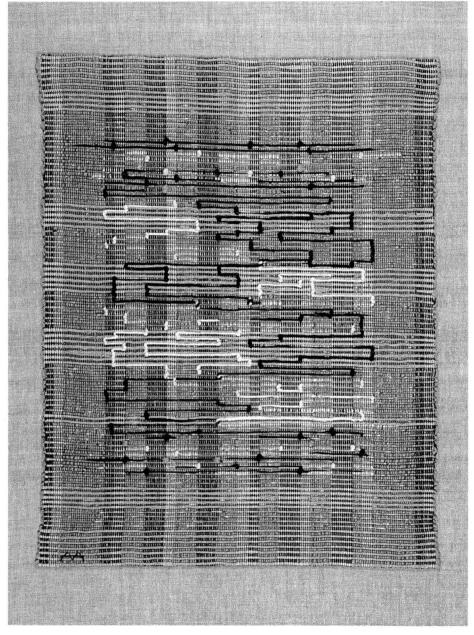

86 *Right* Anni Albers's pictorial weavings are mounted for display on a rigid background. Her *Black-White-Gold I* dates from 1950.

87 In her pictorial weavings Anni Albers assigns equal importance to the
warp and the weft. Both carry an intensely personal message.
Intersecting was executed in 1962.

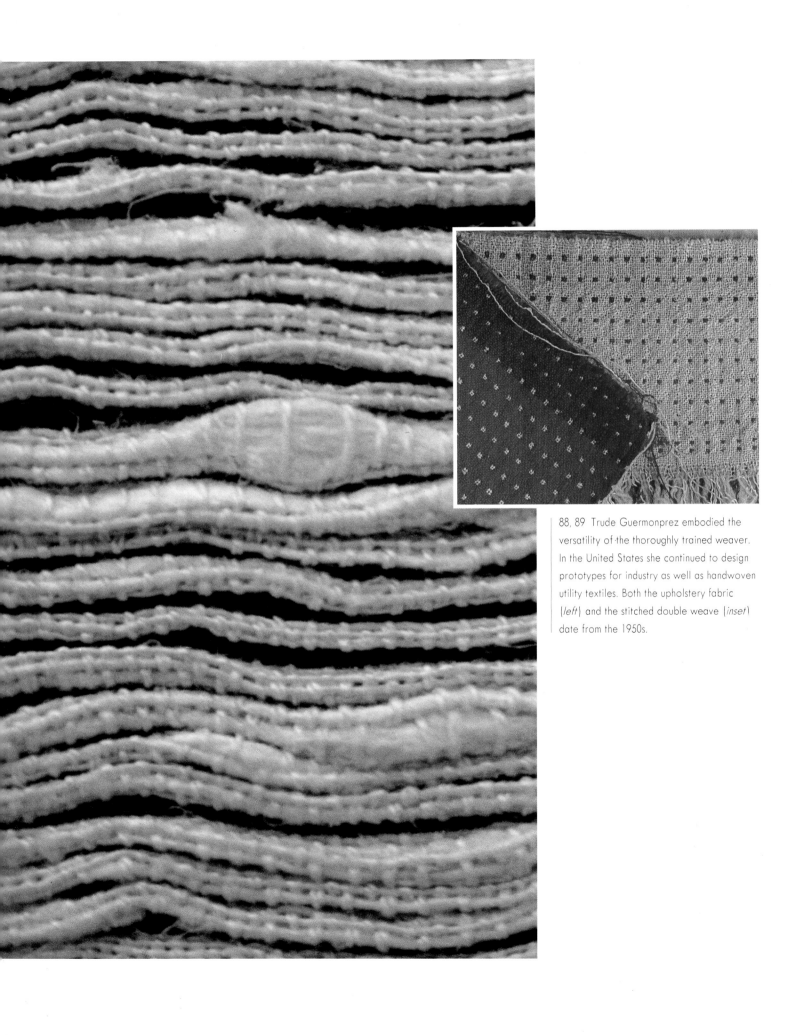

88, 89 Trude Guermonprez embodied the versatility of the thoroughly trained weaver. In the United States she continued to design prototypes for industry as well as handwoven utility textiles. Both the upholstery fabric (*left*) and the stitched double weave (*inset*) date from the 1950s.

91 Guermonprez always forged new ground. In *We Are But Two Shadows* of 1971 (*above*) she stencilled the warps of her double-woven hanging.

90 Trude Guermonprez was gravely ill when she executed her last hanging, *Mandy's Motto* (*left*), in 1975. Undiminished in spirit, she experimented with graphics, inlay, printed fabrics and flag strips combined with double-weave. The hanging is a wistful summation of a life affected by circumstances beyond personal control.

92, 93 With her tubular hangings in nylon monofilament, Kay Sekimachi pioneered the exploration of three-dimensional space. Warp and weft of her multilayered constructions are equal partners in shaping autonomous sculptural forms. Her work was included in the seminal 1969 'Wall Hangings Exhibition' at the Museum of Modern Art. Her latest work includes forms made from fusing left-over warp ends, scraps of handwoven fabric, linen threads and rice paper. Her two versions of *Amiyose* in clear monofilament, quadruple and tubular weave were both produced in 1965.

Opposite

94 *Left* *The Queen* of 1962 is one of Lenore Tawney's 'woven forms' which, although created on the loom, no longer adheres to the rectilinear format dictated by it.

95 *Above right* In *Morning Redness* of 1974 Tawney explored the theme of the circle in the square. Her symbolism refers not only to the inner self, but also, through incorporation of manuscripts, to the thoughts of those who went before.

96 *Below right* Tawney's abstractions, like *Four Petaled Flower II* of 1974, are timeless because they are completely of the present, at the same time invoking memories of the past.

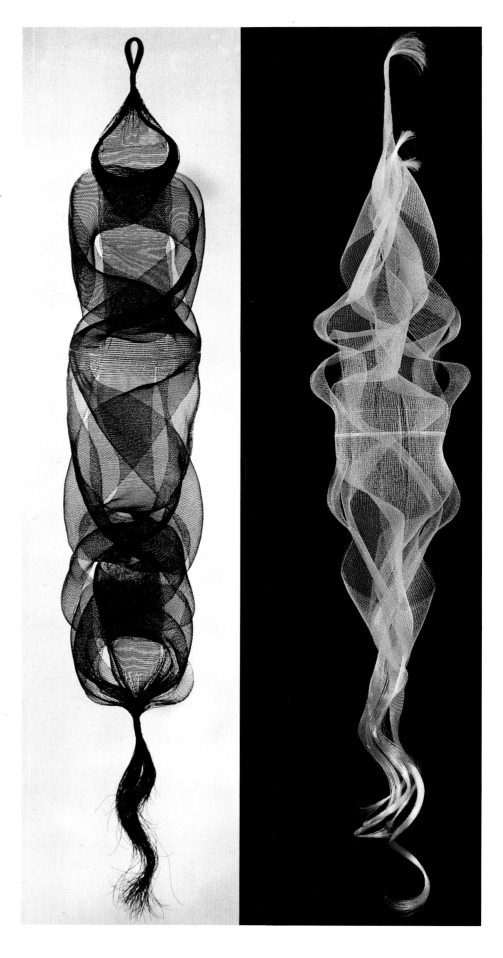

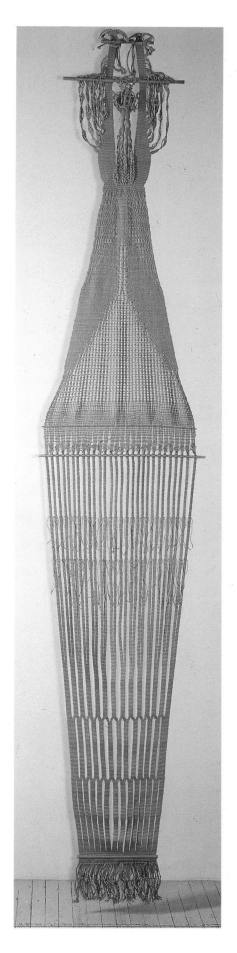
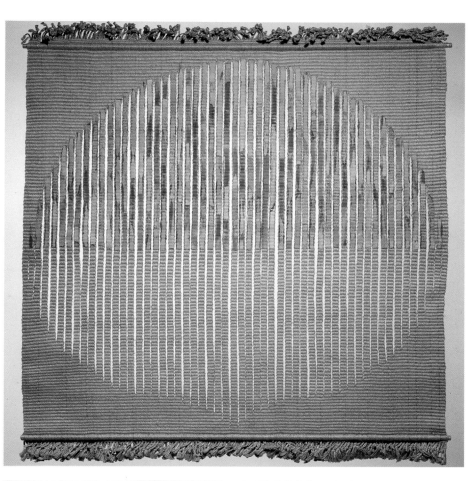
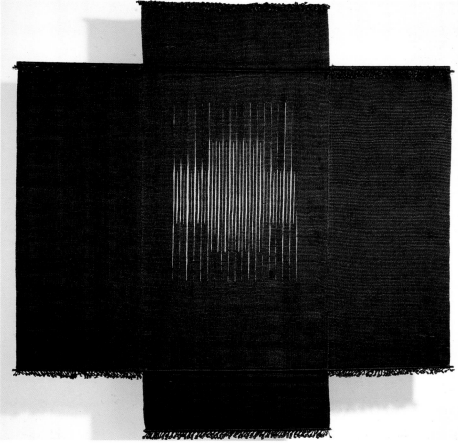

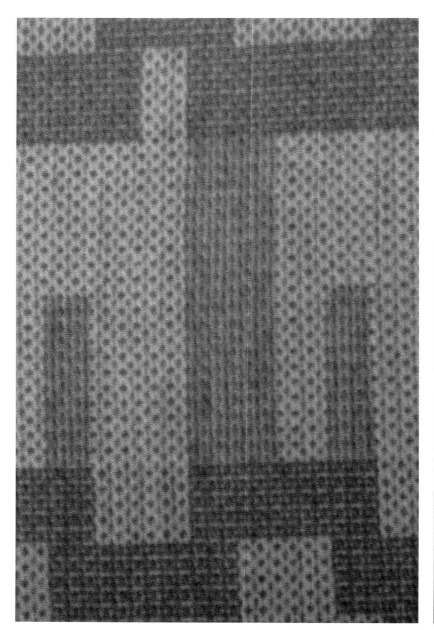

97, 98 Mies van der Rohe, familiar with Marli Ehrman's work for industry, commissioned her to design the curtains for his Lake Shore Drive Apartments in Chicago. *Above left* A fabric sample from her collection for the Raphael Company. *Above* A very similar utility fabric used as a chair covering.

99 *Opposite* This fabric sample by Ehrman was photographed by her friend Ray Pearson at the Chicago School of Design.

100, 101 *Opposite* Two examples of
upholstery fabrics woven by Else
Regensteiner and Julia McVicker and
marketed as fabric co-ordinates by their
studio, Reg/Wick Handwoven Originals.
Cotton, wool, novelty yarns and Lurex, 1948.

102 *Right* The Reg/Wick Studio specialized
in production handweaving as well as
designing for industry. Here is an example of
a leather and cotton upholstery fabric from
1949.

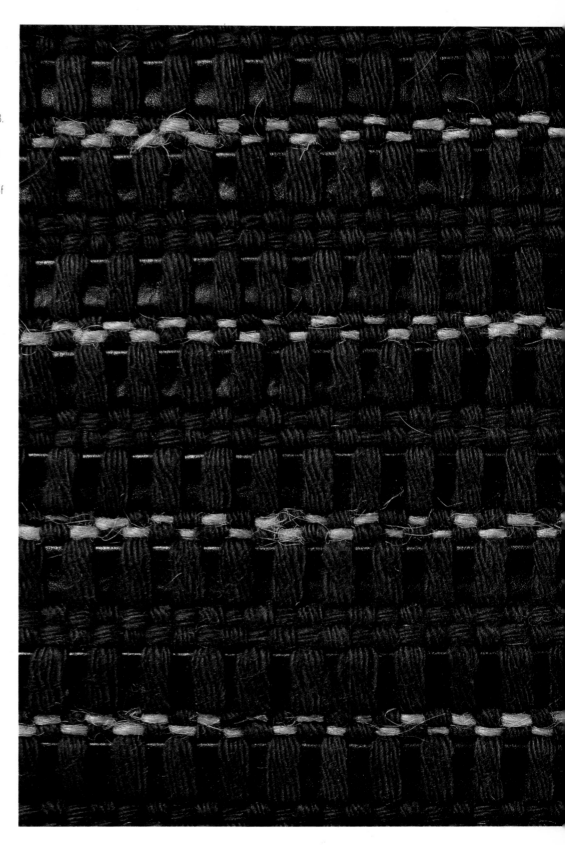

103 *Left* Angelo Testa was one of Marli Ehrman's star students and among the first graduates of the Chicago Institute of Design. *La Ligna*, a damask weave of cotton and rayon, dates from *c.* 1950.

105 *Below* Testa worked closely with interior designers and architects. His casement fabrics fulfilled the need to cover vast expanses of glass windows in modern high-rise interiors.

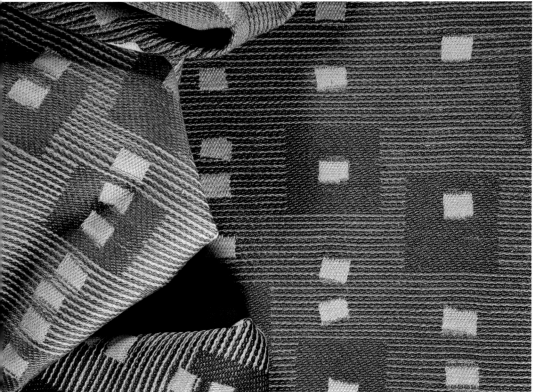

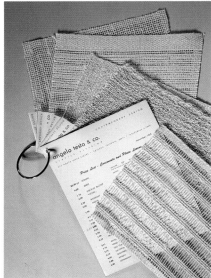

104 *Left* Like most of Testa's fabrics, *Times Square* is reversible. It is a damask weave of cotton and rayon from *c.* 1950.

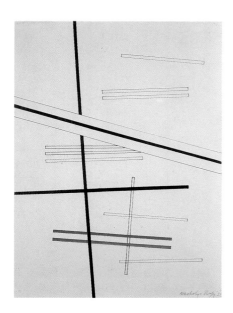

106, 107 Testa was an enthusiastic spokesperson for Bauhaus ideals and an admirer of his teacher László Moholy-Nagy, whose composition of 1923 in black and red ink on paper (*above*) might have been the inspiration for Testa's fabric *Bamboo Stripes* (*right*), a cotton and rayon damask of about 1950.

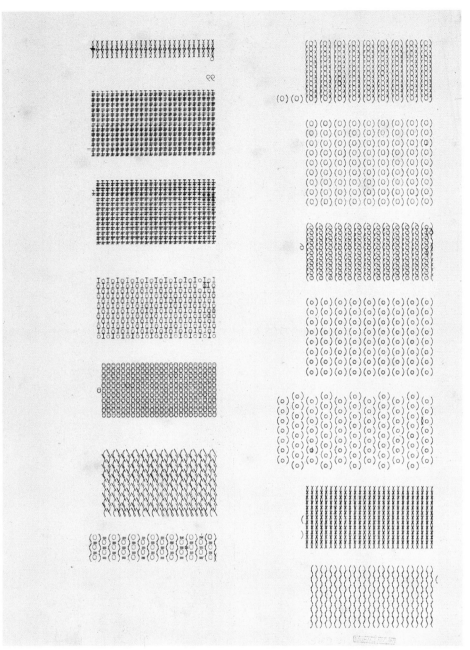

108 When Josef Albers taught at Black Mountain College, his student Ruth Asawa created this design, *Double Sheet* (*detail*, *above*), with a rubber stamp on newsprint in his design class.

109 In 1932, under Lilly Reich, the Weaving Workshop introduced print design. At that time Josef Albers was still at the Bauhaus. Katja and Hajo Rose's playful exercises on the typewriter (*right*) were later transformed into printed fabrics.

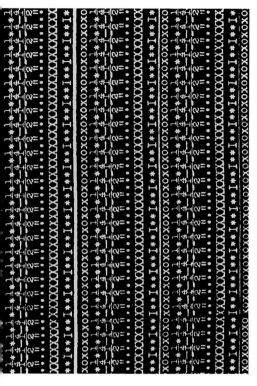

110 The effectiveness of typewriter patterns is evident in *Textile Fractions* (*detail, above*), a silk-screen printed cotton twill, designed by the Viennese-born architect and designer Bernard Rudofsky in 1948 and manufactured by Schiffer Prints, New York.

111 *Right* Alvin Lustig designed *Incantation*, a silk-screen printed fabric on plain linen weave, *c.* 1947. It was produced by Laverne Originals, New York.

112 *chromatic interlocking* is one in a series of nine tapestries by
Herbert Bayer, executed by the Nuremberg Gobelin Works in 1966.

113 Since World War II the Nuremberg Gobelin Works has woven a
number of tapestries based on designs by Bauhäusler, among them
Johannes Itten and Josef Albers. Here is Herbert Bayer's *chromatic
square with circle* of 1968.

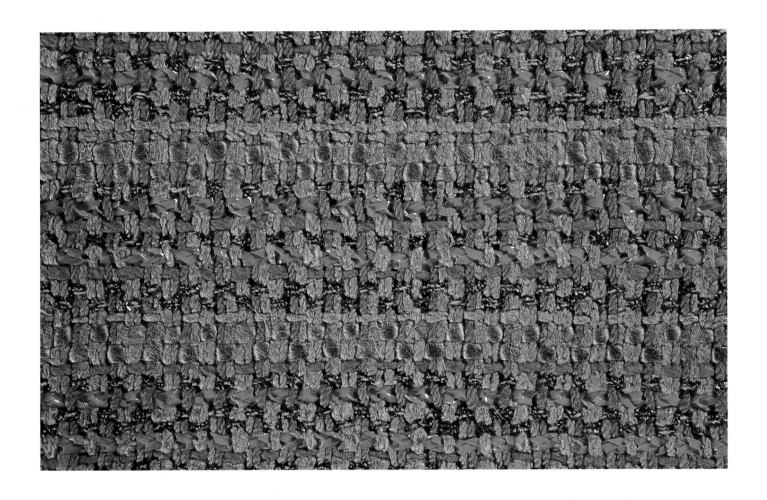

114–117 Dorothy Liebes utilized many Bauhaus innovations in her textiles: Cellophane, plastics, leather, Lurex and novelty yarns. These and her unusual colour combinations assured her a place as an important designer of contemporary American textiles. *Above* Novelty yarns and Cellophane, 1950s. *Left* An example of her rigid weft, 1950s. *Opposite* Unusual combinations of yarns and colours, not complexity of weave construction, are hallmarks of Liebes's designs.

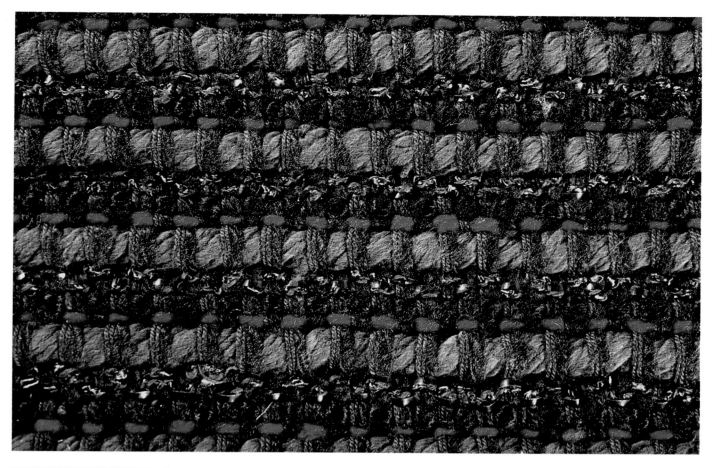

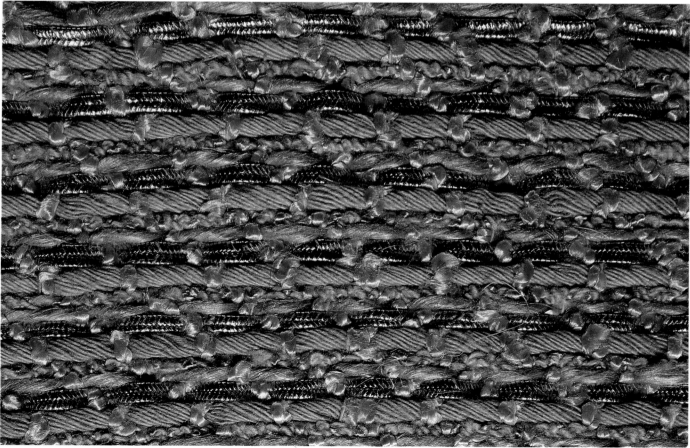

118 *Opposite* A hint of Lurex gives Dorothy Liebes's predictable plaid a lively sparkle.

119 *Right* The pulsating colours of Kroll's *Boogie-Woogie* and the arrangement of the grid is reminiscent of Piet Mondrian's *Broadway Boogie-Woogie*.

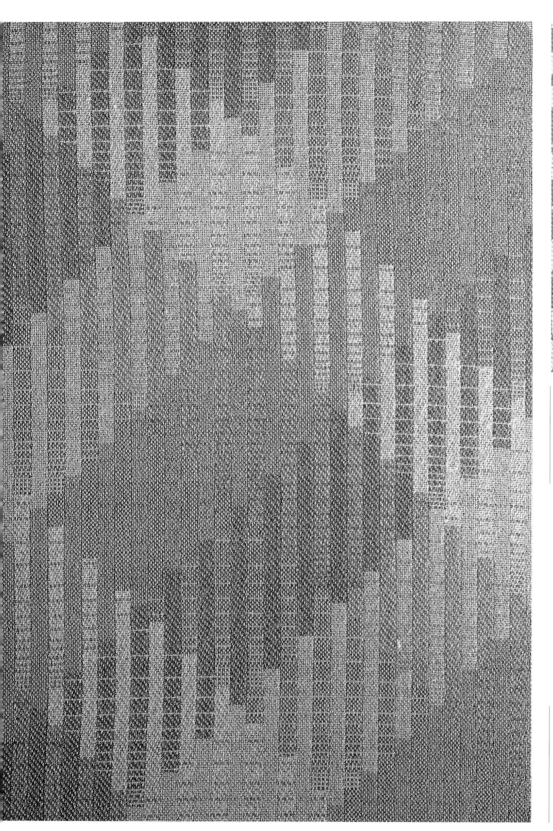

121 *Above* Anni Albers's design *Eclat* for Knoll Textiles was printed on 'Dorset', a 65 per cent cotton and 35 per cent linen fabric, available in twelve different colourways. It is interesting to compare this design to her screen print *GR I* (pl. 85).

120, 122 Boris Kroll was a great admirer of the Bauhaus and, in creating his own fabrics, payed hommage to several designers, acknowledging each by name. In *Channel Plaid* of 1980 (*left*) and *Ponte* of 1976 (*opposite*) he gave credit to the weavings of Anni Albers.

124, 125 Gertrud Arndt's wall hanging of 1927 (*above*) was the
inspiration for Boris Kroll's *Translucence* of 1982 (*right*), which
was manufactured in a variety of colourways.

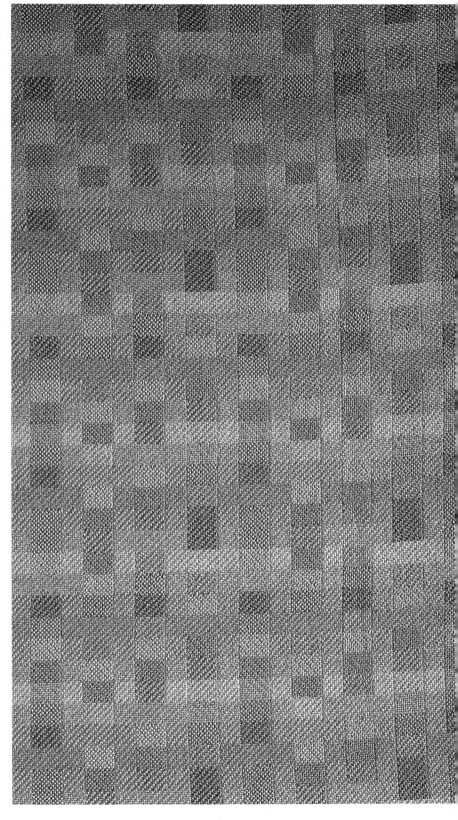

123 *Opposite* With *Gamut* Boris Kroll acknowledged the
Bauhaus painter Lyonel Feininger.

126 *Above* Jack Lenor Larsen's hangings of 1972 in the Sears Bank, Chicago, show the integration of architecture and textiles.

127 *Left* Larsen's *Anagram*, a Jacquard Wilton rug of 1985, has a strong Bauhaus flavour.

128 *Opposite* A utility textile in the best Bauhaus tradition and one of Larsen's best-selling fabrics is *BRNO*, aptly named after Mies van der Rohe's famous Tugendhat House.

129 In 1927 T. Lux Feininger photographed the weavers on the steps of the new Bauhaus building. From left going up the stairs: Léna Bergner; next to her: Grete Reichardt; centre: Gunta Stölzl; next to her: Ljuba Monastirsky; coming down: Otti Berger, Lis Beyer, Elisabeth Müller in the light sweater, Rosa Berger in the dark sweater, Ruth Hollós behind Lisbeth Oestreicher.

130 The Bauhaus staircase today in the restored Dessau building.

131 Roy Lichtenstein modelled his *Bauhaus Stairway* of 1988 on a painting of the same name by Oskar Schlemmer that was in turn based on Feininger's photo of the weavers.

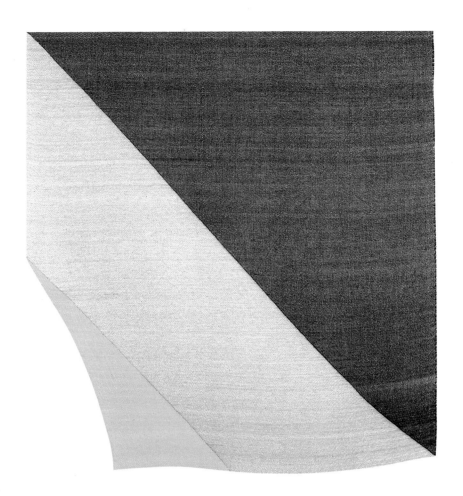

132, 133 Margot Rolf, a student of Greten Neter-Kähler and Kitty van der Mijll Dekker, succeeded the latter at the Gerrit Rietveld Academy in 1974 and continues the Bauhaus tradition in the Netherlands. Rolf's consummate craftsmanship, her carefully chosen colours and her deliberate distortions – seen here in *Smiling Square I* (*left*) and *Westwind* – startle the viewer into recognizing unexpected possibilities in geometric shapes.

chapter 11

a new frontier

Lore Kadden Lindenfeld in the Weaving
Studio at Black Mountain College, *c.* 1946.

The United States and the Bauhaus were linked by crosscurrents of ideas that had their genesis in events before World War I and continued until Hitler's rise to power. In 1910, when Frank Lloyd Wright visited Germany, he startled visitors to the Academy of Art in Berlin with his extraordinary architectural drawings. The effect of his work on an impressionable young Walter Gropius is well known. A similar encounter, but in reverse – the 1913 New York Armory Show – introduced many Americans for the first time to the European avant-garde. Among the exhibitors were the future Bauhaus master, Wassily Kandinsky, and a young American painter, already thoroughly conversant with Modernism, Katherine S. Dreier. She was also one of the first Americans to visit the Bauhaus.

Dreier was a complex person. She was a second-generation American fiercely loyal to her German roots, a suffragette, an artist and friend to the international avant-garde – her friendship with Marcel Duchamp lasted from 1916 until her death in 1952 – and an extremely astute collector. In 1920, with Duchamp and Man Ray, Dreier founded the Société Anonyme in New York, a group that aimed at introducing Americans to Modernism. It became one of the largest private art collections in the United States. Dreier maintained a studio in Paris and until the outbreak of World War II made annual trips to Europe, where she hobnobbed with the élite of contemporary art. When she visited the Weimar Bauhaus in 1922, she purchased works directly from Paul Klee and Wassily Kandinsky, then continued her shopping spree in Berlin at Herwarth Walden's Der Sturm gallery, where Gropius had encountered Moholy-Nagy's work. At the 'Erste Russische Kunstausstellung' a gouache by Liubov Popova, whom Dreier had identified in the catalogue's margin as a 'lady painter', cost her 62,500 Marks. A year later, at the height of the inflation, she bought Paul Klee's *Destruction and Hope* for 80,000 Marks.[2]

Through Dreier's visits the Bauhaus established valuable contacts with America long before Philip Johnson and Alfred H. Barr, Jr., 'discovered' the institution. In 1922 Kandinsky became honorary vice-president of the Société Anonyme which, a year later, gave him his first solo exhibition in the States, to be followed, in 1924, by one for Paul Klee. Dreier corresponded with several Bauhäusler, travelled with Lucia Moholy-Nagy and befriended the Hildebrandts, who remained on the periphery of the institution. She bought a painting from Lily and sent Hans a list of names for his book *Die Frau als Künstlerin*. Her attempts to get them a visa during the Nazi era, however, failed. In 1926 Dreier organized the Brooklyn Museum's 'International Exhibition of Modern Art', which opened in November with more than 300 works by 106 contemporary artists from 19 countries.[3] The accompanying catalogue carried a full-page advertisement for the

This full-page advertisement appeared in the catalogue for the 'International Exhibition of Modern Art' which was organized by Katherine S. Dreier and which took place at the Brooklyn Museum in 1926.

Bauhaus which would not have passed Gropius's scrutiny, had he seen it. It billed the school as an 'Academy of Arts and Krafts', a description that was anathema to the Bauhaus at any time, but even more so after its move to Dessau. It listed the Pottery Workshop, which no longer existed, Lothar Schreyer, who had left in 1923, and Georg Muche, who was form master of the Weaving Workshop and was not teaching architecture as the advertisement stated. The metamorphosis of 'craft' into the teutonic 'Kraft' not only changed the meaning – *Kraft* is power or strength in German – but is also evocative of later Nazi sloganeering. Dreier's pro-German sentiments rendered her curiously myopic to the unfolding events in Germany. Thus she viewed the 'Degenerate Art' exhibition as nothing more than typical government hostility toward modern art. Dreier's collection, however, chronicled like no other the American, European and Latin American avant-garde. She bought Constructivists, Cubists, Dadaists, Expressionists, Neoplasticists and Surrealists and was one of the few collectors to include women artists. She owned works by twenty-seven women and nine Bauhäusler. [4]

Dreier's connection to the Bauhaus continued through her nephew, Theodore Dreier, co-founder of Black Mountain College. When he consulted her about the hiring of Josef Albers, whom she had not met before, she was initially opposed to it. Later, she participated with Albers in college events and joint exhibitions. Dreier's commitment to Modernism never waned.

The Bauhaus had other influential contacts in the United States. As early as the Weimar years, the Gropiuses had befriended the American journalist Dorothy Thompson, who followed the development of the school with interest. As Berlin correspondent for the *New York Evening Post* she kept her American readers abreast of cultural and political events and had also reported on the opening of the Dessau Bauhaus. [5] She was enthusiastically supportive of progressive causes, and her apartment in Berlin became a salon for European literary and artistic circles. As 'one of the most influential political journalists in America – her name was known everywhere', [6] Thompson later sponsored a number of German refugees by providing affidavits, housing, clothing and monetary gifts. In 1939, on short-wave radio aimed at the German-American community, Joseph Goebbels denounced Thompson as 'an enemy of Germany'. [7]

One of the best contacts for Americans interested in contemporary German art was the art dealer J.B. Neumann. He sold art to both Alfred H. Barr, Jr., and Philip Johnson, who relied on his judgment, and all three visited those German galleries that he suggested. During their 1927 sojourn in Germany, Neumann proposed a stop-over at the Dessau Bauhaus. For Barr and Johnson the visit was akin to an epiphany. They met Gropius and most of the Bauhaus masters, sat in on classes and were especially bedazzled by the *Vorkurs* and Josef Albers's teaching methodology. Three years later Neumann accompanied Barr on his travels through Germany, assisting in the selection of art works for an exhibition to be held at the Museum of Modern Art. 1930 was also the year the 'Modern Wall Hanging' exhibition opened in his own gallery in Munich. The rise of Nazism put an end to Neumann's career in Germany but not in the United States, where, now an immigrant himself, he became director of the New Art Circle, a gallery in New York. As one of the few venues for geometric abstract art in the forties, this gallery also exhibited works by Josef Albers. Neumann remained a steadfast champion of Modernism. In 1944 he gave Katherine S. Dreier, with whom he had been acquainted since 1923, nine prints by German Expressionist artists for the Société's collection.[8] He became associated with Black Mountain College through its European faculty and gave a two-week course there on art appreciation during the summer session in 1945.[9]

While the interaction between a relatively small group of people with shared aesthetic values had been a source of pleasure before 1933, after the establishment of the Nazi regime it took on enormous political importance. One's career and, in too many cases, one's life depended on such contacts. Less than a month after the Bauhaus closed, Anni and Josef Albers, the first Bauhäusler to come to America, received, through Philip Johnson, the offer to teach at Black Mountain College. Donations from Museum of Modern Art trustees covered the Alberses' travel expenses and their salary for the first year. It was a leap of faith on the part of the college and a courageous move to transplant a prominent artist and teacher from a world-renowned institution in the German metropolis to a small, experimental, brand new school in the rural South. The Alberses had no idea where the school was located; moreover, Josef Albers knew no English. Norman Weston, a student, remembered the day of their arrival: 'Of course, they didn't have a hundred words of English between them, and Anni had most of those.'[10] The initial publicity focused on Anni Albers, simply because she was able to communicate in the limited English she had learned from a nanny as a girl. 'The tall, slim and vivacious Frau Albers looks more like a student than the leader of a movement,' wrote the *New York Sun* in December 1933, 'and speaks English slowly and solemnly, much as a child recites a poem "by heart".' The paper heralded 'Frau Anni Albers, [as] one of the foremost designers of textiles in Europe and a leader in the movement started by the famous Bauhaus in Dessau, Germany, to revive the art of textile weaving.'[11] At Black Mountain, Anni Albers became her husband's spokesperson and also translated in his classes until his own English improved. Both embraced their new community – 'we liked it from the start'[12] – and both contributed to the reputation of Black Mountain College as a creative force in American arts. 'Under Josef Albers', wrote Mary Emma Harris, 'Black Mountain became a spiritual heir to and center for the transmission of Bauhaus ideas.'[13]

Unlike the Bauhaus, whose mission it had been to better society through the integration of art and design, Black Mountain College had no defined role for the artist. As a liberal arts college, it recognized the arts as central to the individual, enhancing all experiences. For M.C. Richards, who taught English, there was 'a co-presence as it were, the availability of the arts, the participation in the act of making, the inter-relationship of the arts' as well as 'a three-fold approach to life and learning: the studio arts, the intellectual disciplines and community work, which not only changed my life but began to form the foundation toward a philosophy of wholeness.'[14] For these reasons Black Mountain attracted an outstanding faculty and an equally committed student body, one of the many similarities between the two institutions. There were others.

Black Mountain College was founded in 1933, at a time of great uncertainty. 'Outside was the world I came from, a tangle of hopelessness, of undirected energy, of cross purposes. Inside here . . . was confusion, too, I thought, but certainly not hopelessness or aimlessness, rather exuberance with its own kind of confusion.'[15] This description sums up the Europe Anni Albers left behind and the community she was now embracing, but she was talking about neither, she was describing her arrival at the Bauhaus a decade earlier. Like the German institution Black Mountain was a progressive co-educational school with a strong emphasis on community, it provided an alternative to entrenched academia, and was committed to self-directed studies as the only way to prepare young people for adult life. Bauhaus students took their examinations before the guilds, Black Mountain students were tested by outside examiners. Both institutions were havens for the intellectually and spiritually curious. Both embraced diversity, Black Mountain by hiring an unprecedented number of foreign refugees – 'the splendid offerings that Hitler gave the New World'[16] – and, as a southern institution at the height of segregation, by addressing the issue of racism. Although apolitical, Black Mountain, like the Bauhaus, was perceived as too liberal, radical and even Communist. It experienced the same chronic financial shortages. And, as is inevitable in a group of strong-willed personalities, there were cliques and factionalism. What Otti Berger said of the Bauhaus – 'we moderns felt rather important inside its cloistered walls'[17] – was equally true of Black Mountain College.

The opportunity to teach in and direct the Weaving Workshop at Black Mountain College launched Anni Albers's career. After her graduation from the Bauhaus she had continued to weave at home but, unlike Otti Berger, Margaret Leischner, Benita Otte and a host of other weavers now firmly ensconced in jobs in industry or teaching, Anni Albers was not involved in either. She was not, as the *New York Sun* called her twice, 'the leader of a movement'. She would only become that in America.

Hampered initially by a lack of facilities, Albers began her teaching at Black Mountain by assigning preliminary weaving studies made from found objects. A direct continuation of the Bauhaus *Vorkurs*, these exercises sensitized students to the material and the possibilities inherent in the structure of woven surfaces. Albers encouraged playful exploration, the kind she had enjoyed during her own student days, but she also believed in teaching sound technical skills. She emphasized weave construction, fibre identification, incorporation, not superimposition, of plastics, metals and other materials and finishes, and familiarity with the latest research in textiles. Although students wove and sold functional items, such as apparel fabric, table-cloths, place-mats and curtains – the Weaving Workshop at Black Mountain became self-supporting – formal projects involved textiles for aeroplanes, public halls, dormitories and the stage. The hand loom was to be the designer's tool. 'One of the areas that was stressed was not to become a craftsman but to be a person who would influence the larger scope of

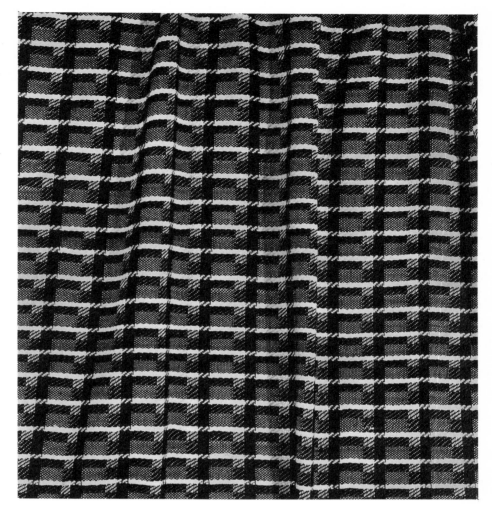

The Workshop at Black Mountain College became self-supporting. This is an example of the functional fabrics woven in the studio. It is clearly visible on Kadden Lindenfeld's loom on page 161.

design, and primarily in industry. Anni Albers was an exceptional teacher in that she had a totally intellectual approach and she was very articulate.'[18] She shared with her husband a reputation for sound pedagogical principles and discipline, a well-defined, sometimes inflexible, point of view and a certain remoteness, no doubt the result of cultural differences. Nevertheless, she invited young people to her house at night for stimulating discussions,[19] which made them 'conscious of the fact that Black Mountain was also a meeting point of European and American avant-garde thinking'.[20] She could be blunt and tell a student that 'six weeks in the summer is not enough to learn weaving', so that Ruth Asawa, now a prominent artist in San Francisco, enrolled instead in Josef Albers's design course. It not only lengthened her intended summer course into three years at Black Mountain College, but also changed her future.[21]

Acculturation, mastering a new language, teaching and the duties and pleasures of communal life did not prevent Anni Albers from embarking on a multifaceted, rich professional path. A watershed for the Alberses was a trip to Mexico in 1936. It was the first of more than a dozen visits to the Southwest, Central America and Mexico, where they would later spend two sabbatical leaves. The discovery of pre-Columbian art affected them deeply and in very different ways. As a technician and as an artist, Anni Albers experienced a close kinship with the weavers of Mexico and ancient Peru. Their work affirmed her own inclinations toward complexity of construction and clarity of design,[22] which is evident in all of her undertakings. As a highly intellectual person, she was blessed with the gift of conveying her message, whether in weaving, teaching or writing, by distilling it into its essence. She was suspicious of obfuscation in design – 'the original characteristics may be diluted by some additional ones that might counteract them' – and in expression: 'If you try to speak or write clearly, you are thought to lack profundity; while the impenetrable verbiage of today's writing on art, for instance, is respected for the very reason, I suspect, that it is beyond understanding and therefore is believed to be too highly advanced for the unassuming reader's grasp. Simplicity', she wrote, 'is not simpleness but clarified vision.'[23]

Despite Black Mountain's geographic isolation it attracted painters, writers, musicians and dancers. Like her husband, Anni Albers was very much at the centre of artistic life. Occasional travels, the only luxury she afforded herself, not only widened her circle of acquaintances but introduced her to her new country. In 1937, the year she enthusiastically embraced American citizenship, Albers showed her work in Chicago, lectured to women's groups and assisted in assembling material, including her own, for the 1938 Bauhaus Exhibition at the Museum of Modern Art. She also contributed an essay on the Bauhaus Weaving Workshop to the catalogue. Although the exhibition did not represent the history of the institution in its entirety – it ended with Gropius's departure in 1928 – public awareness and recognition of what has become known as the International Style can be dated to this event. For Anni Albers it marked her long association with the Museum of Modern Art, which began with Barr's and Johnson's visits to Germany in 1927 and has continued to the present. In 1944 she directed a seminar on textile design and in 1949 the Museum gave her – the first weaver ever – a solo show. She advised her friend Edgar Kaufmann, Jr., director of the Department of Industrial Design, on the 'Good Design' exhibitions, which were held every year between 1950 and 1955 and which were instrumental in fostering awareness of design aesthetics. Sponsored jointly by the Museum and the Chicago Merchandise Mart, they reached audiences in New York and the Midwest, as well as in Europe, Latin America and Asia. Over the years, Albers served as juror for a number of exhibitions. In 1969, when, in response to the emerging fiber arts, the Museum of Modern Art mounted its important 'Wall Hangings' exhibition, it 'revised' its 'concept of this craft . . . to view the work within the context of twentieth-century art.'[24] Although neither Gunta Stölzl's nor Anni Albers's works bore any resemblance to the other pieces, their inclusion in the show acknowledged the weavings as pioneering breakthroughs in the field. This respect for the two weavers has never waned. In 1990 the Museum of Modern Art honoured Stölzl's and Albers's 'creative experiments in material, structure, and color'[25] by displaying their fabrics from its permanent collection.

Like no other European weaver – and there were a number who contributed immeasurably to American textile design – Anni Albers's rapid rise to pre-eminence was reinforced by her visibility as a writer. From the Industrial

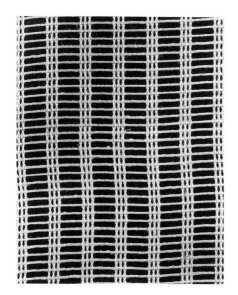

Anni Albers's linen casement fabric, *Rail*, was designed for Knoll International.

Revolution to the 1930s, handweaving languished in the United States. Although practised in some rural areas as a means to improve the standard of living, it was hardly more than physical therapy or the occasional hobby. This changed with the arrival of European refugees, and by the forties and fifties handweaving as an avocation was becoming increasingly popular. Handweavers' guilds – not to be confused with their professional European counterparts – proliferated across the country as a means of contact between interested weavers. Weaving rapidly developed into an exhilarating pastime tied mainly to the nostalgia of recreating traditional patterns. With few exceptions, married, middle-class women formed the backbone of this burgeoning movement, since they had the time and the financial resources to afford looms, materials, instruction and study trips. Although most were college-educated, few had formal backgrounds in the visual arts or design, a possible reason for the general animosity toward contemporary weaving. The European weavers' professional attitude and intellectual inquisitiveness were puzzling to their American counterparts. As early as 1928, the year Walter Gropius visited the States for the first time, he remarked that 'intellectual collaboration between American men and women was unknown.'[26] In the forties Anni Albers was a generation ahead and, while she was respected among peers, her writings and lectures could create quite a stir among amateur weavers. Nevertheless, she was instrumental in stimulating national discussion about the role of weaving.

In a particularly controversial article in *The Weaver* in 1941 – 'Handweaving Today – Textile Work at Black Mountain College' – she explored weaving and industry and weaving as art, as a leisure-time occupation 'and as a source of income in rural communities.'[27] The response was astounding. The sheer quantity and emotional outpouring of readers' letters prompted the magazine to allot Mary M. Atwater space for a rebuttal entitled 'It's Pretty – But Is It Art?'. Atwater, a respected handweaver and as prolific a writer as Anni Albers, was the originator of the 'Shuttle Craft Guild Bulletin', a home weaving study course, with which she reached a wide audience of weavers. She also authored the *Shuttle Craft Book of American Handweaving*, a 'recipe' book of patterns with threading and treadling instructions which has become a standard work. Widowed, with some training in art but none in weaving, she made the latter her livelihood. She operated her business from her home and became a sought-after, popular workshop leader on the guild circuit. A conservative traditionalist, she firmly linked weaving to its American roots by expanding on the endless varieties of coverlet patterns. The concept of connecting weaving to industry, to architecture or art, or to the philosophies of Kandinsky and Klee was literally foreign to her. Unencumbered by the background Anni Albers brought to her writing, Atwater issued authoritative and categorical statements which must have reassured many a bewildered reader. Thus she summed up 'Mrs. Albers' opinion as expressed in her article: (1) the making of ''models'' for industry – I fancy industry would consider this a big joke! – (2) for some rather vague ''educational'' value, and (3) for profit or money. None of these things appear to me to be the ''why'' of handweaving – today or any day.' For Atwater, the matter was straightforward:

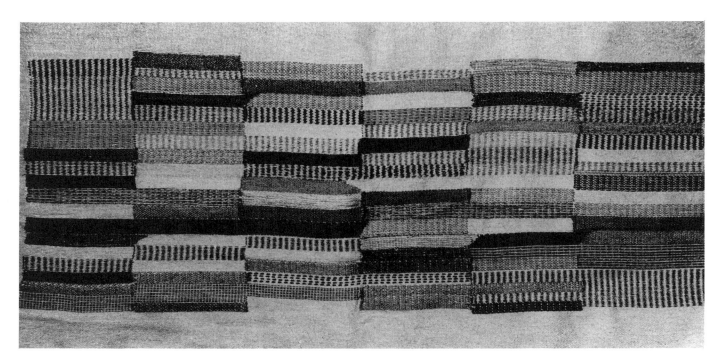

Anni Albers wove this untitled wall hanging in 1934, soon after her arrival at Black Mountain College.

'essentially we weave because we like to do it, and in a secondary way, because we like to have our own beautiful textiles, made with our own hands, for the greater comfort and seemliness of our lives.'[28]

By the late forties the published discourse on weaving was reaching a more elevated plane. The field still accommodated the nostalgia of amateurs but an increasing number of professionals addressed the present and anticipated the future. The 'Good Design' exhibitions – the first opened in Chicago in January 1950 – 'considered only progressive design: evocations of the past are not eligible.'[29] More than 150 exhibitors working in the home furnishings field responded to the challenge and generated tremendous excitement regarding handwoven textiles. Not a year passed without a major exhibition or competition.[30] Events spanned the entire country, from the West Coast to the East Coast. A regular column in *Handweaver & Craftsman* was simply entitled 'Covering the Exhibition Circuit'. Even an incomplete roster of jurors for these events reveals distinguished names from all areas of design.[31] Announcements and reviews of textile shows appeared routinely alongside fine arts events and revealed a strong European presence.

Architecture was not a part of the Black Mountain curriculum, but Anni Albers continued to explore its relationship with textiles. Like Gottfried Semper, the eminent nineteenth-century theoretician, she believed that weaving and architecture are historically linked, that 'the pliable plane' preceded the solid walls of buildings. She saw affinities between the construction and structure of textiles and the erection of buildings. Her abiding interest in the subject was grounded in her education at the Weaving Workshop, her exposure to the theories of the Bauhaus architects, her collaboration with Hannes Meyer and admiration for Mies van der Rohe, as well as her interest in archaeological discoveries. Architecture and textiles became a recurrent theme in her writings which promoted a reorientation among American textile designers. Prestigious magazines such as *Art and Architecture* gave textiles serious consideration, not least because Anni Albers took every opportunity to remind designers 'that textiles for interior use can be regarded as architectural elements.'[32] By pointing to historical connections – the tents of nomads or medieval tapestries as movable walls – yet brilliantly articulating the demands of Modernism, Albers gained the respect of architects and designers alike. 'Instead of decorative additaments [sic]' she advocated textiles as 'a counterpart to solid walls.'[33] Albers's writing on textiles and architecture coincided with the expansion of Modernism in America, the period from the thirties to the sixties. Four other influential lay critics, Catherine Bauer, Jane Jacobs, Sybil Moholy-Nagy and Ada Louise Huxtable, wrote at the same time and shared 'certain characteristics: besides being female, all have wielded an impressive amount of influence . . . through writing and related activities. Many of their articles have appeared in professional

The *Magazine of Art* carried a page of exhibition announcements in February 1949. It attests to a happy co-existence of fine and 'Everyday Art'. Marli Ehrman and her students Else Regensteiner, Julia McVicker ('reg/wick') and Angelo Testa are represented as well as Anni Albers's student Lore Kadden Lindenfeld.

in the everyday art gallery

modern textiles

135 hand-made and machine made fabrics are now being shown in the Everyday Art Gallery. Represented in this comprehensive exhibition of MODERN TEXTILES are the following designers, weavers, and textile mills from all over the country:

designers and weavers

Ruth Adler, hand prints; Ben Boldwin, hand prints; Michael L. Belangie, woven fabrics produced by Menlo Textiles; Arthur Brill, woven fabrics produced by Golding Decorative Fabrics; Frannie Dressel, hand prints; Marli Ehrman, hand woven fabrics; Elenhank Designers, hand prints; Ann Franke, woven fabrics produced by Fife Fabrics and Cohn-Hall-Marx; Lillian Garrett, woven fabrics produced by Louisville Textiles; Alexander Girard, hand prints; June Groff, hand prints; Ernest Haeckel, hand woven fabrics; Lore Kadden, hand woven fabrics; Ray Komei, prints produced by Laverne Originals; Estelle & Erwine Laverne, prints produced by Laverne Originals; Dorothy Liebes, woven fabrics produced by Goodall Fabrics; Stig Lindberg, prints produced by Knoll Associates; Alvin Lustig, prints produced by Laverne Originals; Alix & Warren Mackenzie, hand prints; Paeter & Wells, hand prints; Shirle Rapson, prints produced by Knoll Associates; Naomi Raymond, prints produced by Knoll Associates; Reg-Wick (Regensteiner & McVicker), hand woven fabrics; Ben Rose, hand prints; Robert Sailors, hand woven and power loomed fabrics; Don Smith, prints produced by Walter & Co.; Marianne Strengell, hand woven and power loomed fabrics and prints for Knoll Associates; Angelo Testa, hand prints; Henning Watterston, woven fabrics produced by Henod Textiles and Menlo Textiles.

mills and distributors

Celanese Corporation of America, Arundell Clarke, Don Cooper, Cohn-Hall-Marx, Dan River Mills, Fife Fabrics, Goley & Lord, Golding Decorative Fabrics, Goodall Fabrics, Henod Textiles, Itosca Fabrics, Knoll Associates, Laverne Originals, Louisville Textiles, Manart Textile Co., Menlo Textiles, Thortel Fireproof Fabrics, D. N. & E. Walter & Co.

modern textiles will be shown through march 27

made in minnesota

MADE IN MINNESOTA, an exhibition of modern consumer goods of fine design being manufactured in the state today, will be held here from June to October of 1949. A survey is now being conducted by the Walker Art Center to discover available well-designed products. The exhibition will feature household equipment of all kinds: furniture, decorative objects, toys, sporting goods, and many other products. Manufacturers are requested to submit photographs and drawings for consideration and selection in this design survey. MADE IN MINNESOTA is one of the important events celebrating the Minnesota Centennial.

minnesota art activities

paul burlin

During the month of January, an exhibition of the paintings and drawings of PAUL BURLIN was held at the University Gallery. Mr. Burlin is conducting classes in painting for advanced students at the University of Minnesota during the winter quarter. He is the first of a series of Visiting Artists in the Department of Fine Arts. Paul Burlin participated in the historic Armory Show of 1913, and has received notable recognition as a painter. His paintings are represented in the collections of a number of museums, including the Whitney Museum of American Art, The Museum of Modern Art, the Denver Art Museum, and many private collections.

YOUNG MAN ALONE WITH HIS FACE by Paul Burlin

collection of the Whitney Museum

max beckmann

The first comprehensive exhibition in this country of the work of MAX BECKMANN, outstanding German Expressionist painter, is currently being shown at the Minneapolis Institute of Arts. The exhibition was organized and circulated by the St. Louis City Art Museum under the direction of Perry T. Rathbone, who spoke at the opening of the exhibition in Minneapolis. Mr. Beckmann, who recently arrived in the United States, is now Artist-in-Residence at Washington University in St. Louis. The development and scope of forty years of Beckmann's work are presented in 150 oils, drawings, watercolors, and prints in this retrospective exhibition, which may be seen through February 17.

MAX BECKMANN at the preview of his exhibition in Minneapolis

In 1947 Anni Albers created this gouache entitled *Knot II*.

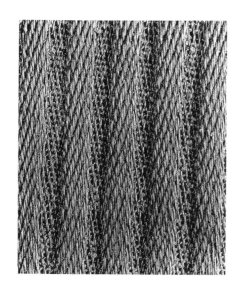

This is an example of a structural fabric. It was designed by Anni Albers in the late forties.

architectural journals; some almost exclusively so.'[34] This assessment is applicable to Albers as well. In 1961 the American Institute of Architects honoured Anni Albers with its gold medal in craftsmanship.

The Alberses left Black Mountain College in 1949 and a year later Josef Albers began his long association with Yale University in New Haven, Connecticut. During the next decades Anni Albers, now freed from the constraints of academic duties, became involved in a great variety of activities. Individual and group exhibitions featured her work, her books and articles introduced broad audiences to new ideas, she received requests to conduct seminars, to teach and consult, and she designed prototypes for industry. Yet she always found time to pursue her art. Soon after her arrival at Black Mountain, Anni Albers executed a small untitled wall hanging which was a departure from her crisp, hard-edged work in Germany. Although still geometric, it has a tactile quality that invites touching, a reflection, possibly, of her rustic, rural environment. An expansion, a looseness, is also evident in a gouache of 1947, *Knot II*. Like the primal element in all weaving, the intertwined lines express interconnection as much as individuality, fusion as much as freedom, a coming together in open-endedness. Albers worked on a series of weavings which she categorized as 'pictorial'. Neither architectural elements nor prototypes for designs, they are individual works of art, to be displayed framed or mounted on a rigid backing. Although the style of these pictorial weavings is uniquely that of Anni Albers, the technique was developed in the Weaving Workshop. The Bauhaus weavers considered the move away from traditional tapestries with their invisible warp, toward equality of warp and weft to be one of their early breakthroughs. A representative example is Else Mögelin's *Red Deer* of 1929 (pl. 76), a hanging of restrained elegance and beautiful proportions. One can argue that hers, too, is a pictorial hanging. In each case, Mögelin's and Albers's, the possibilities of woven expression are enriched by the artists' innovative and personal styles. This is evident in Anni Albers's *Black-White-Gold I* of 1950 (pl. 86), *Open Letter* of 1958 and *Intersecting* of 1962 (pl. 87). Although seemingly simple, they are complex constructions in which every individual thread has been assigned to carry a message. Parts of the surface appear to be floating, conveying both flatness and dimensionality. These are cryptic works which strike a chord in the viewer. Reminiscent of runic scripts, of ancient writings in the collective unconscious, they are at once mysterious and universal.

Thirty years after her arrival in the United States Anni Albers experienced yet another major change. She discovered for herself an entirely new medium, print-making. At the Tamarind Lithography Workshop in Los Angeles, where 'as a useless wife, I was just hanging around',[35] Albers was prodded by June Wayne, the director, to try her hand at lithography. A fellowship a year later set her on the course that would make her abandon weaving – she gave away her looms in 1970 – and fulfil her creative energy in a new way. Her lithographs and later screen prints suggest patterns on graph paper. Only upon closer scrutiny does one recognize the spatial ambiguity and the absence of patterned repetition. Can one discern the echo of the figure-ground, light-dark emphasis of the *Vorkurs*? Is there

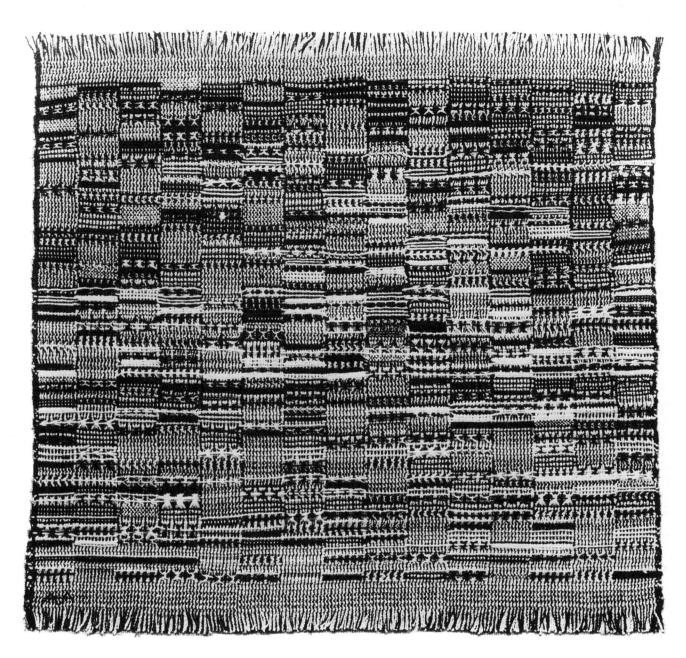

Open Letter, a pictorial weaving by Anni Albers, was executed in 1958.

a memory of Paul Klee's abstract shapes? Anni Albers is not effusive – 'people tell me that my graphic work reminds them of weaving. I can't see it, of course, because I am too near to it'[36] – and neither is her graphic art. It shares with her weaving the self-effacing qualities she associated with good design. Albers derived tremendous satisfaction from print-making. It gave her the freedom of expression she had yearned for as a young woman, the opportunity she had hoped to find at the Bauhaus when she entered it in search of art. Once there, she discovered that 'when the work is made with threads, it's considered a craft; when it's on paper, it's considered art.'[37] In America Anni Albers had the chance to lay the groundwork for the release of textiles from the prison of rigid, preconceived functions and the move toward the multiplicity of expression that would occur in the seventies. In opening eyes and minds Anni Albers led the way.

chapter 12

the legacy

In her final weaving (pl. 90), a red, white and blue hanging with insertions of the American flag – *Mandy's Motto* – Trude Guermonprez paid tribute to her adopted country and its folk wisdom. The use of graphics is only one aspect of Guermonprez's avant-garde creativity. This work is symbolic of much more. It is a leitmotif, a summation of the odysseys forced on European Jews and intellectuals by the Hitler regime, of personal and political suffering, but also of hope and trust in new beginnings.

> *The wind don't blow one way all the time.*
>
> MANDY[1]

Marli Ehrman at the Institute of Design in Chicago, *c.* 1945.

When Trude Jalowetz Guermonprez arrived at Black Mountain College in 1947, she did not know that it would become for her, no longer a refugee, what it had been to her family and others: a gateway to a new life. In 1933 Guermonprez went to the Netherlands, her parents and sister to America and Black Mountain College. Neither knew the whereabouts of the other during the War, which Guermonprez spent in hiding. Her marriage to Paul Guermonprez, a resistance fighter, ended tragically when he was executed by the Nazis. The strength to overcome such adversity and to prosper in spite of it, she attributed to 'the deeper values and sensitivities [that] came from a parental home where all forms of art were an integral part of life.'[2] Now, after the sudden death of her father, Heinrich Jalowetz, a musicologist and conductor and a beloved presence at Black Mountain College, she had come for a visit. Anni Albers, about to take sabbatical leave, could not have hoped for a better replacement and asked Guermonprez to stay. Trained at Burg Giebichenstein in Halle under Bauhäusler Benita Otte and Gerhard Marcks and at the School of Textile Engineering in Berlin, Guermonprez embodied Bauhaus ideals. In the Netherlands she had worked as a production handweaver, a free-lance designer and as head of the design department at Het Paapje Company. Two grants, one before and one after the War, took her to Scandinavia, where she studied indigenous weaving techniques. Instead of returning to Europe, she agreed to step in for Anni Albers. She never went back but stayed as a consultant in weaving and, in 1948, joined the faculty of Black Mountain College.

It is clear from the accounts of her students that Guermonprez 'was simply extraordinary as a teacher. She had a special gift of making the process of weaving logical.' Lore Kadden Lindenfeld relates that Guermonprez more than Albers – 'Albers's concern was with the development of ideas, not with small details' – would explain weave constructions in such a way that they became totally clear and could be taken into other directions. 'I learned from her how to think independently.' Lindenfeld and Guermonprez were close in age and developed a special bond. They shared not only the experience of the refugee but an appreciation of the opportunity to begin anew. 'I certainly wish I had not lived through that time in Germany and been uprooted; to suddenly find myself where

nobody knows you and nobody has been waiting for you either. But on the other hand, I had the chance to study at Black Mountain College, I had the support of people here, and Trude, too, was appreciated. She became a very honoured member of the profession. Sometimes, the difficult things that happen make you really want to do something with your life. I don't know about another country — but here, we were able to do that.'[3]

Albers and Guermonprez intended to expand the programme at Black Mountain to include production weaving, in which they were experts. It never came to fruition since both left in 1949. Yet each designed prototypes for industry and so did their student, Lore Kadden Lindenfeld, who graduated from the college in August 1948. Marli Ehrman, her outside examiner, required five papers, a four-hour oral examination on questions of weave construction, colour and design, and an exhibition of her work. Lindenfeld's achievements were close to the expectations of the original Bauhaus Weaving Workshop, where Ehrman herself had taken a similar examination in the twenties: 'her woven fabrics, samples, and larger pieces are proof of her thorough knowledge of fabric construction, of the design elements involved, and of her clear thinking in planning and creating new materials. Her craftsmanship is excellent. Her intelligent theoretical studies, her great interest in experimentation, and her intense effort in finding new solutions have given her an unusual understanding in her chosen field.'[4]

Lindenfeld was one of the first women in the United States to work for industry, and was especially unusual in her desire to learn all the technical processes. In 1950 *Mademoiselle* published an article on job opportunities for textile designers: 'Another woolen house, Forstmann, has a young woman, Lore Kadden, who learned weaving from Anni Albers at Black Mountain College. . . . Once in, she asked and received permission to take the training program for young male

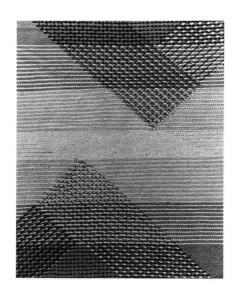

In addition to designing functional fabrics, Lore Kadden Lindenfeld has woven individual tapestries, such as *Reflection II*.

employees – which teaches trainees what happens to wool between sheep's back and customer's. Five days a week she treks out to the mill . . . Saturdays she shops the Fifth Avenue windows, visits galleries and museums.'[5] Lindenfeld not only designed for Forstmann but also for Herbert Meyer, John Walther Fabrics and Kanmak Textiles. Like Anni Albers and Trude Guermonprez, her versatility as an artist and designer is in the true Bauhaus tradition. From fabrics for mass production to individual hangings, she has expressed herself in new materials and forms. She has taught, published, lectured and brought the textile traditions of other cultures, especially those of Japan, to the attention of wide audiences.

When Trude Guermonprez left Black Mountain in 1949, she exchanged the exquisite mountains of North Carolina for the equally spectacular valley of Armstrong Forest near Guerneville, California. It is hard to imagine that these two remote rural communities had become gathering places for displaced Bauhäusler. Pond Farm, like Black Mountain, but on a more intimate scale, was home to refugee artists, and Guermonprez was eager to accept an invitation from Marguerite Wildenhain, a friend since Guermonprez's student days at Burg Giebichenstein in Germany. In 1933 the municipal authorities in Halle dismissed Wildenhain, a Jew, from her position as director of the Pottery Workshop. There was strong protest from the faculty and from Gerhard Marcks, a former master at the Weimar Bauhaus and the director of the school. In retaliation against this courageous move, the institution was forced to divest itself of all former Bauhäusler, including Benita Otte, the head of the Weaving Department. Wildenhain fled to neutral Putten, a small Dutch town, where, with her husband Frans Wildenhain, she set up a pottery studio. Their work not only gained them individual recognition but also won their host country second prize in the 1937 World Exhibition in Paris. As Wildenhain's life was threatened once again, she received an offer for a position in America from Gordon Herr, a California architect. She was able to leave the Netherlands in 1940; her husband was denied a visa.

Gordon Herr had journeyed to Europe in 1939 in search of like-minded participants for a community of artists that he and his wife Jane, a writer, were planning to establish. When Wildenhain arrived, Pond Farm was no more than a dream, and the War years were difficult, even in safe California. Together with the Herrs she remodelled an old barn into studio space, while single-handedly building her own house. By 1949, Herr's signature building, the Hexagon House, had been completed and Pond Farm became a viable school and community. It was the year Trude Guermonprez joined the core faculty. The teaching methodology at Pond Farm was consciously modelled on Bauhaus precepts, since Wildenhain shared Gropius's belief that art cannot be taught except by total immersion. Not surprisingly, the school also adopted another Bauhaus tenet, the close relationship between craft, design and architecture. For Guermonprez, the years at Pond Farm were rewarding. She firmly established her professional reputation as an outstanding teacher and innovative weaver. Her personal life was enriched by John Elsesser, an architect-builder, whom she married in 1951. Pond Farm, although short-lived, was of major importance to the arts in

California. Like the Bauhaus and Black Mountain it had pursued noble goals and in so doing had captured the imagination of a new generation. Its closure in 1953 was caused partly by the death of Jane Herr, the unifying force among so many disparate people, and partly by conflicts endemic to educational experiments. 'In the end,' wrote Tim Tivoli Steele, the grandson of Pond Farm's founders, 'the trait that all the artists had relied on to survive the War and follow their visions – the strength of their personalities – would also contribute to the demise of the Workshops. . . . The years of hell had hardened their tendencies to never give in. . . . Marguerite Wildenhain and Trude Guermonprez also had been forced to defend their roles in the Bauhaus movement, which was derided by the Nazis as ''degenerate'' and ''Jewish-Bolshevist''.'[6]

After a teaching stint at the San Francisco Art Institute, Trude Guermonprez joined the faculty of the California College of Arts and Crafts in 1952. From 1960 until her death in 1976 she chaired its Weaving Department. As Kay Sekimachi, today one of California's most distinguished fiber artists, relates, all her previous teachers had taught 'from the book, but Guermonprez opened my eyes, opened up a whole new field, which had been narrow before.' Sekimachi had been weaving since 1949. In 1951 she met Guermonprez at Pond Farm and, although she did not study with her until 1953, she was 'overwhelmed' by her presence. From designing industrial prototypes to individual works of art, Guermonprez presented the medium as a range of possibilities never envisioned before.[7] As painters study the technique of old masters, Guermonprez asked students to analyse complex structures and compound weaves such as those of Anni Albers (pl. 48). Sekimachi's double and triple weaves (pls 92 and 93) may seem far removed from Albers's restrained compositions but each is the result of complete technical mastery and individual artistic expression. The overlapping planes of Sekimachi's three-dimensional works are as subtle, complex and visually

View of Pond Farm, near Guerneville, California, c. 1950.

stimulating as Anni Albers's light and dark contrasts. Her use of nylon monofilament represents the Bauhaus ideal of working with contemporary materials. Weavers trained in the Bauhaus manner gave their students a dual gift: sound technical grounding and the courage to experiment. This emboldened young people to find themselves and pursue their own artistic vision. The disdain for any form of copying, a veritable credo at the original Bauhaus, remained inviolate. Seen from the vantage point of history, this criterion has separated passing fad from lasting achievement. Sekimachi and a host of other 'third generation' Bauhäusler are not clones of their teachers but voices with a message of their own.

In her experiments with new forms of weaving, Guermonprez never abandoned the loom. Her sculptural space hangings remained loom-controlled. She shared with Bauhaus weavers a sensitivity for the expressive quality of the warp, which she emphasized by painting, stencilling or resist printing. She incorporated 'painterly' touches as naturally as graphics and was able to communicate equally forcefully in small hangings as in large architectural commissions. In a tribute to her teacher and friend, Kay Sekimachi quoted one of Guermonprez's favourite poets, who invoked the solitary bird that 'flies to the highest point'.[8] Trude Guermonprez's odyssey ended in California, but her influence continued: it was she who defined the textile arts for the West Coast.

In the middle of the country, in Chicago, the Association of Arts and Industries established a New Bauhaus in 1937 and appointed László Moholy-Nagy as director and Walter Gropius as consultant. Although it closed a year later, it reopened in 1939 as the School of Design and received academic accreditation as the Institute of Design in 1944. Moholy-Nagy's death in 1946 profoundly changed the school, and in 1949 it was incorporated into the Illinois Institute of Technology. Like the Bauhaus, the Institute of Design was fraught with internal and external problems, not the least of which were financial. Much has been written about the Institute, but hardly anything about its Weaving Workshop. Records documenting the time under Moholy-Nagy fell victim to personal vendettas and destruction.[9] It is nearly impossible to reconstruct the history of the Textile Department and to restore, even in a small way, some measure of verity. 'As far as the Weaving Workshop and its natural extension, interior architecture, are concerned, it is the sparseness if not non-existence of documents that prevents us from giving it all the space it deserves. Like the Bauhaus, it attracted almost exclusively women and was led until 1947 by the only woman on the faculty.'[10]

As is evident from surviving correspondence, Moholy-Nagy had intended to appoint Otti Berger as head of the Weaving Workshop. Her forced detention in Yugoslavia and inability to get a visa ended her prospects for emigration. Instead, it was her friend Marli Ehrman who assumed the position. Like Berger, Ehrman, who was Marie Helene Heimann as a student, had taken the *Vorkurs* under Moholy-Nagy. Born in Berlin and educated there as well as at a private school in Switzerland, Ehrman studied at the Bauhaus from 1923 until 1926. She then worked for another year in the Experimental Workshop as an independent assistant. She passed her journeyman's examination in Glauchau in 1927 but

Nathan Lerner photographed this fabric by Marli Ehrman, c. 1943.

continued studies at the Universities of Jena and Weimar and qualified as a teacher in Hamburg in 1931. As a Jew, she was dismissed from her teaching position in Holstein in 1933, but found work at the Herzl School in Berlin where she met her husband, Eliezer Ehrman. They emigrated to the United States in 1938 and spent a difficult first year during which Ehrman took positions as a governess. Moholy-Nagy's offer in 1939 to join his school gave her a new start.

The Weaving Workshop held to the same philosophies as had been practised in Germany: free experimentation – 'exploring the material from its source, taking demands and directions from its basic substance'[11] – discarding all preconceived ideas, focusing on mass production and design for industry. In contrast to the German Workshop, fashion and print design were incorporated from the beginning. As in Weimar, students were encouraged to sample the wares of other workshops. Myron Kozman, an architect and one of the first five graduates of the Illinois Institute of Technology, remembers how 'we majored in everything! Moholy imbued us with the fact that everything is related. We didn't have to specialize unless we chose to.'[12] Kozman had enrolled in the Light and Color Workshop and rose from student to instructor. After Moholy's death he taught sculpture, serigraphy, lithography, visual fundamentals, packaging, graphic design and colour. It is not surprising then that such versatility should include curiosity about weaving: 'Marli taught me how to weave – one of my many rich Bauhaus experiences.'[13] Nathan Lerner, who was with Moholy 'from the beginning to the end' and who became acting director after his death, confirms the infectious enthusiasm and 'Moholy's instinctive understanding of students' intentions. You had a problem – you solved it!'[14]

The Weaving Workshop at the Institute of Design existed until 1947 when it was discontinued by Moholy-Nagy's successor, Serge Chermayeff.[15] Although several accounts attest to Chermayeff's interest in weaving, it cannot be substantiated. The evidence points to the contrary.[16] Nevertheless, during the eight years of the Weaving Workshop's existence, 'the creative years, the Institute of Design had an enormous influence on weaving, reaching far beyond the city limits of Chicago.'[17] In part, this was due to the close contact among European weavers and to Moholy-Nagy's energetic outreach. From 23 June to 3 August 1940 he arranged for a 'Session of the Chicago School of Design (Bauhaus) at Mills College' in Oakland, California. The rigorous programme of forty hours a week included the basic workshop and photography with Moholy-Nagy, modelling and drawing with Robert Jay Wolff, colour with Gyorgy Kepes and weaving with Marli Ehrman. Ehrman explained that the programme 'would include the basic workshop training as we give it in the first year preliminary course.' An exhibition of 'Bauhaus art, circulated by the Museum of Modern Art' was held preceding and during the summer session.[18] Interaction was common among schools with Bauhaus connections. In 1949, Claire Falkenstein, a faculty member at Mills College, participated in a summer session at Pond Farm.[19] Trude Guermonprez returned to Black Mountain College for a seminar, and Marli Ehrman taught two summer sessions there, a welcome escape from hot Chicago.[20] She also served as Black Mountain's outside examiner in weaving.

In 1941 Marli Ehrman won first prize in the 'Organic Design' competition sponsored by the Museum of Modern Art, one of many awards she received during her distinguished career. Her prototypes for a number of textile firms were mass produced and marketed throughout the United States. She often collaborated on commissions for residential and commercial interiors with Marianne Willisch, the Austrian-born interior designer, who taught night classes at the Institute of Design. However, the interior of the Oak Park Public Library was Ehrman's individual achievement and 'a highlight in her career'.[21] For Mies van der Rohe's Lake Shore Drive Apartments she designed the curtain fabric.[22] In 1956 she founded the Elm Shop in Oak Park, an avant-garde source for modern design, which she directed until her retirement.

Ehrman's reputation and the respect she commanded from the design community was twofold: she was an outstanding weaver-designer and an equally gifted teacher. As a pedagogue, she was at home in the sophisticated setting of a highly advanced art school for professionals, but she was equally committed to teaching children and adults at Hull House, a settlement school founded in 1889 by Jane Addams in a neighbourhood of Mexican, Italian and Greek immigrants. Students at the Chicago Institute of Design experienced the closure of the textile department as a tragedy. Almost immediately they incorporated themselves as the 'Marli-Weavers', aiming to 'preserve the spirit of the former class and to promote the study of handweaving and design among its members by stimulating, encouraging and increasing interest in the development and execution of new handweaving techniques.[23] The 'Marli-Weavers', in existence from 1947 until 1991, met once a month for study assignments and organized many exhibitions, some in prestigious institutions such as the Art Institute of Chicago. Ehrman, their inspiration, like Albers and Guermonprez, had been able to awaken the innate talent of each weaver, their divergent careers reflections of their own rather than their teachers' temperaments. Former students, such as Lenore Tawney and Claire Zeisler took weaving into the realm of sculpture and fiber art; Angelo Testa became a major presence in the textile industry; Else Regensteiner and Julia McVicker established a custom-weaving studio for interior fabrics.

Else Regensteiner left Germany in 1936 and, soon after Marli Ehrman's arrival in Chicago, met her at a gathering of friends. She recalled that they were immediately drawn to each other and that as recent immigrants 'it was natural to talk about our experiences and aspirations in our new surroundings.' Ehrman invited Regensteiner to become her assistant at the Institute of Design, although Regensteiner's degree from the Frauenschule in Munich was in teaching and not in weaving. Moholy-Nagy agreed to an arrangement whereby Regensteiner would help out with spooling, warping and threading looms in exchange for instruction. Regensteiner discovered a natural talent for textiles and Ehrman soon promoted her to custom weaving on dobby looms with fly shuttles. It gave her the experience in production work so important in her later business venture. By this time, Regensteiner was committed to textile design and relished 'the Bauhaus influence and atmosphere which encouraged conscious and unconscious learning. It was never a craft environment, but a fusion with industrial design and art.' Ehrman encouraged Regensteiner to take courses with Anni and Josef Albers at Black Mountain College which 'became a lasting experience and creative influence in my development as a weaver and textile designer. The Bauhaus conception stayed with me and carried over into my approach to weaving and teaching.'[24]

In 1942 Else Regensteiner joined Marli Ehrman as an instructor at the Institute of Design and in 1945 she joined the staff of the Art Department at the School of the Chicago Art Institute. In many ways the Weaving Department, which she established in 1957 and directed until her retirement in 1971, carried on Moholy's ideal of instruction. There, she trained young people to become professionals, but she also reached a broad cross-section of avocational weavers by conducting workshops across the country. She waged a tireless campaign in favour of inventiveness and exploration as opposed to weaving from recipes. As a director of the Handweavers Guild of America she fostered the concept of quality even for amateurs and established the 'Certificate of Excellence', which has to be earned and which attests to a weaver's technical competence. She founded the Midwest Designer-Craftsmen, a group of professionals in the Midwest organized to foster standards and guidelines for craftspeople, arrange exhibitions, workshops, symposia, gallery outlets, etc., and is the author of books which have become classics in the field.[25] Her interest in textiles of other cultures resulted in study tours abroad and culminated in her collaboration, from 1972 to 1978, with the American Farm School in Thessaloniki, Greece. She taught Greek girls to become self-sufficient by utilizing modern, high-volume techniques yet retaining respect for indigenous designs. A woman of extraordinary energy and enthusiasm, Regensteiner spent a lifetime disseminating Bauhaus ideas. Yet she was also a prolific weaver. From 1945 to 1980 she and Julia McVicker, a fellow student from the Institute of Design, operated the flourishing 'reg/wick' custom studio. The success of 'reg/wick' coincided with the building boom in modern offices and residences. Vast expanses of glass fronts proved to be transmitters not only of light but of cold as well. Here, the ubiquitous casement fabric of the period satisfied the longing for the tactile, the sensuous and the visual. In addition, there were orders for co-ordinates, complementary, not matching, upholstery and curtain material that was custom-dyed.[26] For years, the Stiffel Company used 'reg/wick' fabrics for its lampshades. The two women designed in the Bauhaus tradition, 'directly on the loom, because thorough technical knowledge allows the freedom to expand and get away from the expected.'[27] Fabrics from the 'reg/wick' studio were included in the Museum of Modern Art's 'Good Design' exhibitions and other national shows and won Regensteiner and McVicker numerous prizes. In 1954 the Smithsonian Institution organized a travelling exhibition, 'American Craftsmen', which was greeted by such an 'extraordinary response' that it was extended into 1955 because it proved impossible to 'fill all demands from museums within one year'.[28] The 'reg/wick' studio also designed prototypes for industry – 'a challenge since we had to work within the framework of restrictions'.[29]

Unlike Regensteiner and McVicker, the first student to graduate from the Institute of Design, Angelo Testa, worked almost exclusively for industry. He studied with Marli Ehrman, and, like her, was drawn to the structural qualities in weaving. The motivating force behind Testa's work as a textile designer was the relationship of fabrics to architecture. 'Testa has been concerned with maximizing a sense of space by using the most minimal geometric elements' in his fabrics, wrote Charlotte Moser a year before Testa's death in 1984.[30] Although his own firm, Angelo Testa and Company, was enormously successful, he also worked as a designer for major national companies.[31] Prints were as important to him as woven fabrics. It was, in fact, a printed textile, a free-form design of three overlapping shapes, that launched his career. Created in 1942 and called *Little Man*, it appeared in newspapers and magazines throughout the United States.

A transplant from New England, Testa became a convinced Chicagoan – 'there is a very human quality here you can relate to' – and his indebtedness to Moholy-Nagy and the ideals of the Bauhaus remained a recurring theme. He shared with his teacher an unbounded energy and enthusiasm. 'I have never been bored. And if I come close, I quickly go to my loom and weave.'[32] Testa was especially interested in producing good design for the mass market and for dormitories, schools, institutions and hotels. His 'Budget Package' offered custom weaves and special prints as 'correlates', fabrics for bedspreads, upholstery and curtains, available in specified colours. These could be mixed and matched in endless combinations by the client or an interior designer, thus providing an individual look while keeping the price to a minimum. Many of his designs have the solid, anonymous quality of the typical functional Bauhaus fabric. To others he brings a definite American quality. In *Times Square* (pl. 104), for instance, he gives an otherwise geometric design an off-beat, rhythmic kick. In *La Ligna* (pl. 103) he uses the early Bauhaus colours of red, black and white, but the damask weave

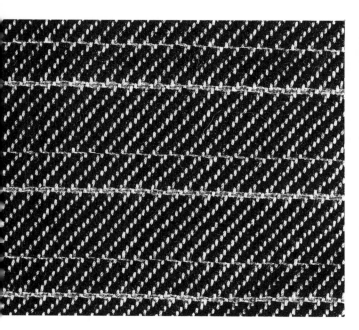

reg/wick

Custom Hand Weaving
Designing for Power Looms

Elsa Regensteiner / Julia McVicker

dilutes and softens the effect, and the pattern, despite its rigid lines, appears fluid. It is not difficult to see Moholy's influence in *Bamboo Stripe* (pl. 107).

Testa was a prolific and visible presence, a crusader and spokesman for the Bauhaus, especially when it came under attack and experienced increasingly adverse criticism. 'The Bauhaus has been blamed for this sterile visual environment that we live in. This is an unforgivable transgression of truth. The Bauhaus did not condemn nor outlaw ornamentation. [It believed] that honesty of approach in the use of materials and of technology in the development of ornamentation would substantiate the creation of a visual experience that equates to man today.'[33] His death at the age of sixty-two was a great loss for the American textile industry.

Of Lenore Tawney, another student at the Chicago Institute of Design, Else Regensteiner said, 'observing her, I knew immediately that she would become one of the top weavers and a great artist.'[34] From 1946 to 1947 Tawney studied with László Moholy-Nagy, Emerson Woelffer, Marli Ehrman and Alexander Archipenko. She continued to work with Archipenko in Chicago and in his studio in Woodstock, New York, until 1948. Several years of travelling took her abroad but she resumed her studies in weaving with Martta Taipale at the Penland School of Craft in North Carolina. Lenore Tawney's involvement with textiles defies definition and, most of all, categorization. She began every task with an open, cleared mind, a *tabula rasa*, a state that both Gropius and Moholy-Nagy envisioned as the ideal precondition for creativity.

In the early sixties Tawney encountered two extremely divergent but intricately beautiful aspects of textiles: hand-manipulated gauze weaves and the complex cord system of the industrial Jacquard loom. Under the guidance of Lili Blumenau, Tawney explored ancient Peruvian gauze, double and triple weaves. Blumenau, like Anni Albers and Gunta Stölzl before her, was fascinated by the extraordinary complexity of ancient Peruvian constructions, which were in her care from 1944 to 1950 when she served as curator of textiles for New York's Cooper Union Museum. Lili Blumenau was educated in Berlin and spent the Hitler years in Paris. She emigrated to the United States after the War and enrolled as the first female student at the New York School of Textile Technology. In 1948 she started the Weaving Workshop at Teachers College, New York, and in 1952, the Weaving Department at the Fashion Institute of Technology, also in New York. Strongly influenced by the Bauhaus, Lili Blumenau contributed to the field of American textiles as a lecturer, as an author of articles and books and through exhibitions of her work. When the First World Congress of Craftsmen met in New York in 1964, participants paid a visit to a Jacquard mill in New Jersey. Blumenau was familiar with this aspect of textile production, but for Lenore Tawney it was a revelation. The ingenuity of the Jacquard loom's mechanics made as profound an impression on Tawney as Peruvian hand manipulation. She recalled that 'it was the most thrilling thing to see the threads moving and trembling like music.' During 1964 Tawney travelled once a week to Philadelphia to study the mechanics of the Jacquard loom at the Textile Institute.[35] The result was a series of exquisite line drawings on graph paper.

Lenore Tawney has a rare gift – empathy – the ability to see, to absorb and to be deeply moved, whether by weavers of ancient cultures, contemporary artist-friends or Eastern contemplative thought. In her quiet, very private, but wholly directed search for artistic expression she became a pioneer. Tawney's early work shimmers with colour and expressive line. Diaphanous warps hold fluid wefts, as handmade paper holds calligraphy. In the early sixties she moved away from colour and abstract compositions. She used instead natural linen to emphasize the structure and outline of her creations, free-form shapes suspended in space. 'The new work', she explained, 'is called *Woven Forms*. It is sculptural.'[36] The regal presence of these forms and their names – *Inside the Earth – A Mountain*, *The King* and *The Queen* (pl. 94) – command awe. As Erika Billeter points out, 'These are works that changed the face of textile art; they have no precursors.'[37] If in the past the law of weaving had been the intersecting of threads at right angles, the rectilinear form, she was intent on offering a redefinition and coaxing the medium into new directions, 'something in me knowing what I was doing.'[38] Although Tawney was in the forefront of the fiber art explosion, the movement she helped to create cannot contain her. The plethora of poor adaptations with their unfortunate sloppiness and mimicry are devoid of Tawney's aesthetic sensibilities, her intellectual rigour, emotional grounding and sound technical expertise. Her encounters with Moholy-Nagy, Archipenko, Ehrman, Taipala and Blumenau were crucial, a meeting of the mind and heart with kindred spirits, but one suspects that Tawney would have made her contribution to art anyway. Hers is a unique artistic vision.

America has been enriched by its immigrants and the contribution of their students. Black Mountain College, Pond Farm, the Institute of Design in Chicago and the city that nurtured it have been fertile ground for all manner of talent. The loyalty has been fierce. 'Chicago is my home town – more than my native Munich where I was born', said Else Regensteiner. 'Chicago has provided my background and my beginning as a weaver, and the exciting, teeming city has given me the stimulation of a lifetime.'[39] 'Everything I have achieved during the fifty years of my career had its source in the Bauhaus philosophy and the guidance of Marli Ehrman.'[40] Angelo Testa echoed these sentiments: 'Whatever success I have enjoyed in my varied areas of work I totally owe to Moholy-Nagy's inspiration and to the Bauhaus philosophy. The Universal Truths that were revealed to me are as valid and as vital today as they were over fifty years ago when they were conceived.'[41] Myron Kozman, who lived his professional life in Milwaukee and Missouri, said that 'in my teaching, I have always introduced the Bauhaus educational philosophy. Turmoil – yes, but insignificant compared to the impact of the Bauhaus philosophy on design and education, and I choose to emphasize that which changed my entire life.'[42] Nathan Lerner is brief: 'Of course, I see myself as a Bauhäusler.'[43] In 1992, fifty-five years after the founding of the Chicago Bauhaus, its dispersed alumni returned for a reunion, still active, vital and youthful in spirit.

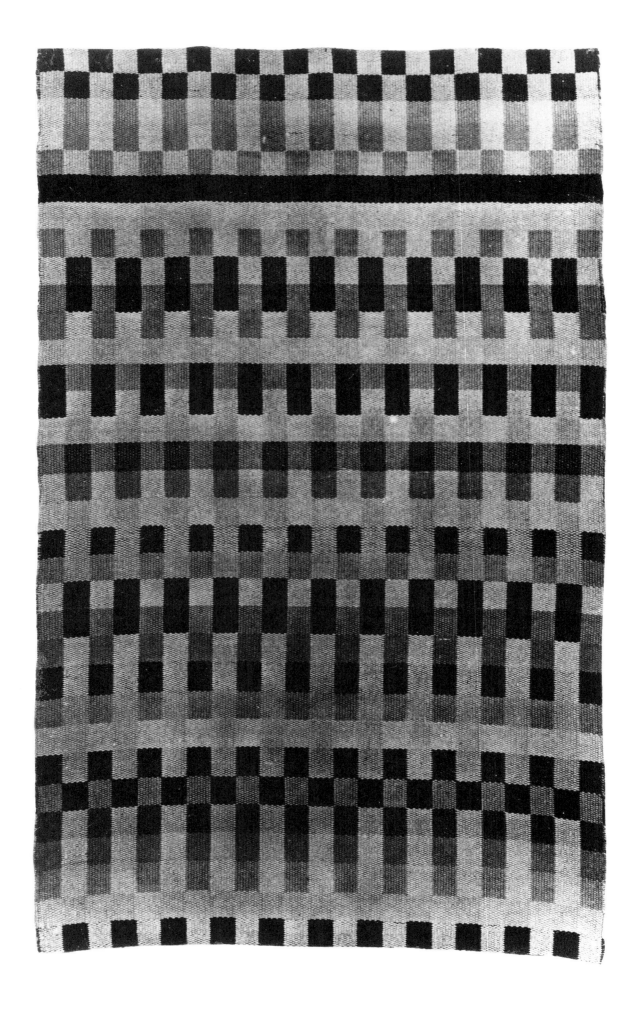

bauhaus style

When Ernst Kallai wrote in 1930, 'What is urgently needed is reform. . .',[2] he was pleading for deliverance from the Bauhaus style. He was not the first to do so. In 1923, only four years after the Bauhaus had been established, Paul Westheim commented on the difference between students from traditional arts and crafts schools, where they 'are plagued with stylizing cabbage leaves from nature,' and Bauhaus students, who 'plague themselves with stylizing squares from ideas. Three days in Weimar and one can never look at a square again for the rest of one's life.'[3] Hannes Meyer, in his 1928 letter of resignation had scathingly commented on the 'colored geometry' and the 'tragicomic situation' that as the director of the institution he had to fight 'against the Bauhaus style.'[4]

> We aimed at realizing standards of excellence, not creating transient novelties.
> WALTER GROPIUS, 1965[1]

Anni and Josef Albers in a photograph of 1955.

Kallai noted correctly that the Bauhaus was not alone among various reform attempts in the international Modernist movement. But the effectiveness with which it disseminated its ideas and its success, he felt, were grounded in Bauhaus experimentation. In the ten years of its existence it had reached 'even the remotest corners of the country. Today everybody knows about it.' Kallai's list of what was perceived as Bauhaus style in 1930 is worth repeating: 'Houses with lots of glass and shining metal: Bauhaus style. The same is true of home hygiene without home atmosphere: Bauhaus style. Tubular steel armchair frames: Bauhaus style. Lamp with nickel-coated body and a disk of opaque glass as lamp shade: Bauhaus style. Wallpaper patterned in cubes: Bauhaus style. No painting on the wall: Bauhaus style. Incomprehensible painting on the wall: Bauhaus style. Printing with sans-serif letters and bold rules: Bauhaus style. everything written in small letters: bauhaus style. EVERYTHING EXPRESSED IN BIG CAPITALS: BAUHAUS STYLE. Bauhaus style: one word for everything.'[5] Today, after so many years, the confusion remains. Modernism is still elusive. Mies van der Rohe's Barcelona chair has been described as contemporary, modern, classic and antique, according to the point of view. Does a Bauhaus style exist?

Walter Gropius was most emphatic in stating that it does not. In his opinion, one shared by most contemporary design historians, indiscriminate critics appropriated as Bauhaus style anything geometric, functional and modern. What they failed to recognize was that style cannot be detached from meaning, and that the Bauhaus philosophy was opposed to aesthetic dogmatism and instead strove to invest contemporary architecture and interiors with a humanizing effect. Stylistic Bauhaus characteristics are the result of cross-fertilization between art and technology, or of standard, repeated units and Gropius's belief that 'form elements of typical shape should be repeated in series',[6] in other words, simplicity in multiplicity. This holds true for fabrics as it does for architecture.

Opposite Anni Albers wove this wall hanging in 1928. It is an example of what is often called 'the Bauhaus style'.

Bauhaus textiles share a unified stylistic approach but not a style in itself. They are forthright and progress-oriented in their acceptance of novel fibres, advances in technology and contemporary machine aesthetic. Colours, either primary or restricted to restrained neutrals, are chosen as ancillary to their intended environment. The natural vertical/horizontal nature of weaving lends itself to geometric and textural units as well as to stripes and small repeat effects. Above all, Bauhaus textiles stress structure, a structure not superimposed but instead one derived from intimate knowledge of the capability of the material itself. Despite these affinities, each Bauhaus textile is a unique design invested not only with visual but with symbolic content as well. Like any other activity at the Bauhaus, weaving was an intellectual undertaking comprising virtuosic technique and a thorough understanding of the contemporary design aesthetic. The intellectual character of Bauhaus weaving is precisely what sets it apart from mere craft. Bauhaus fabrics have expanded the definition of textiles because they transcend trendiness.

Gropius enticed young people to come to his school at a desperate time in European history. Idealistic and full of hope, they were eager to break with tradition and break new ground. The weavers followed the lead of the painters and workshop masters. During the Weimar years, experimentation and encouragement of individual achievement was paramount. During the Dessau years the orientation was toward industry. In both cases, Gropius felt that 'a breach has been made with the past', that 'the morphology of dead styles has been destroyed;' and that 'we are returning to honesty of thought and feeling'.[7] The struggle to define themselves as professionals and not as dilettantes, as they were commonly perceived, was hard and confusing for this first generation of female designers. Over a period of fourteen years, the original Weaving Workshop attracted but a handful of men.[8] Most of these only sampled the craft. Of the two who graduated neither achieved the stature of those who changed 'woman's work' into a respectable profession for both genders. A firm sense of identity is indispensable for charting a new course, and it emerged only slowly. It paralleled the shift from playful exploration to a coherence of style based not on optical imitation of reality but on simplification, abstraction and structure. Gropius saw the development of standard types as freeing. 'In all great epochs of history the existence of standards – that is the conscious adoption of type-forms – has been the criterion of a polite and well-ordered society; for it is a commonplace that repetition of the same things for the same purposes exercises a settling and civilizing influence on men's minds.'[9] Although the repetitiveness of the craft itself was initially held against the weavers as a typically feminine and, therefore, inferior trait, Lenore Tawney was able to bring it back to its 'civilizing influence' and transform it into the exact opposite: 'meditation – the source of her creativity.'[10]

The goal of the Bauhaus was the unity of design as a whole, not the conscious creation of one style or – notwithstanding the flat roof – one kind of architecture. In its method of construction and its intimate relationship with the building, weaving is close to architecture. As a medium it had to be divested of historicist

ornament to harmonize with modern structures; technically it had to fulfil the requirements of contemporary needs. It was essential to learn the craft not as an end in itself but as a prerequisite for developing prototypes. Just as it had become an anachronism as a means of production, the hand loom changed into the designer's tool for experimentation, and it continues to serve the artist. Through choice of colour and material, the skilled weaver uses it to transform the appearance of the same structure, creating diversity within the unity of the pattern. To accept and integrate new materials with differing properties was an exhilarating challenge eagerly pursued by Bauhaus weavers. Like buildings with pretentious exterior veneers, textiles are dishonest if yarns are superimposed, held together by a backing rather than by sound construction. Moreover, the Bauhaus had a strong inhibition against any form of copying. The achievements of the Weaving Workshop had no precedent. It embraced the machine age, developed technical proficiency, utilized new materials and met consumer needs. Bauhaus textiles were designed to fulfil their intended aesthetical and functional purpose and as such they share an attitude rather than a style.

What has now become commonplace – geometric designs in stacked units, light/dark juxtapositions and transposed elements in a multiplicity of variations – was explored for the first time by Bauhaus weavers in the twenties. Examples are

Ruth Hollós's viscose blanket of 1927, Anni Albers's hanging of 1928, an anonymous cotton rug for a child's room dating from 1929 and a variety of functional fabrics. The weavers developed a language of design which, although new at the time, has become timeless. Their textiles can be broadly categorized as 'modern', the way buildings are 'baroque' or 'rococo'. Like good architecture, they communicate a *Zeitgeist* that involves the user as much as the creator, and today these weavings trigger the pleasure of recognition. Don Page's double-weave hanging acknowledges Anni Albers, his mentor at Black Mountain College, but at the same time he offers his personal restatement of a modern theme. In 1931 Katja Rose, inspired by *Vorkurs* exercises, experimented with patterns derived from her typewriter (pl. 109). In Josef Albers's course at Black Mountain College, Ruth Asawa used a rubber stamp on newsprint to great effect (pl. 108). Nearly two decades later, Bernard Rudofsky and Alvin Lustig, both teachers of summer sessions at Black Mountain College, offered their versions, one an adaptation of Katja Rose's 'typescript', the other a playful paraphrasing of themes by Paul Klee (pls 110 and 111). Herbert Bayer's tapestries (pls 112 and 113) explore chromatic interlocking and the relationship of the circle to the square. Individual interpretations or Bauhaus style?

It is astonishing how quickly the émigré weavers affected the quality and appearance of American textiles. Their influence on students was not the only reason for this. They were also highly visible in national exhibitions. Anni Albers's reputation was such that after only six years in the United States she was asked to exhibit at the 'Golden Gate International Exposition' in San Francisco. The invitation came from Dorothy Liebes who was the director of the Division of Decorative Arts. 'This is an exciting age in which to create!', wrote Liebes in the catalogue. 'The weaver, whether of fabric, tapestry or rug, has never before possessed so rich and varied a palette. The amazing development of synthetic yarns means that texture and appearance of fabric is no longer limited by the characteristics of natural fibres such as flax, silk, wool and cotton. Consider the shining Cellophanes, dull acetates, lacquered plastics, treated leathers, artificial horsehair, non-tarnishable metals and glass threads!'[11] She was describing the pioneering efforts of the Bauhaus weavers of more than a decade earlier. How much these tenets had penetrated the North American continent is evident when one realizes that it is Dorothy Liebes, not Anni Albers, who wrote: 'What makes a fabric modern? Essentially that it is created in terms of today with material of today, within a whole set of conditioning factors. Chief of these are function, architecture and related textures.'[12]

Dorothy Liebes was strongly influenced by the Bauhaus and was among the first Americans to adapt handweaving to mass production. After she opened her studio in San Francisco in 1930 she specialized in custom handwoven fabrics for architects and designers. In 1935 she met Frank Lloyd Wright, who advocated the acceptance of machines in contemporary society. That same year she was awarded two major architectural commissions for California public buildings. Her contacts with the textile industry started in 1940. Eight years later she moved her design studio to New York and from 1958 on she concentrated solely on designs for industry (pls 114–117). In the course of her career Liebes designed for most major textile companies. Although her name has become synonymous with Lurex (metallic yarns) she is equally well known for her unusual, daring colour combinations. Liebes's simple weave structures lack Albers's highly technical sophistication and architectonic approach to pattern. Where Liebes's attitude toward colour is emotional, Albers's is intellectual. Their commonality lies in their uninhibited exploration and use of new material, including rigid wefts for blinds and room dividers, and their unequivocal acceptance of power looms.

Bauhaus-inspired textiles became mainstream in the fifties and sixties with the shift from production handweaving to power-weaving. Among the gifted young designers who had started as handweavers was Boris Kroll. He had been introduced to the Bauhaus philosophy by his friend Robert J. Wolff, an abstract painter and dean at Moholy-Nagy's Institute of Design in Chicago from 1938 to 1942. They met while Wolff was head of the Art Department at Brooklyn College, from which he retired in 1978. Kroll's company was noted for its Jacquard designs and developed into one of America's largest textile manufacturers, with showrooms across the country. At all times Kroll was intimately involved in the design process. He loved the hand loom for its responsiveness to 'innovative ideas. There is nothing I can't do as an experiment.'[13] Kroll interpreted several designs by Bauhaus weavers, always crediting the originator. His *Channel Plaid* (pl. 120) of 1980 pays homage to the ideas of Anni Albers, not to any specific design. It is, however, interesting to compare it to her screenprint, *GR I* (pl. 85) of 1970, or to *Eclat* (pl. 121), her first print design on fabric for Knoll Textiles. Knoll advertised *Eclat* in 1976 as 'meticulous weighing and arranging, to achieve satisfying totalities and visual resting places'. Knoll added that, although *Eclat* at first glance seems devoid of repeats, it 'demands a second look.'[14] Boris Kroll's *Translucence* (pl. 125), which, like all his Jacquard weaves, came in a variety of colourways, was inspired by Gertrud Arndt's wall hanging of 1927 (pl. 124). Kroll fabrics were meticulously designed and of the highest quality. After Kroll's death in 1991 the company was acquired by Scalamandré, of which it is now an affiliate.

Another gifted designer of contemporary textiles, first on the hand loom, then as principal of his own company, is Jack Lenor Larsen. Deeply cognizant of past innovators, Larsen has championed excellence in design as author, lecturer and museum consultant. It is in this spirit that he created the 'Masterworks Twentieth Century Collection'. Larsen admired Gunta Stölzl, whom he knew personally. In 1986, to coincide with the opening of the Metropolitan Museum of Art's new wing for twentieth-century art, he donated his collection of original Bauhaus textiles to the Museum.[15] In the 1950s he pleaded with designers 'not to imitate the work of pioneers . . . to recall that ''modern'' is not a style but the philosophic upholding of self-expression.'[16] Larsen's own career is testimony to this creed. When the Paris Museum of Decorative Arts honoured him in 1981 with a thirty-year retrospective exhibition, it featured the range of his achievements, from prints and knits to woven textiles, and especially his close association with architectural projects.

Jack Lenor Larsen is a graduate of Cranbrook Academy which was founded in 1932 by Eliel Saarinen in Bloomfield Hills, Michigan. Cranbrook represents the Scandinavian rather than the Bauhaus influence in America, and has made important contributions to the American design aesthetic. Textile design at Cranbrook was shaped by the Finnish weaver Marianne Strengell, who came to the school in 1937 and headed the department from 1942 until her retirement in 1961. At Cranbrook 'architecture was the mother of the arts. There was a hierarchy which went from architecture to painting, sculpture and then the minor arts. Nevertheless, there was a wonderful feeling of integration and a respectful understanding of each medium.'[17] Strengell, a forceful presence in textile circles, nurtured some of the best-known American designers. Reflecting the general climate during the fifties and sixties, she favoured functional textiles and discouraged the weaving of wall hangings. Yet many of her students later distinguished themselves in art weaving.

One of these is Yvonne Pacanovsky Bobrowicz, who not only studied with Strengell but with Anni Albers as well. She describes herself as belonging to the 'transitional' group of weavers who started their careers as designers of utility fabrics but later moved into weaving as art. Bobrowicz at first followed in Strengell's footsteps, weaving the then typical three-yard lengths for architects and showrooms and samples intended for mass production. At the time when the demand for interior fabrics reached its peak, weaving emerged as an art form, and the younger generation of weavers began to define their careers either as industrial designers, such as Kroll and Larsen, or as fiber artists, such as Bobrowicz.

By the late sixties weavers, attempting to fit into a hierarchy of set rules, were struggling with semantics. Artist-craftsman, designer-weaver, fabric engineer, hand-artist were but a few of the awkward labels. Designer was clear-cut. But what about the weaver who created a unique work of art? Anni Albers gave this considerable thought and repeatedly confronted the issue. 'Whenever I find myself listed as a craftsman or . . . as an artist-craftsman, I feel that I have to explain myself to myself or occasionally, as here, to others. For when taking a rather long look at the past, at what craftsmen made centuries ago – even thousands of years ago – all over the world, I feel an unworthy latecomer, perhaps belonging to an almost obsolete species. These ancient craftsmen were artists, no hyphen needed.'[18]

It was inevitable that a fiber revolution would occur. From the very beginning, the Bauhaus believed that the warp was as important as the weft and need not be hidden, that, indeed, it could be expressive in its own right. It was an entirely new concept and changed textile design for ever. Exposed to this philosophy, students of Bauhaus weavers took it a step further, liberating the medium from all preconceived conventions. The Museum of Modern Art was the first mainstream institution to recognize the fiber art movement and in 1969 mounted an exhibition of this new approach to weaving. Again semantics got in the way, for its title, 'Wall Hangings', did not accommodate stacked units or sculptural forms hung in space. Four years later Jack Lenor Larsen and Mildred Constantine coined a new term when they published the now classic *beyond craft: the art fabric*, an oversize volume, its title in lower-case Bauhaus graphics. Both the museum catalogue and the book acknowledged the debt to the Bauhaus. Critical assessments faintly echoed what had been debated at the Dessau Bauhaus in the twenties: the shift from colour to structure, the use of new materials, the manipulation of threads. The difference was primarily in scale – structure as bas-relief or sculpture – and in the end use – functional versus non-functional. Many of the weavers included in the exhibition and the book had studied either first-hand with Albers and Stölzl or with teachers trained by them. In the Bauhaus tradition of free experimentation the weavers were finally free to choose a technique, a medium, new materials. If this did not immediately change their status into un-hyphenated artists, the art establishment was at last taking note. Fibres had been squarely placed into the context of twentieth-century art.

Neither Anni Albers nor Gunta Stölzl participated in the fiber art revolution. After a full career of designing first non-functional, then functional textiles, each returned to weaving individual hangings as works of art, but they continued to relate them to the wall, not to space. Just before textiles received recognition as art, Anni Albers divested herself of her looms and took up graphics as a medium. Her feelings about fiber art were mixed, possibly because so much of it displayed dearth of vision and poverty of craftsmanship.[19] Of course, she recognized those deficiencies in art as well: 'today a painter can just squeeze a tube and his obedient medium permits him to use it any way he likes – with care, without care, splashing it if he wishes. This outer unrestraint does not provide him with the stimulation and source for inventiveness that may come in the course of struggling with a hard-to-handle material. It rather permits him unrestraint in turn, in every form or formlessness. . . . convulsion is mistaken for revelation.' After participating on the jury of a textile exhibition, she was overwhelmed by the sheer quantity of questionable submissions – '2,500 objects were submitted, and I confess I still have not recovered from the shock that 2,450 senseless, useless things gave me. . . . their standards seem to have become obscured. They belong to a twilight zone, not quite art, not really useful.'[20]

Anni Albers never lived in a twilight zone. She was too strong a person, her standards too unwavering to embrace much of what she saw. To her, art was a constant, linked to the past, looking forward to the future. The forms changed but not the inner necessity. She would have preferred it if her struggle with the material, the years of intellectual and emotional involvement with the medium, had been recognized as art. 'Today it is the artist who in many instances is continuing the direct work with a material, with a challenging material; and it is here, I believe, that the true craftsman is found – inventive as ever, ingenious, intuitive, skillful, worthy of linking us with the past. His work is concerned with meaningful form, finding significant terms for newly unfolding areas of awareness. And dealing with visual matter, the stuff the world is made of, the inherent discipline of matter acts as a regulative force: not everything "goes".'[21] She has been proven right. The shooting stars, the passing phenomena have been unable to sustain the initial moment of attention.

Weaving is beginning to exist in a broader context without the isolating absolutes. Space installations and miniature textiles of exquisite technical virtuosity can co-exist. Monumentality and the need to look closely, to experience intimacy, are not mutually exclusive. Designing for industry remains paramount. 'Seldom are the art-conscious ideas of the artist applicable to production', says Jack Lenor Larsen. 'There's been a definite swing of the pendulum to design from "art fabric" in recent years.'[22] The world has become smaller but the opportunities for textile designers have expanded. From the Biennale in Lausanne to the design studio in Tokyo, art and technology still form a unity. The search for proportion and enduring aesthetics which the Bauhaus weavers initiated has become global.

In pursuing his vision of the *Gesamtkunstwerk* Gropius had hoped for an 'exalted craftsman', a person free to work 'without the class distinctions that raise an arrogant barrier between craftsman and artist'. He created a school in which students learned by doing. This concept was known to the Greeks as *techne*. 'Art is not an idea *followed* by technical expression;' writes Edmund Burke Feldman, 'art is idea and materials simultaneously united by technique. The notion of technique as subordinate to idea is a philosophic error that has bedeviled aesthetics and art criticism for a long time. In criticism we cannot afford to ignore craft or technique because making and forming processes are expressive or satisfying in themselves.'[23]

Transient novelties were not the aim of the Bauhaus, nor was it a single style. In the fourteen years of its existence the Weaving Workshop wrestled with the endless possibilities of expression and the complexities that the medium offers. 'We wanted to develop the greatest variety of fabrics',[24] said Gunta Stölzl. With deep respect for the natural limitations of the craft, Bauhaus weavers experimented but never imitated. Reverence for other textile traditions was paramount and Stölzl instilled this in her students. 'The Copts, the Peruvians, the early Gothic weavers adhered to limitations. . . . they were not alienated from spiritual and material grounding.'[25] Stölzl wanted her students to have 'love of the material' and to share her own 'anticipatory imagination'.[26]

They came with more: determination. At the Bauhaus they had entered uncharted territory. Tenacity was the foundation of their growth into competent professionals. This, and their vision and strength of character, the weavers took with them when they were forced once again to embark into the unknown. They had developed into pioneers at home, they would become pioneers abroad. In Weimar, Dessau, Berlin, Amsterdam, London, Black Mountain, Chicago, Pond Farm and Oakland, Bauhaus women directed weaving departments that explored ideas and techniques and art and technology, and upheld the principle of learning and teaching. They shared with a new generation of students their unshakable faith in the creative powers of the individual. The fundamental transformation of textiles from mere craft into an integral part of the contemporary design aesthetic had already occurred. They had made it happen.

notes

Prelims and Introduction
1. Otti Berger quoted in Wingler, 1969 (from 'Interviews mit Bauhäuslern', *bauhaus* magazine 1928, numbers 2–3 and 4), p. 528.
2. Herbert Bayer quoted in Cohen, 1984, p. 338.
3. Lucia Moholy, 'Fragen der Interpretation' in Neumann, 1985, p. 290.
4. See Radewaldt (Ph.D. dissertation), 1986. This is an admirable compilation of facts and data.
5. In a letter to 'Former Members of the Bauhaus', dated 30 October 1946, Ise and Walter Gropius asked more than thirty American Bauhäusler to contribute $5.00 or $10.00 a month for 'a group effort to help our old friends to get safely through the worst period of starvation.' Chicago Historical Society.

Chapter 1
1. Schlemmer, 1990, p. 300.
2. Wingler, 1969, p. 31.

Chapter 2
1. Ditty by Oskar Schlemmer in use throughout the Bauhaus years to describe the Weaving Workshop. Author's translation. Typewritten manuscript at the Bauhaus Archive, Berlin. 'Wo Wolle ist,/ ist auch ein Weib/ das webt,/ und sei es nur zum Zeitvertreib.'
2. Callen, 1970.
3. Wingler, 1969, p. 33.
4. Franciscono, 1971, p. 250.
5. Minutes of the Master Council, dated 20 September 1920, p. 10, Bauhaus Archive, Berlin.
6. Circular to the Master Council, dated 15 March 1921, Bauhaus Archive, Berlin.
7. Herkner (Master's dissertation), 1984, p. 43, Landesgewerbeamt Baden-Württemberg, 1989.
8. *Gunta Stölzl: Weberei am Bauhaus und aus eigener Werkstatt*, p. 107.
9. Wingler, 1969, p. 22.
10. Weltge-Wortmann, 1987, p. 21.
11. *Florence Henri*, 1990.
12. Soupault, 1988.
13. Gunta Sharon-Stölzl, 'Die Entwicklung der Bauhausweberei' in *bauhaus* magazine, No. 2 (July 1931).
14. Marianne Brandt in Neumann, 1985, p. 158.
15. Sharon-Stölzl, op. cit.
16. Stölzl in *OFFSET Buch und Werbekunst*, Leipzig, No. 7 (1926), as quoted in Wingler, 1969, p. 116.
17. Gunta Stadler-Stölzl, 'Mehr Wagnis als Planung: Die Textilwerkstatt des Bauhauses 1919–1931' in *Werk*, Vol. 55, No. 11 (1968).
18. Wingler, 1969, p. 31.

Chapter 3
1. *bauhaus* magazine, No. 2 (July 1931).
2. Gunta Stadler-Stölzl, 'Mehr Wagnis als Planung: Die Textilwerkstatt des Bauhauses 1919–1931' in *Werk*, Vol. 55, No. 11 (1968).
3. Anni Albers in conversation with the author, 21 February 1987.
4. Anni Albers in conversation with the author, 21 February 1987.
5. Monica Bella-Broner in conversation with the author, 1 December 1991.
6. Muche, 1965, p. 166.
7. Claire Kosterlitz (Traute Wagner) in conversation with the author, 25 May 1991.
8. *Anni Albers*, 1977, p. 6.
9. Rotzler, 1978, p. 24.
10. Stadler-Stölzl, op. cit.
11. Anni Albers in conversation with the author, 21 February 1987.
12. Kandinsky, 1977, p. 32.

Chapter 4
1. Will Grohmann in *bauhaus* magazine, No. 2 (July 1931).
2. H.E. von Berlepsch, 'Endlich ein Umschwung' in *Deutsche Kunst und Dekoration* (October 1887), p. 3.
3. Whitford, 1987, p. 9.
4. Kandinsky, 1977, p. 47.
5. Ibid.
6. Schlemmer, 1990, p. 117.
7. Ibid., p. 152.
8. Albers, 1961, p. 2.
9. Kandinsky, 1977, p. 55.
10. Gunta Stölzl, 'Weberei am Bauhaus' in *OFFSET Buch und Werbekunst*, No. 5 (1926).

Chapter 5
1. Gunta Stadler-Stölzl, 'Mehr Wagnis als Planung: Die Textilwerkstatt des Bauhauses 1919–1931' in *Werk*, Vol. 55, No. 11 (1968).
2. Rotzler, 1978, p. 32.
3. Ibid.
4. *La Revue Moderne Illustrée des Arts et de la Vie*, 26e Année, No. 2 (30 January 1926), p. 26.
5. Quoted in *Gunta Stölzl: Weberei am Bauhaus und aus eigener Werkstatt*, 1987, p. 10.
6. *Johannes Itten*, 1973–1977, n.p.
7. The appliqué belonged to Hanna Bekker vom Rath, artist, patron and collector of works by avant-garde artists. She owned numerous works by her close friend Ida Kerkovius, among them several textiles. Most of these, according to Bekker vom Rath's daughter, Dr Barbara Bekker Rawling (letter to the author), had deteriorated over time. This appliqué, now in the Bauhaus Archive in Berlin, was published for the first time in *Experiment Bauhaus*, 1988, p. 76, along with a detailed description of the piece.

Chapter 6
1. Gunta Stölzl, 'Über die Bauhausweberei' in *Gunta Stölzl: Weberei am Bauhaus und aus eigener Werkstatt*, 1987, p. 99.
2. Benita Koch-Otte in *Vom Geheimnis der Farbe: Benita Koch-Otte*, 1972, p. 14.
3. Anni Albers in conversation with the author, 21 February 1987.
4. *Georg Muche*, 1980, p. 11.
5. Muche, 1965, p. 168.
6. Ibid.
7. Schlemmer often borrowed money from Otte, once to pay back Kandinsky. She maintained an active correspondence with a number of Bauhäusler after leaving the school. Schlemmer repeatedly refers to her in his letters and diaries (Schlemmer, 1990).
8. Koch-Otte, op. cit., p. 13.
9. Claire Kosterlitz (Traute Wagner) in conversation with the author, 25 May 1991.
10. Marguerite Wildenhain, 8 February 1972, in Koch-Otte, op. cit., p. 30.
11. Gunta Stölzl in a letter to her brother, dated 12 November 1925, Bauhaus Archive, Berlin.
12. Gunta Stölzl in a letter to her brother, dated 20 June 1933, Bauhaus Archive, Berlin.
13. Fritz Wichert, 'Ein Haus, Das Sehnsucht Erweckt' in *Frankfurter Zeitung* (10 October 1923) as quoted in *Georg Muche*, 1980, p. 40.
14. Magdalena Droste, 'Die Werkstatt für Weberei' in *Experiment Bauhaus*, 1988, p. 75. This hanging was considered anonymous, but is attributed to Mögelin by Droste.
15. Gunta Stölzl in a letter to Dr Charles Kuhn, 2 August 1949, Busch-Reisinger Archives, Cambridge, Mass.

Chapter 7
1. Günther Freiherr von Bechmann quoting Rudolf von Delius in 'Das Bauhaus in Dessau. Die Arbeit' in *Velhagen & Klasings Monatshefte*, Vol. 2, No. 7 (1927).
2. Wingler, 1969, p. 461.
3. Ise Gropius in letters to Linnea Martin, 26 January 1974 and 26 February 1974. The information in both letters, according to Mrs Gropius, is based on her own diary entries of 1926.
4. Ibid.
5. Isaacs, 1985, p. 354.
6. Ise Gropius in a letter to Linnea Martin, 6 January 1974.
7. Quoted in *Gunta Stölzl: Weberei am Bauhaus und aus eigener Werkstatt*, 1987, p. 119.
8. Ibid., p. 126.
9. Schlemmer, 1990, p. 168. Stölzl's name appears variously as 'Gunda' or 'Gunta'.
10. Ibid.
11. Isaacs, 1985, p. 409.
12. *Gunta Stölzl: Weberei am Bauhaus und aus eigener Werkstatt*, 1987, pp. 114 and 115.
13. Bauhaus Archive, Berlin.
14. Claire Kosterlitz (Traute Wagner) in conversation with the author, 25 May 1991.
15. Claire Kosterlitz in conversation with the author, 5 August 1991.
16. Gunta Stölzl in Mairet, 1939, p. 117.
17. Ibid., p. 114.
18. Bauhaus diploma of Ruth Hollós, Bauhaus Archive, Berlin.
19. *la tessitura del bauhaus 1919/1933*, 1985, p. 50.
20. Anni Albers in conversation with the author, 21 February 1987.
21. Minutes of the Master Council, 26 October 1920, Bauhaus Archive, Berlin.
22. Minutes of the Master Council, 7 February 1921, Bauhaus Archive, Berlin.
23. *Gunta Stölzl: Weberei am Bauhaus und aus eigener Werkstatt*, 1987, p. 121.

24. Anni Albers in conversation with the author, 21 February 1987.
25. Otti Berger in a letter dated 13 May 1932. Permission to borrow the pieces was granted on 24 May 1932. Bauhaus Archive, Berlin.
26. Karl-Heinz Hüter, 1976, as quoted in *Gunta Stölzl: Weberei am Bauhaus und aus eigener Werkstatt*, 1987, p. 120.
27. Minutes of the Master Council, 7 April 1922, Bauhaus Archive, Berlin.
28. Mies van der Rohe in a letter to Otti Berger, 9 May 1932, Bauhaus Archive, Berlin.
29. Gunta Stölzl in a letter to her brother dated 11 November 1925, Bauhaus Archive, Berlin.
30. Ibid.
31. Gunta Stölzl in letters to her brother dated 11 December 1927 and 3 March 1928, Bauhaus Archive, Berlin.
32. Gunta Stölzl in a letter to her brother dated 5 December 1928, Bauhaus Archive, Berlin.
33. Ise Gropius in a letter to Linnea Martin, 26 January 1974.

Chapter 8
1. Albers, 1961, p. 59.
2. Gunta Stölzl in Mairet, 1939, p. 113.
3. Gunta Stölzl, 'Weberei am Bauhaus' in *OFF-SET Buch und Werbekunst*, No. 7 (1926), p. 405.
4. Anni Albers in conversation with the author, 21 February 1987.
5. Isaacs, 1991, p. 94.
6. Cited in Isaacs, p. 120.
7. Partial list of marriages between Bauhäusler:
   Lotte Beese – Mart Stam
   Lou Bekenkamp – Hinnerk Scheper
   Lis Beyer – Hans Volger
   Martha Erps – Marcel Breuer
   Anni Fleischmann – Josef Albers
   Elsa Franke – Georg Muche
   Gertrud Hantschk – Alfred Arndt
   Ruth Hollós – Erich Consemüller
   Kitty van der Mijll Dekker –
       Hermann Fischer
   Greten Neter-Kähler – Hermann Fischer
   Helene Nonné – Joost Schmidt
   Benita Otte – Heinrich Koch
   Hilde Reindl – Karl Cieluszek
   Käthe Schmidt – Hajo Rose
   Gunta Stölzl – Arieh Sharon.
   Fischer, a graduate of the Bauhaus, was married to two weavers: Neter-Kähler and, after their divorce, to van der Mijll Dekker. Among the relationships that did not lead to marriage were:
   Otti Berger – Ludwig Hilberseimer
   Lilly Reich – Ludwig Mies van der Rohe.
8. This theory is put forward by Magdalena Droste in *Gunta Stölzl: Weberei am Bauhaus und aus eigener Werkstatt*, 1987, p. 19, and in *Frauen im Design*, 1989, p. 192.
9. *Alen Müller-Hellwig*, 1976.
10. Gunta Stölzl, 'Weberei am Bauhaus' in *OFF-SET*, op. cit.
11. Wingler, 1969, pp. 116 and 117.
12. Hildebrandt, 1928, p. 24.
13. Ibid., p. 34.
14. Ibid., p. 24.
15. Ibid., p. 30.
16. Albers, 1961, p. 19.

17. Sigrid Weltge in *The Bauhaus Weaving Workshop*, 1987.
18. Albers, op. cit., p. 18.
19. Gunta Stölzl, 'die entwicklung der bauhaus-weberei' in *Bauhaus Zeitschrift für Gestaltung*, Vol. 7, No. 2 (1931).
20. Ibid.
21. Anni Albers in conversation with the author, 21 February 1987.
22. *Gunta Stölzl: Weberei am Bauhaus und aus eigener Werkstatt*, 1987, p. 131.

Chapter 9
1. Gunta Stölzl in a letter to her brother dated 16 March 1928, Bauhaus Archive, Berlin.
2. Wingler, 1969, p. 136.
3. Conrads, 1989, p. 119.
4. Dearstyne, 1986, p. 208.
5. Isaacs, 1991, p. 138.
6. Schlemmer, 1990, p. 225.
7. Wingler, 1969, p. 141.
8. Schlemmer, 1990, p. 192.
9. Léna Meyer-Bergner, 'Unterricht bei Klee' in *Form + Zweck Zeitschrift für industrielle Formgestaltung*, No. 3 (1979).
10. Ibid.
11. Klaus-Jürgen Winkler, 'Léna Meyer-Bergner' in *Form + Zweck Zeitschrift für industrielle Formgestaltung*, No. 5 (1981).
12. Ibid.
13. Ibid.
14. Letter from Hermann Lange, Vereinigte Seidenwebereien AG, addressed to Gunta Stölzl, head of the Weaving Workshop, 17 April 1929, Bauhaus Archive, Berlin.
15. Galerie J.B. Neumann und G. Franke, Munich, Briennerstrasse 10, Am Wittelsbacher Palais. Bauhaus Archive, Berlin.
16. Gunta Stölzl in a letter to her brother dated 12 May 1928. Bauhaus Archive, Berlin.
17. Gunta Stölzl in a letter to her brother dated 21 December 1927. Bauhaus Archive, Berlin.
18. Anni Albers believed that the Bauhaus, while respecting her expertise, regarded her as a wife first and a professional second. She was surprised to find that she had actually served as acting director of the workshop: 'If it is written down, it must be true.' In conversation with the author, 21 February 1987.
19. *Bauhaus Berlin*, 1985, pp. 192 and 193.
20. Ise Gropius in a letter to Dr Charles Kuhn dated 3 October 1951, Busch-Reisinger Archives, Harvard University, Cambridge, Mass.
21. Moholy-Nagy, 1947, p. 42.
22. Otti Berger, 'Weberei und Raumgestaltung', typescript in the Busch-Reisinger Archives, Harvard University, Cambridge, Mass.
   Berger typed the address of her Berlin studio under the title but did not date the article. It is possible that it was written for the special issue of *bauhaus* magazine dedicated to Gunta Stölzl. In June 1931 Berger received two requests for such an article with suggestions for possible titles, such as 'What is the Weaving Workshop?', 'What did the Weaving Workshop mean to us?' After an urgent reminder to send the manuscript, which she apparently did, she received notification that there was no space, after all. 'We could

therefore not use your essay. I hope very much that this will not interfere with our friendship.' Letters in Bauhaus Archive, Berlin.
23. Anni Albers in conversation with the author, 21 February 1987.
24. Albers, 1961, p. 27.
25. Wingler, 1969, p. 164.
26. Ibid.
27. Hannes Meyer in a letter from Moscow to Lisbeth Oestreicher dated 3 June 1935, Bauhaus Archive, Berlin.
28. Gunta Stölzl in a letter to her brother dated 5 June 1930, Bauhaus Archive, Berlin.
29. Letter from Otti Berger and other members of the Weaving Workshop to Grete Reichardt, Ilse Voigt and Herbert von Arend, dated 5 July 1930. Bauhaus Archive, Berlin.
30. Gunta Stölzl in a letter to her brother dated 14 December 1930, Bauhaus Archive, Berlin.
31. Gunta Stölzl in a letter to her brother dated 4 March 1931, Bauhaus Archive, Berlin.
32. Ibid.
33. Walter Gropius in a letter to Gunta Stölzl, dated 17 April 1931, courtesy of Stölzl Estate.
34. *Symbol, Zeitschrift für Bildende Kunst und Lyrik*, No. 36 (1981), unpaged.
35. Marlies and Bernd Gronwald, 'Margaretha Reichardt (1907–1984). Bauhaustradition und schöpferisches Wirken in der Gegenwart' in *Wissenschaftliche Zeitschrift der Hochschule für Architektur und Bauwesen Weimar*, No. 2A (1985), pp. 91–93.
36. *Bauhaus Berlin*, op. cit., p. 62.

Chapter 10
1. Hans Kessler describing the events surrounding the closure of the Dessau Bauhaus in a letter to his mother, quoted in *Bauhaus Berlin*, 1985, p. 164.
2. Combined advertisement of the companies M. van Delden, C.E. Baumgärtel and Gebr. Rasch for Bauhaus fabrics and wallpapers. Among other firms who purchased prototypes were: Deutsche Werkstätten-Textil GmbH, Dresden, Mechanische Weberei Pausa, Stuttgart, Hoffmann, Fischer & Co., Zwickau.
3. Muthesius, 1903.
4. The magazine *Deutsche Kunst und Dekoration* promoted ideas on dress reform and publicized, among others, Henry van de Velde's and Else Oppler's designs. Maria van de Velde contributed an 'Album of Modern Ladies' Dresses Designed by Artists'; Alfred Mohrbutter 'The Dress of Woman'.
5. Annelise Fleischmann (Anni Albers), 'Economic Living' in Supplement of *Neue Frauenkleidung und Frauenkultur*, Karlsruhe, 1924.
6. Otti Berger in a letter to Mies van der Rohe dated 9 November 1931, Bauhaus Archive, Berlin.
7. Schulze, 1985, p. 144.
8. Mia Seeger quoted in Günther, 1988, p. 13. Günther's scholarly monograph provides new information based on interviews with Reich's friends and relatives and on documents in the Mies van der Rohe Archive at the Museum of Modern Art, New York.

9. Schlemmer, 1990, pp. 311 and 312.
10. Gunta Stölzl in a letter to her brother dated 22 July 1933, Bauhaus Archive, Berlin.
11. Gunta Stölzl in a letter to her brother dated 20 June 1933, Bauhaus Archive, Berlin.
12. Schlemmer, 1990, p. 403.
13. Letter of recommendation for Otti Berger signed by Gunta Stölzl-Sharon, director of the Bauhaus Weaving Workshop, and Prof. Kandinsky, acting director, dated 9 September 1930, Bauhaus Archive, Berlin.
14. Otti Berger in a letter to the Fremdenamt Berlin, dated 12 January 1933, Bauhaus Archive, Berlin.
15. Otti Berger in a letter to the Reichskammer der Bildenden Künste, Berlin, dated 12 December 1933, Bauhaus Archive, Berlin.
16. Letter to Otti Berger, dated 11 September 1935, Bauhaus Archive, Berlin. 'Auf Ihre Interventionen hin, Ihnen die Aufnahme in die Reichsbehördekammer der bildenden Künste zu gestatten, hat die zuständige Behörde leider geantwortet, dass nach den Paragraphen 4 und 10 des Reichskulturkammergesetzes Ihrem Ansuchen bestimmungsgemäss bedauerlicherweise nicht stattgegeben werden kann, da Sie ausländische Nichtarierin sind.'
17. Registered letter to Otti Berger from the president of the Reichskammer der Bildenden Künste, dated 23 May 1936, Bauhaus Archive, Berlin. 'Nach dem Ergebnis meiner Prüfung der in Ihren persönlichen Eigenschaften begründeten Tatsachen besitzen Sie nicht die erforderliche Eignung und Zuverlässigkeit im Sinne des Paragraphen 10 der ersten Verordnung zur Durchführung des Reichskulturkammergesetzes vom 1. November 1933 (RGBL. I, S. 797). Da Sie die Voraussetzung zur Mitgliedschaft in der Reichskammer der bildenden Künste nicht erfüllen, lehne ich Ihren Aufnahmeantrag ab und untersage die weitere Ausübung des Berufes als Kunsthandwerkerin, sowie die Führung dieser Berufszeichnung.'
18. Letter to Otti Berger from der Kirchensteuerstelle des Finanzamtes Berlin, dated 22 March 1937, Bauhaus Archive, Berlin.
19. Letter to Otti Berger dated 5 June 1929, Bauhaus Archive, Berlin.
20. Fabrics by Otti Berger in International Textiles, Vol. 11, No. 15 (1934), p. 12, Busch-Reisinger Archives, Cambridge, Mass.
21. Domus: L'Arte Nella Casa, Vol. 14, No. 95 (November 1935), pp. 28 and 29, Busch-Reisinger Archives, Cambridge, Mass.
22. According to Anni Albers, Berger's deafness was of great concern to her and the source of much sadness. Anni Albers in conversation with the author, 21 February 1987.
23. Otti Berger in a letter to Slava, from Gordon Street, London, without date, Bauhaus Archive, Berlin.
24. Otti Berger in a letter to Alexander Dorner, from Belsize Square, London, 24 June 1937, Busch-Reisinger Archives, Cambridge, Mass.
25. Otti Berger in a letter to Slava, from Lucia Moholy's residence, Mecklenburg Square, London, 23 June 1938, Busch-Reisinger Archives, Cambridge, Mass.
26. Correspondence between Ise Gropius, Ludwig Hilberseimer, Hanna Lindemann and Charles Kuhn, October to December 1951, Busch-Reisinger Archives, Cambridge, Mass.
27. Ludwig Hilberseimer to Hanna Lindemann, 26 October 1951, Busch-Reisinger Archives, Cambridge, Mass.
28. Bauhaus Berlin, 1985, p. 229.
29. Walter Gropius in a letter to Lilly Hildebrandt, quoted in Isaacs, 1985, p. 251.
30. Friedl Dicker's life and career is documented in two excellent catalogues:
Franz Singer – Friedl Dicker: Bauhaus in Wien, 1989, and Vom Bauhaus nach Terezin: Friedl Dicker-Brandeis und die Kinderzeichnungen aus dem Ghetto-Lager Theresienstadt, 1991.
31. Claire Kosterlitz (Traute Wagner) in conversation with the author, 25 May 1991.
32. Joyce Storey in conversation with the author. Storey was a student in Manchester when she met Leischner, 'a notable person in textile circles', at openings of the Cotton Board and Red Rose Guild exhibitions around 1944. Storey herself went on to become one of the foremost authorities in the field of printed textiles. Her Manual of Textile Printing, Thames and Hudson, London, 1974, is a classic in the field.
33. Donald Tomlinson in his obituary of Margaret Leischner, 1970, Bauhaus Archive, Berlin. Tomlinson was the second director of the Colour, Design and Style Centre, as well as the head of the Department of Textiles and Fashion at Birmingham Polytechnic.

Chapter 11
1. Alexander Schawinsky in a letter from Black Mountain College, dated 6 January 1937, to Ise and Walter Gropius, quoted in Bauhaus Berlin, 1985, p. 225.
2. The Société Anonyme and the Dreier Bequest at Yale University, 1984, pp. 379 and 534.
3. Ibid., p. 758.
4. Ibid., p. 746. (Albers, Bauer, Baumeister, Drewes, Feininger, Kandinsky, Klee, Moholy-Nagy, Muche.)
5. Isaacs, 1991, p. 321.
6. Zuckmayer, 1966, p. 465.
7. Ibid., p. 481.
8. The Société Anonyme and the Dreier Bequest at Yale University, 1984, p. 767.
9. Harris, 1987, p. 99.
10. Quoted in Lane, 1990.
11. New York Sun, 4 December 1933, p. 34.
12. Anni Albers in conversation with the author, 21 February 1987.
13. Harris, 1987.
14. M.C. Richards in conversation with the author, 15 June 1992.
15. Anni Albers in a typed statement dated May 1947, Busch-Reisinger Archives, Cambridge, Mass.
16. Quoted in Harris, 1987, p. 53.
17. Otti Berger in a letter to Slava from London, without date (1937 or 1938), Bauhaus Archive, Berlin.
18. Lore Kadden Lindenfeld in conversation with the author, 2 April 1987.
19. Else Regensteiner, who took a summer course with Albers in the early forties, derived great pleasure from these gatherings at which Trude Guermonprez's mother, Johanna Jalowetz, was often present. In conversation with the author, February 1992.
20. Lore Kadden Lindenfeld in conversation with the author, 2 April 1987.
21. Ruth Asawa in conversation with the author, 20 June 1992.
22. Anni Albers in conversation with the author, 21 February 1987.
23. Albers, 1965, p. 47.
24. Wall Hangings, 1969, unpaged.
25. Gunta Stölzl – Anni Albers, 1990.
26. Isaacs, 1991, p. 146.
27. Anni Albers, 'Handweaving Today – Textile Work at Black Mountain College' in The Weaver, Vol. 6, No. 1 (January–February 1941), pp. 1–4.
28. Mary M. Atwater, 'It's Pretty – But Is It Art?' in The Weaver, Vol. 6, No. 3 (July–August 1941), pp. 13 and 14.
29. Edgar Kaufmann, Jr., 'The Handweaver's Place in the US Textile Market' in Handweaver & Craftsman, Vol. 5, No. 4 (Fall 1954).
30. Among the many events were the Young Americans Exhibition (exhibitors had to be under the age of thirty), the International Textile Exhibitions, the American Institute of Decorators' Decoration and Annual Home Furnishings Competitions, the Detroit Institute of Art's International Carpet Competitions, the Biannual Exhibitions for Textiles and Ceramics at Cranbrook, 'One Hundred Museum Selections' and the Museum of Modern Art's 'Textiles USA'.
31. Jurors for handweaving competitions included the architects Philip C. Johnson, Alexander Girard and Eero Saarinen, fashion designer Claire McCardell, Curator of Decorative Arts at the Chicago Art Institute Meyric Rogers, designers Charles and Ray Eames and textile designers Anni Albers and Marianne Strengell.
32. Anni Albers in Art and Architecture (March 1948), unpaged.
33. Albers, 1961, p. 23. (Essay written 1957.)
34. Women in American Architecture, 1977, p. 136.
35. Anni Albers in conversation with Gene Baro in Anni Albers, 1977, p. 7.
36. Anni Albers in conversation with the author, 21 February 1987.
37. Anni Albers in conversation with Gene Baro in Anni Albers, 1977, p. 8.

Chapter 12
1. Mandy's Motto, tapestry by Trude Guermonprez, double-weave and inlay hanging, printed fabric and flag strips, 1975, 54 ins x 32 ins, collection of John Elsesser. Mandy was Trude Guermonprez's cleaning woman.
2. Trude Guermonprez as quoted in The Tapestries of Trude Guermonprez, 1982, p. 5.

3. Lore Kadden Lindenfeld in conversation with the author, 12 November 1991.
4. Report of the outside examiner, Marli Ehrman, and recommendation for graduation from Black Mountain College, 27 August 1948. Collection Lore Kadden Lindenfeld.
5. Polly Weaver, 'Jobs Looming. Jobs and Futures for the Artist-Weaver' in *Mademoiselle* (July 1950), p. 117.
6. *School of the Pond Farm Workshops*, 1992, unpaged. Tim Tivoli Steele's essay is a comprehensive summary of Pond Farm. I am indebted to him for sharing additional information with me.
7. Kay Sekimachi in conversation with the author, 21 June 1992.
8. Carlos Castaneda as quoted in Kay Sekimachi, 'Trude Remembered' in *The Tapestries of Trude Guermonprez*, 1982, p. 23.
9. Correspondence (over a period of several months in 1991) between the author and Per Pearson, son of Elmer Raymond Pearson (1921–86). Pearson studied with Moholy-Nagy and later became associate professor at the Institute of Design. He taught the foundation course as well as three-dimensional and industrial design. When Jay Doblin succeeded Chermayeff as director, a number of members of staff resigned in protest. Pearson, who was tenured, stayed on and rescued material which, he claimed, was deliberately discarded to obliterate Moholy-Nagy's legacy. The Pearson papers have been deposited in the archives of the Chicago Historical Society and were made available to the author in February 1992, although they had not yet been catalogued.
10. Findeli (Ph.D. dissertation), 1989, p. 183. Findeli 'found very little material on the Chicago Weaving Workshop' (in a letter to the author). On the other hand, his dissertation is unique in that it refers to the Weaving Workshop at all.
11. Keynote address by Else Regensteiner at the Midwest Weavers' Conference, Lake Forest, 1980.
12. Myron Kozman in a letter to the author, 1 November 1991.
13. Myron Kozman in a letter to the author, 29 November 1991.
14. Nathan Lerner in conversation with the author, 13 February 1992.
15. In a letter to Marli Ehrman, dated 14 February 1947, Chermayeff explained that closing the workshop 'until November 1950' was due to lack of space. 'I am sure you will agree that a textile department of which we would all be proud should not be a poor sister to other departments.' In the same letter he offered Ehrman the workshop equipment: 'it would be wicked to let our good loom equipment lie idle, we would place this at your disposal for any private instruction or other uses you would care to put it to.' Letter in the Chicago Historical Society.
16. Conversations and correspondence with Per Pearson, Nathan Lerner, Myron Kozman, Nancy Spiegel and Else Regensteiner in 1991 and 1992.

17. Keynote address by Else Regensteiner at the Midwest Weavers' Conference, Lake Forest, 1980.
18. Typescript in the archives of the Mills College Art Gallery, Oakland, California. I am indebted to its director, Katherine B. Crum, for locating documents.
19. *School of the Pond Farm Workshops*, 1992.
20. Frank Ehrman, Marli Ehrman's son, recalled idyllic weeks at Black Mountain College while his mother taught weaving. In conversation with the author, 12 February 1992.
21. The author is grateful to Nancy Spiegel for sharing information about her friendship with Marli Ehrman, as well as a letter from Eliezer Ehrman, dated 23 December 1985, which contains the quoted passage.
22. Mies van der Rohe's requirement for his famous apartment complex was matching window curtains for the glass front to give the exterior of the building a uniform look. According to Nancy Spiegel, some residents objected to this uniformity and asked Ehrman to design a second set of curtains to be hung facing toward the inside of the apartment. In conversation with the author, 25 September 1991.
23. Ilse Etta Uhlman, 'The Marli-Weavers of Chicago' in *Handweaver & Craftsman*, Vol. 4, No. 5 (Winter 1952–53), p. 9.
24. Else Regensteiner in a letter to the author, 27 June 1991.
25. *The Art of Weaving*, Schiffer Publishing Ltd (3rd revised edition, 1986; French edition, 1979; German edition, 1987). *Weaver's Study Course Sourcebook for Ideas and Techniques*, Schiffer Publishing Ltd (3rd edition, 1987; Dutch edition, 1981). *Geometric Design in Weaving*, Schiffer Publishing Ltd (1986). *Program for a Weaving Study Group*, a booklet published by The Handweavers Guild of America, Hartford (1974).
26. Regensteiner and McVicker rented facilities at a commercial Chicago dye-house. Regensteiner in conversation with the author, February 1992.
27. Else Regensteiner in conversation with the author, February 1992.
28. Letter from Anne Marie H. Pope, Chief of the Traveling Exhibition Service, Smithsonian Institution, to 'reg/wick', 2 June 1954.
29. Regensteiner in conversation with the author, February 1992.
30. Charlotte Moser, 'Fabric Designers Display Integrity of their Dyed-in-the-Wool Art Form' in *Chicago Sunday Times*, 1 May 1983.
31. A sampling of companies for whom Testa designed reads like a 'Who's Who' of the American industry: Ames Plastic Company, Artek-Pascoe Company, Beach Products, Bradley Lamps, Chatham Mills, Cohn, Edward Field, Everfast, Fixler Brothers, Forester Textile Mills, Geneva Kitchen Cabinets, Golding Bros, Greeff, Hall, Hartmann Luggage, Henry Regnery Publishing Company, Herman Miller, IBM, International Container Corporation, Joanna Western Mills, Knoll Associates, Leacock Co., Lions

International, Marx and Company, Monsanto, Plastron Corporation, Raymour, Santa Fe Railroad, Schumacher, Simmons, St Regis Paper Company, Sunbeam Corporation, TWA and V'Soske.
32. 'Angelo Testa: A Deeply Woven Impact on Fabrics' in *Chicago Tribune* (1 May 1983).
33. *Angelo Testa*, 1983.
34. Else Regensteiner in conversation with the author, February 1992.
35. Lenore Tawney in conversation with the author, 25 June 1992. The Textile Institute, founded in 1884, was renamed the Philadelphia College of Textiles and Science in 1960 and is the oldest private textile college in the United States. Since its mission is to train students for industry, its laboratories have always been equipped with current industrial looms, knitting machines and related textile machinery.
36. Lenore Tawney quoted in Kathleen Nugent Mangan, *Messages from a Journey: Lenore Tawney*, 1990, p. 24.
37. Erika Billeter, 'A Very Personal Word for L.T.' in *Messages from a Journey: Lenore Tawney*, 1990, p. 41.
38. Lenore Tawney, quoted in Kathleen Nugent Mangan, *Messages from a Journey: Lenore Tawney*, exh. cat., 1990, p. 24.
39. Keynote address by Else Regensteiner at the Midwest Weavers' Conference, Lake Forest, 1980.
40. Else Regensteiner in a letter to the author, 27 June 1991.
41. *Angelo Testa*, 1983.
42. Myron Kozman in a letter to the author, 1 November 1991.
43. Nathan Lerner in conversation with the author, 13 February 1992.

Chapter 13
1. Gropius, 1965, p. 54.
2. Ernst Kallai, 'Ten Years of Bauhaus' in *Die Weltbühne*, Berlin, No. 21 (January 1930), reprinted in Wingler, 1969, p. 163.
3. Paul Westheim, 'Comments on the "Squaring" of the Bauhaus' in *Das Kunstblatt*, Potsdam, Vol. 8 (1923), p. 319, reprinted in Wingler, 1969, p. 69.
4. Wingler, 1969, p. 164.
5. Kallai, op. cit., p. 161.
6. *Bauhaus 1919–1928*, 1938, p. 29.
7. Gropius, 1965, p. 19.
8. Herbert von Arend, Friedrich Wilhelm Bogler, Max Enderlin, Hermann Fischer, Emil Hartwig, Gerhard Kadow, Max Peiffer-Watenphul, Vincent Weber. Only Herbert von Arend and Gerhard Kadow received a diploma. Hermann Fischer was first married to Greten Neter-Kähler, later to Kitty van der Mijll-Dekker. He collaborated with both women in their handweaving studio in the Netherlands. Max Peiffer-Watenphul had special dispensation from Gropius to attend all workshops. He was a gifted artist but did not specialize in weaving.
9. Gropius, 1965, p. 37.
10. Erika Billeter in *Messages from a Journey: Lenore Tawney*, 1990, p. 39.
11. Dorothy Liebes, 'Modern Textiles in Decora-

tive Arts' in *Decorative Arts*, 1939, p. 92.
12. Ibid., p. 93.
13. E.C. Boris Kroll, 'Fifty Years in Business' in *Interior Design* (April 1982), Vol. 53, No. 4, p. 233.
14. Knoll Textiles, New York. News Release dated 3 October 1976.
15. Jack Lenor Larsen in conversation with the author, 19 September 1991.

16. Jack Lenor Larsen, 'The International Textile Exhibition' in *Handweaver & Craftsman*, Vol. 4, No. 5 (Winter 1952–53), p. 58.
17. Yvonne Pacanovsky Bobrowicz in conversation with the author, 13 July 1992.
18. Albers, 1961, p. 62.
19. Anni Albers in conversation with the author, 21 February 1987.
20. Albers, 1961, pp. 62 and 63.

21. Albers, 1961, p. 63.
22. Jack Lenor Larsen in an interview with Charles Talley in *Surface Design Journal*, Vol. 14, No. 4 (Summer 1990), p. 8.
23. Feldman, 1987, p. 490.
24. Gunta Stölzl in Neumann, 1970, p. 129.
25. Gunta Stölzl, in *bauhaus zeitschrift für gestaltung*, Vol. 7, No. 2 (July 1931), p. 4.
26. Ibid.

bibliography

Books

Albers, Anni, *On Designing*, Wesleyan University Press, Middletown, Conn., 1961.
——, *On Weaving*, Wesleyan University Press, Middletown, Conn., 1965.
Bauhaus Berlin: Auflösung Dessau 1932, Schliessung Berlin 1933. Bauhäusler und Drittes Reich, Weingarten and Bauhaus Archive, Berlin, 1985.
Callen, Anthea, *Women of the Arts & Crafts Movement: 1870–1914*, Pantheon Books, New York, 1970.
Cohen, Arthur A., *herbert bayer: the complete works*, The MIT Press, Cambridge, Mass., 1984.
Conrads, Ulrich (ed.), *Programs and Manifestoes on 20th-Century Architecture*, The MIT Press, Cambridge, Mass., 1989.
Constantine, Mildred, and Larsen, Jack Lenor, *beyond craft: the art fabric*, Van Nostrand Reinhold Company, New York, 1973.
Dearstyne, Howard (David Spaeth, ed.), *Inside the Bauhaus*, Rizzoli, New York, 1986.
Droste, Magdalena, *bauhaus: 1919–1933*, Bauhaus Archive, Benedikt Taschen Verlag, Cologne, 1990.
Feldman, Edmund Burke, *Varieties of Visual Experience*, Prentice-Hall, Inc. – Harry N. Abrams, Inc., New York, 1987.
Franciscono, Marcel, *Walter Gropius and the Creation of the Bauhaus in Weimar: The Ideals and Artistic Theories of its Founding Years*, University of Illinois Press, Urbana, Chicago, London, 1971.
Grohn, Christian, *Die Bauhaus-Idee*, Gebr. Mann Verlag, Berlin, 1991.
Gropius, Walter, *the new architecture and the bauhaus*, The MIT Press, Cambridge, Mass., 1965.
Günther, Sonja, *Lilly Reich, 1885–1947: Innenarchitektin Designerin Ausstellungsgestalterin*, Deutsche Verlagsanstalt, Stuttgart, 1988.
Harris, Mary Emma, *The Arts at Black Mountain College*, The MIT Press, Cambridge, Mass., 1987.
Hildebrandt, Hans, *Die Frau als Künstlerin*, Mosse Verlag, Berlin, 1928.
Isaacs, Reginald R., *Walter Gropius: Der Mensch und sein Werk*, 3 vols, Ullstein Verlag, Frankfurt, Berlin, Vienna, 1985.
——, *Walter Gropius: An Illustrated Biography of the Creator of the Bauhaus*, Little, Brown, and Company, Bulfinch Press, Boston, Toronto, London, 1991.
Kandinsky, Nina, *Kandinsky und ich*, Droemersche Verlagsanstalt Th. Knaur Nachf., Munich, 1987.
Kandinsky, Wassily, *Concerning the Spiritual in Art*, Dover Publications, New York, 1977. Originally published as *Über das Geistige in der Kunst*, R. Piper, Munich, 1912.
——, *Point and Line to Plane*, Dover Publications, New York, 1979.
Kandinsky, Wassily, and Marc, Franz, *The Blaue Reiter Almanac*, Da Capo Press, Inc., New York, 1989.
Kepes, Gyorgy (ed.), *Education of Vision*, George Braziller, New York, 1965.
Klee, Paul (introduction by Herbert Read), *On Modern Art*, Faber and Faber, London, 1937.
——, *Pedagogical Sketchbook*, Praeger Paperbacks, New York, 1953.
——, *The Diaries of Paul Klee: 1898–1918*, University of California Press, Berkeley, 1968.

——, *Kunst-Lehre*, Reclam-Verlag, Leipzig, 1991.
Lane, Barbara Miller, *Architecture and Politics in Germany 1918–1945*, Harvard University Press, Cambridge, Mass., 1968, London, 1985.
Lane, Mervin (ed.), *Black Mountain College: Sprouted Seeds: An Anthology of Personal Accounts*, The University of Tennessee Press, Knoxville, Tenn., 1990.
Mairet, Ethel, *Handweaving Today*, Faber and Faber, London, 1939.
Moholy-Nagy, László, *Vision in Motion*, Paul Theobald, Chicago, 1947.
Moholy-Nagy, Sybil, *Experiment in Totality* (2nd ed., introduction by W. Gropius), The MIT Press, Cambridge, Mass., 1969.
Muche, Georg, *Blickpunkt*, Verlag Ernst Wasmuth, Tübingen, 1965.
Muthesius, Anna, *Das Eigenkleid der Frau*, Kramer & Baum, Krefeld, 1903.
Naylor, Gillian, *The Bauhaus Reassessed: Sources and Design Theory*, E.P. Dutton, New York, The Herbert Press, London, 1985.
Neumann, Eckhard, *Bauhaus and Bauhaus People*, Van Nostrand Reinhold Company, New York, 1970.
——, *Bauhaus und Bauhäusler: Erinnerungen und Bekenntnisse*, DuMont, Cologne, 1985.
Passuth, Krisztina, *Moholy-Nagy*, Thames and Hudson, New York, 1985, London, 1987.
Poling, Clark V., *Kandinksy's Teaching at the Bauhaus: Color Theory and Analytical Drawing*, Rizzoli, New York, 1986.
Roters, Eberhard, *Maler am Bauhaus*, Rembrandt Verlag, Berlin, 1965.
Rotzler, Willy (ed.), *Johannes Itten Werke und Schriften*, catalogue raisonné by Anneliese Itten, Orell Füssli Verlag, Zurich, 1978.
Schlemmer, Oskar, *Oskar Schlemmer Idealist der Form: Briefe – Tagebücher – Schriften*, Reclam-Verlag, Leipzig, 1990.
Schlemmer, Tut (ed.), *The Letters and Diaries of Oskar Schlemmer*, Wesleyan University Press, Middletown, Conn., 1972, Northwestern University Press, Evanston, Ill., 1990.
Schulze, Franz, *Mies van der Rohe: A Critical Biography*, The University of Chicago Press, Chicago, 1985.
Soupault, Ré, *Eine Frau Allein Gehört Allen: Fotos aus dem 'Quartier Reservé' in Tunis*, Verlag das Wunderhorn, Heidelberg, 1988.
Völker, Angela, *Die Stoffe der Wiener Werkstätte 1910–1932*, Verlag Christian Brandstätter, Vienna, 1990.
Wangler, Wolfgang, *bauhaus-weberei am beispiel der lisbeth oestreicher*, Verlag der Zeitschrift 'Symbol', Cologne, 1985.
Weiss, Peg, *Kandinsky in Munich: The Formative Jugendstil Years*, Princeton University Press, Princeton, New Jersey, 1979.
Weltge-Wortmann, Sigrid, *Die Ersten Maler in Worpswede*, Worpsweder Verlag, Worpswede, 1987.
Whitford, Frank, *Understanding Abstract Art*, E.P. Dutton, New York, 1987.
——, *Bauhaus*, Thames and Hudson, London and New York, 1984.
Wilk, Christopher, *Marcel Breuer: Furniture and Interiors*, The Museum of Modern Art, New York, 1981.
Wingler, Hans, *Bauhaus in America: Repercussion and Further Development*, Bauhaus Archive, Berlin, 1972.

Wingler, Hans Maria, *The Bauhaus: Weimar Dessau Berlin Chicago*, The MIT Press, Cambridge, Mass., 1969.

Wolfe, Tom, *From Bauhaus to Our House*, Farrar Straus Giroux, New York, 1981, Cape, London, 1982.

Wünsche, Konrad, *Bauhaus: Versuche, das Leben zu Ordnen*, Verlag Klaus Wagenbach, Berlin, 1989.

Zuckmayer, Carl, *Als Wär's ein Stück von Mir*, S. Fischer Verlag, Frankfurt, 1966.

Exhibition Catalogues

(Albers, A.) *Anni Albers*, Gene Baro (with an essay by Nicholas Fox Weber), Brooklyn Museum, Brooklyn, NY, 1977.

Anni Albers: Prints and Drawings (with an essay by Marion L. Buzzard), University Art Gallery, University of California, Riverside, 1980.

The Woven and Graphic Art of Anni Albers, Smithsonian Institution Press, Washington, D.C., 1985.

See also Stölzl

(Albers, J.) *Josef Albers: A Retrospective*, Solomon R. Guggenheim Museum, New York, 1988.

(Arndt) *Alfred Arndt – Gertrud Arndt: Zwei Künstler aus dem Bauhaus*, Museum Ostdeutsche Galerie, Regensburg, 1991.

Bauhaus 1919–1928, Museum of Modern Art, New York, 1938.

bauhaus de weverij: en haar invloed in nederland, Nederlands Textielmuseum, Tilburg, 1988.

bauhaus: masters and students, the, Barry Friedman Ltd, New York, 1988.

Bauhaus Utopien: Arbeiten auf Papier, Wulf Herzogenrath, Edition Cantz, Stuttgart, 1988.

The Bauhaus Weaving Workshop: Source and Influence for American Textiles, Sigrid Weltge, Philadelphia College of Textiles and Science, 1987.

(Bayer) *Herbert Bayer: Kunst und Design in Amerika 1938–1985*, Bauhaus Archive, Berlin, 1986.

Decorative Arts, Official Catalog, Department of Fine Arts, Division of Decorative Arts, Golden Gate International Exposition, San Francisco, 1939.

'Degenerate Art': The Fate of the Avant-Garde in Nazi Germany, Los Angeles County Museum of Art, 1991.

Design 1935–1965: What Modern Was, Le Musée des Arts Décoratifs de Montréal, Harry N. Abrams, New York, 1991.

(Dicker-Brandeis) *Vom Bauhaus nach Terezin: Friedl Dicker-Brandeis und die Kinderzeichnungen aus dem Ghetto-Lager Theresienstadt*, Jüdisches Museum Frankfurt am Main, 1991.

See also Singer

Experiment Bauhaus, Bauhaus Archive, Berlin (West) zu Gast im Bauhaus Dessau, Berlin, 1988.

Frauen im Design: Berufsbilder und Lebenswege seit 1900, Landesgewerbeamt Baden-Württemberg, 1989.

(Gropius) *Walter Gropius*, Winfried Nerdinger, Gebr. Mann Verlag, Berlin, 1985.

(Guermonprez) *The Tapestries of Trude Guermonprez*, The Oakland Museum, Oakland, Ca., 1982.

(Henri) *Florence Henri: Artist-Photographer of the Avant-Garde*, Diana C. Du Pont, San Francisco Museum of Modern Art, 1990.

(Itten) *Johannes Itten. Der Unterricht: Grundlagen der Kunsterziehung*, catalogue of a travelling exhibition, 1973–1977.

(Koch-Otte) *Vom Geheimnis der Farbe: Benita Koch-Otte*, Werkstatt Lydda in Bethel, Bielefeld, 1972.

Farblehre und Weberei: Benita Koch-Otte, Bielefeld.

Moholy-Nagy: A New Vision for Chicago, Illinois State Museum, Springfield and Chicago, 1990.

(Muche) *Georg Muche: Das Künstlerische Werk 1921–1927*, Bauhaus Archive, Berlin, Gebr. Mann Verlag, 1980.

(Müller-Hellwig) *Alen Müller-Hellwig*, Museum für Kunst und Kulturgeschichte der Hansestadt Lübeck, 1976.

new bauhaus in Chicago: 50 Jahre Bauhausnachfolge in Chicago, Bauhaus Archive Argon, 1987.

(Rose) *Katja Rose Weberei*, Bauhaus Archive, Berlin, 1983.

School of the Pond Farm Workshops: An Artists' Refuge, Tim Tivoli Steele, a report from the San Francisco Craft and Folk Art Museum, Fort Mason, San Francisco, Ca., Vol. 10, No. 2 (1992).

(Singer) *Franz Singer – Friedl Dicker: Bauhaus in Wien*, Hochschule für Angewandte Kunst in Wien, 1989.

The Société Anonyme and the Dreier Bequest at Yale University: A Catalogue Raisonné, Yale University Press, New Haven, Conn., and London, 1984.

(Stölzl) *Gunta Stölzl – Anni Albers* (with an essay by Matilda McQuaid), The Museum of Modern Art, New York, 1990.

Gunta Stölzl: Weberei am Bauhaus und aus eigener Werkstatt, Bauhaus Archive, Berlin, Kupfergraben Verlag, 1987.

(Tawney) *Messages from a Journey: Lenore Tawney*, American Craft Museum, New York, 1990.

la tessitura del bauhaus 1919/1933 nelle collezioni della Repubblica Democratica Tedesca, Cataloghi Marilio, Venice, 1985.

(Testa) *Angelo Testa: 40 Years as a Designer/Painter/Weaver*, College of Architecture, Art and Urban Planning, University of Illinois at Chicago, 1983.

Wall Hangings, Mildred Constantine and Jack Lenor Larsen, The Museum of Modern Art, New York, 1969.

Women in American Architecture: A Historic and Contemporary Perspective, Susana Torre (ed.), Whitney Library of Design, Watson-Guptill Publications, New York, 1977.

Ph.D. Dissertations

Findeli, Alain, *Du Bauhaus à Chicago: Les Années d'Enseignement de László Moholy-Nagy: Tome II: Amérique*, University of Paris VIII, 1989.

Radewaldt, Ingrid, *Bauhaustextilien 1919–1933*, University of Hamburg, 1986.

Master's Dissertations

Herkner, Maria, *Die Entwicklung der Keramischen Abteilung des Staatlichen Bauhauses Weimar von 1920–1924*, University of Leipzig, 1984.

Martin, Linnea S., *The History and Development of the Bauhaus Weaving Workshop, 1919–1933*, The Pennsylvania State University, State College, Pa., 1976.

Newspapers and Magazines

Art and Architecture (March 1948).

bauhaus zeitschrift für gestaltung, Vol. 7, No. 2 (July 1931; Bauhaus-Sonderheft 1931/32).

Chicago Sunday Times (1 May 1983).

Chicago Tribune (1 May 1983).

Deutsche Kunst und Dekoration (October 1987).

Domus: L'Arte Nella Casa, Vol. 14, No. 95 (November 1935).

Form + Zweck Zeitschrift für industrielle Formgestaltung, No. 3 (1979).

Form + Zweck Zeitschrift für industrielle Formgestaltung, No. 5 (1981).

Handweaver & Craftsman, Vol. 4, No. 5 (Winter 1952–53).

Handweaver & Craftsman, Vol. 5, No. 4 (Fall 1954).

Interior Design, Vol. 53, No. 4 (April 1982).

International Textiles, Vol. 11, No. 15 (1934).

La Revue Moderne Illustrée des Arts et de la Vie, 26e Année, No. 2 (30 January 1926).

Mademoiselle (July 1950).

Neue Frauenkleidung und Frauenkultur (1924).

New York Sun (4 December 1933).

OFFSET Buch und Werbekunst, No. 7 (1926).

Surface Design Journal, Vol. 14, No. 4 (Summer 1990).

Symbol, Zeitschrift für Bildende Kunst und Lyrik, No. 36 (1981).

Velhagen & Klasings Monatshefte, No. 7, Vol. 2 (1927).

The Weaver, Vol. 6, No. 1 (January–February 1941).

The Weaver, Vol. 6, No. 3 (July–August 1941).

Werk, Vol. 55, No. 11 (1968).

Wissenschaftliche Zeitschrift der Hochschule für Architektur und Bauwesen Weimar, No. 2A (1985).

chronology

1919   1 April: Walter Gropius appointed as director of Weimar's Grand-Ducal Saxon School of Arts and Crafts and Grand-Ducal Saxon Academy of Fine Art; consolidates both institutions into the 'Staatliches Bauhaus, Weimar'. A fully furnished weaving studio remains in the former Arts and Crafts building. The looms are the property of Helene Börner, who taught under Henry van de Velde.

1920   Gunta Stölzl co-founds a 'Women's Department' which becomes the Textile Department under Johannes Itten's artistic direction. The Bauhaus has a total enrolment of 137 students, 59 of them women.

1921   Georg Muche is appointed form master of the Weaving Workshop. Helene Börner remains as craft master. A memorandum to the Master Council urges that women be directed into the Weaving Workshop. First student collaboration with Gropius on the interior of his Sommerfeld House.

1922   First public exhibition of student work. Sales of products from the Pottery and Weaving Workshops contribute to the financial upkeep of the institution. Gunta Stölzl and Benita Otte enrol at the Färberei-Fachschule in Krefeld for a month-long course in dyeing techniques. Following their return, existing facilities are updated and dyeing becomes an in-house operation. The American artist and collector Katherine S. Dreier visits the Bauhaus and purchases directly from Klee and Kandinsky.

1923   Johannes Itten leaves the Bauhaus. Student work is on exhibit in Zurich and at the Leipzig Fair. Preparations for a major exhibition take up most of the year. Approximately 15,000 visitors travel to Weimar between 15 August and 30 September to view the Bauhaus Exhibition under Walter Gropius's new credo 'Art and Technology – a New Unity'. The Weaving Workshop is prominently represented in all exhibitions and in Georg Muche's experimental Haus am Horn. In addition to weavings, Benita Otte is responsible for the architectural drawings of the Haus am Horn and, in collaboration with Ernst Gebhardt, for the design of the kitchen. Publication of *Staatliches Bauhaus Weimar 1919–1923* containing examples from the Weaving Workshop.

1924   Gunta Stölzl and Benita Otte return to Krefeld for advanced instruction in weave technology. First textile prototypes are reproduced by industry. Political pressures from the Thuringian Government prompt the Master Council at its December meeting to vote for the dissolution of the Bauhaus.

1925   The Bauhaus owns and inventories approximately 900 textiles. The Bauhaus moves from Weimar to Dessau. Instruction and workshop activities resume on 1 April in temporary quarters. Helene Börner leaves the Weaving Workshop. Gunta Stölzl becomes craft master.

1926   The official inauguration of Gropius's Dessau Bauhaus Building on 4 and 5 December is attended by 1,500 national and international guests. The county government recognizes the 'Bauhaus Dessau Hochschule für Gestaltung' as an institute of higher education and changes the designation 'master' to 'professor'. The Weaving Workshop is reorganized into a Teaching and Production Workshop with emphasis on industrial textiles. Gunta Stölzl is appointed technical director. Workshops become laboratories.

1927   Georg Muche resigns. Gunta Stölzl is appointed *Jungmeister* (junior master) of the Weaving Workshop with sole responsibility for teaching, the designing of prototypes for industry and production. The Bauhaus establishes an architecture department. Paul Klee teaches special design classes for weavers. The exhibition 'Modern Wall Hangings' opens at the J.B. Neumann Gallery. Alfred H. Barr and Philip Johnson visit the Bauhaus.

1928   Walter Gropius resigns as director effective 31 March and proposes Hannes Meyer as his successor. Herbert Bayer, Marcel Breuer and László Moholy-Nagy also resign. Paul Klee continues his design instruction for weavers. Weaving students intern in industrial mills.

1929   Anni Albers and Otti Berger make the transition from students to assistants at the Weaving Workshop. Anni Albers is acting director from 1 September to 1 November. The Weaving Workshop participates in several important exhibitions. Its income increases through licensing agreements with industry. Anni Albers breaks new technological ground with a sound-proof and light-reflective fabric for Hannes Meyer's Trade Union School in Bernau for which the Weaving Workshop furnishes all interior textiles. Former and current Bauhaus weavers participate in the travelling exhibition 'Ten Years Bauhaus'.

1930   Margaret Leischner becomes head of the Dye Workshop. The Weaving Workshop supplies a variety of companies with prototypes and enters into a formal contract with Polytextil. Hannes Meyer is dismissed as director. The Bauhaus closes in August and reopens in October with Mies van der Rohe as the new director. Otti Berger is in charge of the workshop during the summer vacation. Several students band together against Gunta Stölzl.

1931   Paul Klee leaves the Bauhaus. Gunta Stölzl revises the Workshop curriculum. She resigns effective 30 September. The 1931/32 issue of *bauhaus* magazine is dedicated to Gunta Stölzl. Anni Albers and Margaret Leischner take on responsibilities for the Workshop. Otti Berger is appointed technical and artistic director. Gunta Stölzl moves to Switzerland.

1932   Mies van der Rohe appoints Lilly Reich as director of the Weaving Workshop; Otti Berger becomes her assistant. The Bauhaus leaves Dessau and moves to Berlin. Otti Berger resigns in September and opens a design studio. Companies continue to order prototypes. The workshop introduces printed fabrics. The Berlin Magistrate dismisses Lilly Reich. Otti Berger registers patents for double-weave upholstery fabrics. Eliel Saarinen establishes the Cranbrook Academy of Art in Bloomfield Hills, Michigan.

1933   The Weaving Workshop introduces a revised curriculum and exhibits at the Leipzig Spring Fair. 20 July: the masters vote to dissolve the Bauhaus. 10 August: the Bauhaus closes. Most Bauhäusler are dismissed from positions at other institutions. Otti Berger designs for the de Ploeg Company in the Netherlands (until 1937). Anni and Josef Albers emigrate to the United States and begin to teach at the newly established Black Mountain College, North Carolina, a haven for European political refugees.

1934   Walter Gropius moves to London.

1936   Otti Berger is forbidden to practise her profession.

1937   Otti Berger moves to London. Walter Gropius emigrates to the United States and begins his association with Harvard University, Cambridge, Massachusetts. Establishment of the 'New Bauhaus – American School of Design' in Chicago. Appointment of László Moholy-Nagy as its director. 'Degenerate Art' exhibition in Munich.

1938   Margaret Leischner emigrates to England. Otti Berger is denied a visa for the United States; she designs a collection for Helios, a division of Barlow & Jones. Exhibition 'Bauhaus 1919–1928' at the Museum of Modern Art, New York. Mies van der Rohe, Ludwig Hilberseimer and Walter Peterhans emigrate to Chicago. The New Bauhaus in Chicago closes.

1939   Moholy-Nagy founds the School of Design in Chicago. His faculty includes several former Bauhäusler. Marli Ehrman becomes director of the Textile Department and appoints Else Regensteiner as studio assistant. Regensteiner begins formal studies in weaving. Otti Berger leaves London and returns to her native Yugoslavia; deportation follows. A number of Bauhäusler exhibit at the Golden Gate International Exposition in San Francisco.

1940   The Chicago School of Design holds summer courses at Mills College in Oakland, California.

1941   Marli Ehrman receives first prize in the Organic Design Competition sponsored by the Museum of Modern Art.

1942   Else Regensteiner joins the staff of the Chicago School of Design.

1944   The School of Design is renamed Institute of Design and receives academic accreditation. Otti Berger is murdered at Auschwitz.

1945   Else Regensteiner joins the staff of the Art Department at the School of the Chicago Art Institute.

1946   László Moholy-Nagy dies on 24 November of leukaemia.

1947   Trude Guermonprez arrives at Black Mountain College and substitutes as head of department for Anni Albers, who is on sabbatical leave.

1948   Margaret Leischner becomes senior lecturer and head of the Weaving Department at the Royal College of Art, London. Trude Guermonprez joins the staff of Black Mountain College. Lore Kadden Lindenfeld is the first graduate of the Black Mountain College Textile Department.

1949   Incorporation of the Institute of Design into the Illinois Institute of Technology. Anni Albers, Josef Albers and Trude Guermonprez leave Black Mountain College. Trude Guermonprez joins the faculty at Pond Farm, Guerneville, California. The Museum of Modern Art honours Anni Albers with a solo exhibition.

1950   The first in a series of Good Design exhibitions, co-sponsored by the Museum of Modern Art and the Chicago Merchandise Mart, opens in Chicago. Josef Albers appointed chair of the Department of Design at Yale University, New Haven, Connecticut.

1951   Marli Ehrman designs the curtains for Mies van der Rohe's Lake Shore Drive Apartments, Chicago.

1952   Margaret Leischner becomes a Fellow of the Society of Industrial Artists in England. Trude Guermonprez joins the staff of the California College of Arts and Crafts.

1953   Pond Farm closes.

1954   The Smithsonian Institution organizes the travelling exhibition, 'American Craftsmen'.

1957   Black Mountain College closes. Else Regensteiner establishes and heads the Weaving Department at the School of the Chicago Art Institute.

1960   Trude Guermonprez appointed as Chair of the Textile Department, Head of the Department of Crafts and Head of the Department of Weaving at California College of Arts and Crafts.

1961   Anni Albers receives the gold medal of the American Institute of Architects.

1964   First World Congress of Craftsmen meets in New York. First postwar exhibition of Bauhaus textiles at the Bauhaus Archive in Darmstadt.

1969   'Wall Hanging' exhibition at the Museum of Modern Art. Walter Gropius dies in Boston, Massachusetts.

1970   Margaret Leischner dies in Maplehurst, England.

1976   Gunta Stölzl exhibition at the Bauhaus Archive in Berlin. Trude Guermonprez dies in San Francisco, California.

1982   Marli Ehrman dies in Santa Barbara, California.

1983   Gunta Stölzl dies in Zurich.

1987   Gunta Stölzl Retrospective exhibition at the Bauhaus Archive, Berlin, the Kunstgewerbemuseum, Zurich, and the Gerhard-Marcks-Stiftung, Bremen. Exhibition 'The Bauhaus Weaving Workshop: Source and Influence for American Textiles' at the Philadelphia College of Textiles and Science.

1990   Gunta Stölzl – Anni Albers exhibition at Museum of Modern Art, New York.

illustration acknowledgments

(Abbreviations: *t*-top, *b*-bottom, *l*-left, *r*-right, *c*-centre.)

Collection Anni Albers. Courtesy the Josef Albers Foundation 132*l*

Collection Anni Albers. Courtesy the National Museum of American Art, Smithsonian Institution, Washington DC 103*br* (photo George S. Barrows, Jr.), 105, 171

Collection the Josef Albers Foundation 72, 185

Badisches Landesmuseum, Karlsruhe 29

Bauhaus-Archiv Museum für Gestaltung, Berlin 15, 18*r*, 19 (photo Hermann Kiessling), 24 (photo Gunter Lepkowski), 31, 36*b*, 37, 38*tl* (photo Gunter Lepkowski), 38*tr*, 38*br* (photo Lucia Moholy), 41, 43, 48, 51, 57*tl*, 57*tr*, 59, 60, 61, 62*l*, 62*r*, 66*r*, 69*r* (photo Peterhans), 79*r*, 80*t*, 88, 89, 91*tl*, 91*tr* (photo Werner David Feist), 91*b* (photo Erich Consemüller), 94, 97 (Repro Labor Petersen), 103*tl* (photo Peterhans), 103*tr* (Repro Labor Petersen), 103*bl*, 106, 111, 115, 116, 118, 125, 127*t*, 127*b*, 144*r*, 155*l*, 158

The Busch-Reisinger Museum, Harvard University Art Museums 14 (gift of Julia Feininger); 17, 68 (Margarete Köhler Estate); 39 (gift of Walter Gropius); 84*tl*, 84*bl*, 84*r* (gift of L. Hilberseimer); 187 (gift of the Germanic Museum Association); 73, 82, 96, 108, 114, 123*t*, 123*b*, 124

Courtesy Leo Castelli © Roy Lichtenstein/VAGA, New York 1993 159*r*

Collection Dreppner, Courtesy the National Museum of American Art, Smithsonian Institution, Washington DC 184

Courtesy Frank Ehrman 138*l*, 138*r*, 172

Collection Sylvia and John Elsesser 135*l*, 135*r* (photo courtesy Kay Sekimachi)

Fotoatelier Louis Held, Weimar 9

Hochschule für Architektur und Bauwesen, Weimar 2, 7, 36*t*, 57*bl*, 63

Itten-Archiv, Zurich 1, 26*l*, 26*r*, 27, 28*l*, 28*r*, 30, 54

Collection Lore Kadden Lindenfeld 130*tl*, 130*tr*, 130*br*, 131*tl*, 131*bl*, 131*r*, 161, 165, 174

Courtesy the Knoll Group 152*r*, 167

Kunstsammlungen zu Weimar 25*b*

Jack Lenor Larsen 156*t*, 156*b*, 157

Courtesy Nathan Lerner, Chicago 177

Photo Bruce Miller 69*l*

Misawa Homes' Bauhaus Collection, Japan 20*l*, 66*cl*, 66*bl*, 71*l*, 76*tl*, 76*tr*, 76*b*, 77, 79*tl*, 79*bl*, 104

Musée des Arts Décoratifs de Montréal 145*l* (gift of Geoffrey N. Bradfield, by exchange), 145*r* (gift of Elaine Lustig Cohen)

Museum für Angewandte Kunst, Hamburg 99*bl*, 99*br*

Museum für Kunst und Kulturgeschichte, Lübeck 75

Collection of the Museum of Modern Art, New York 74*r* (Abby Aldrich Rockefeller Fund and Exchange, © 1993 ARS, N.Y./BILD-KUNST, Bonn)

National Museum of American Art, Smithsonian Institution, Washington DC 8*tl*, 8*tr*, 8*bl*, 8*br*, 53, 170*b*

Nürnberger Gobelin-Manufaktur, Kunsthalle Stadt Nürnberg 146, 147

Collection Kenneth Oberman, Brooklyn 136*r* (photo courtesy Kay Sekimachi)

Österreichisches Museum für Angewandte Kunst, Vienna 32

Collection Don Page, New York 129 (photo Claude Stoller)

Collection Philadelphia College of Textiles and Science (photos Rick Echelmeyer) 22*t*, 22*c*, 22*b*, 148*t*, 148*b*, 149*t*, 149*b*, 150, 151, 152*l*, 153, 154, 155*r*

Pond Farm Portfolio. Courtesy Gail Herr Steele 173, 175

Private Collection, Chicago 139

Private Collection, Germany 132*r*

Private Collection, New York. Photo courtesy Barry Friedman Ltd, New York 33, 35, 58, 70, 78*l*, 78*r*, 83*l*, 83*tr*, 85, 143*l*, 162

Courtesy Else Regensteiner 140*l*, 140*r*, 141, 181*tl*, 181*tr*, 181*bl*, 181*br*

Collection Margot Rolf 160*tl*, 160*br*

Collection Kay Sekimachi, California 134*l*, 134*r*

Collection David Simpson, Port Richmond, California 136*l* (photo courtesy Kay Sekimachi)

Städtische Galerie im Lehnbachhaus, Munich, © 1993 ARS, N.Y./ADAGP, Paris 50*t*, 50*c*, 50*b*

Städtische Kunstsammlungen, Chemnitz 65, 67, 87

Gunta Stölzl Estate Photo Archive 18*l*, 20*r*, 21, 25*t*, 40, 46, 71*r*, 74*l*, 83*br*

Courtesy Lenore Tawney/George Erml 137*l*, 137*tr*, 137*br*

Tecnolumen-Archiv, Bremen 45*t*, 45*b*, 80*b*, 81*t*, 81*bl*, 81*br* (photo Jürgen Nogai); 11*t*, 11*b*, 49

Estate of Angelo Testa 142*tl*, 142*bl*, 142*r*, 143*r*

Visum/Dirk Reinartz 12*tl*, 12*tr*, 16, 159*l*

Von Bodelschwinghsche Anstalten, Bethel 23*t*, 23*b*

Collection Traute Wagner-Kosterlitz 86, 107 (photo Beth Emmott)

Courtesy the Walker Art Center 169

Collection Katharine and Nicholas Weber, Bethany, Connecticut 133, 170*t*

Collection Margot L. Wilkie. Courtesy of the National Museum of American Art, Smithsonian Institution, Washington DC 168

Yale University Art Gallery 34 (gift of Collection Société Anonyme, © 1993, N.Y./BILD-KUNST, Bonn)

biographies

Note:
Biographical data has been gathered from many sources – books, articles, catalogues and personal interviews – and is, of necessity, fragmentary in the cases of some weavers. I am grateful for the assistance of many individuals who shared letters, documents and recollections with me. I have relied on and wish to acknowledge Jeannine Fiedler's pioneering compilation of the Bauhaus weavers' biographies in the catalogue *Gunta Stölzl: Weberei am Bauhaus und aus eigener Werkstatt*. Diana C. du Pont's research on *Florence Henri: Artist-Photographer of the Avant-Garde* has been of invaluable help to me.

Anni Albers (née Annelise Fleischmann)
1899 b. Berlin.
1916–19 Studies art in Berlin under Martin Brandenburg. **1919–20** Studies art at the Kunstgewerbeschule (School of Applied Art), Hamburg. **1922–25** Student at the Bauhaus Weaving Workshop, Weimar. **1923** Enters the Weaving Workshop. **1925** Marries Josef Albers. **1927–28** Six week substitute teaching at the Weaving Workshop. **1928–29** Assistant in the Weaving Workshop; acting director of the Workshop from 1 September to 1 November 1929. **1929–30** Develops sound-proof and light-reflective fabric for Hannes Meyer's Trade Union School in Bernau; graduates with Bauhaus diploma No. 10. **1931** Director of the Weaving Workshop for the autumn term. **1933** Emigrates to the United States. **1933–49** Appointed assistant professor of art, Black Mountain College, North Carolina. **1937** Receives United States citizenship. **1949** First weaver to have a solo exhibition at the Museum of Modern Art, New York. **1950** Moves to New Haven, Connecticut; embarks on free-lance career. **1959** Publication of *On Designing*, Pellango Press, New Haven, Connecticut (reprint, Wesleyan University Press, 1961, paperback edition, 1971). **1961** Receives gold medal for Craftsmanship from the American Institute of Architects. **1962** Honoured by Philadelphia Museum College of Art. **1963** Explores print-making. **1964** Attends the Tamarind Lithography Workshop, Los Angeles, on a fellowship. **1965** Publication of *On Weaving*, Wesleyan University Press, Middletown, Connecticut (reprint, 1972, paperback edition, 1974); recipient of Decorative Arts Book Award Citation, given by the National Decorative Arts Committee of the American Life Foundation and Study Institute, for *On Weaving*. **1970** Moves to Orange, Connecticut; career change from weaver to print-maker; publication of *Pre-Columbian Mexican Miniatures: The Josef and Anni Albers Collection*, Praeger, New York. **1972** Receives honorary doctorate in fine arts from the Maryland Institute College of Art, Baltimore. **1973** Receives honorary doctorate in law from York University, Toronto, Canada. **1976** Receives honorary doctorate in fine arts from the Philadelphia College of Art; death of Josef Albers. **1979** Receives honorary doctorate in fine arts from the University of Hartford, Connecticut. **1980** Honoured by the Women's Caucus for Art for outstanding achievement in the fields of weaving, design and print-making; receives gold medal from American Crafts Council for 'uncompromising excellence'. **1990** Receives honorary doctorates in fine arts from the Rhode Island School of Design, Providence, RI, and the Royal College of Art, London.

Gertrud Arndt (née Hantschk)
1903 b. Ratibor, Silesia.
Student at the School of Applied Arts in Erfurt; architectural studies; first photographic experiments. **1923–27** Student at the Bauhaus Weaving Workshop. **1923** Designs and weaves the carpet in Walter Gropius's office for the Bauhaus Exhibition. **1927** Passes her journeyman's examination in Glauchau; marries fellow Bauhäusler Alfred Arndt. **1929–32** Active in the Weaving Workshop under Gunta Stölzl and in the Photography Department under Walter Peterhans. **1932–48** Resides in Thuringia. **1948** Moves to Darmstadt.

Monica Bella-Broner (née Ullmann)
1911 b. Nuremberg, Germany.
Studies at the Loheland School, influenced by Rudolf Steiner. **1929–31** Student at the Bauhaus Weaving Workshop; designs industrial prototypes. **1937–38** Emigrates to Palestine; collaborates with Arieh Sharon. **1939–47** Moves to Los Angeles; establishes a studio for film sets in Hollywood. **1947–49** Film work in Paris. **1949–68** Works in the United States as stylist for the textile industry; illustrates children's books. **1968** Returns to Germany.

Otti Berger
1898 b. Zmajavac, Austro-Hungary; **1944** d. Auschwitz, Poland.
1921–26 Student at the Kunstakademie (Academy of Art), Zagreb. **1927–30** Student at the Bauhaus Weaving Workshop; passes journeyman's examination in Glauchau; receives Bauhaus diploma. **1930–31** Head designer for Fischer & Hoffmann (curtain manufacturers), Zwickau; artistic consultant to Websky, Hartmann and Yiesen (linen and table-cloth manufacturers). **1931–32** Heads the Bauhaus Weaving Workshop under Lilly Reich. **1932–35** Runs independent studio in Berlin; free-lance design; develops patented fabrics; works as a designer for de Ploeg Company, Bergeyk, the Netherlands. **1937–38** Emigrates to England; works as free-lance designer; develops fabrics for Helios, a division of Barlow & Jones, Bolton. **1939** Travels via Prague to Yugoslavia; deportation.

Léna Bergner (married name, Meyer)
1906 b. Coburg, Germany; **1981** d. Baden Soden, Germany.
1923 Student at a school of applied art. **1926–29** Student at the Bauhaus Weaving Workshop as well as at the Graphics Workshop. **1929** Studies at the Dye School in Sorau; heads the Dye Workshop at the Bauhaus; passes journeyman's examination in Glauchau. **1930** Receives Bauhaus diploma; director of the East Prussian Handweaving Studio, Königsberg. **1931–36** Textile designer in the Soviet Union. **1936–39** Specializes in rug weaving in Switzerland. **1939–49** Works as textile and graphic designer in Mexico. **1949** Returns to Switzerland; works as free-lance designer.

Lis Beyer (married name, Volger)
1906 b. Hamburg, Germany; **1973** d. Viersen-Süchteln, Germany.
1925 Enters the Bauhaus Weaving Workshop in Weimar; moves with the Bauhaus to Dessau; attends additional course in dye technology in Krefeld; designs prototypes for industry; passes journeyman's examination in Dessau. **1932–38** Works as director of the Weaving Department of the Max School in Würzburg. **Since 1938** Works as free-lance designer; married to Bauhäusler Hans Volger.

Margarete Bittkow-Köhler
1895 b. Germany; **1965** d. USA.
1919–23 Student at the Bauhaus Weaving Workshop. **1920** Marries the art historian and director of the Kunstsammlungen zu Weimar, Wilhelm Köhler. **1925** At the dissolution of the Weimar Bauhaus Wilhelm Köhler acquires a number of weavings for the Kunstsammlungen zu Weimar. **1932** Emigrates to the United States; Wilhelm Köhler joins the faculty of Harvard University. The Margarete Köhler Estate is at the Busch-Reisinger Museum, Harvard University, Cambridge, Massachusetts.

Yvonne Pacanovsky Bobrowicz
1928 b. Maplewood, New Jersey, USA.
1946–49 Student at Cranbrook Academy of Art (under Marianne Strengell). **1950** Student at Philadelphia Museum College of Art (under Anni Albers). **Since 1950** Runs independent studio; works as free-lance designer, fiber artist. **Since**

1966 Instructor at Drexel University, Philadelphia.

Lis Deinhardt (married name, Schunke)
1899 b. Weimar, Germany.
Student at the School of Arts and Crafts, Weimar. **1921–24** Student at the Bauhaus Weaving Workshop. **1923** Designs the rugs for the gentleman's room in the Haus am Horn, Bauhaus Exhibition. Works as a free-lance painter; collaborates with Gertrud Grunow and later with her husband, Gerhard Schunke, in developing therapeutic healing methods based on Grunow's philosophy.

Friedl Dicker (married name, Brandeis)
1898 b. Vienna; **1944** d. Auschwitz, Poland.
1912–14 Apprenticeship in photography and printing at the Graphische Lehr- und Versuchsanstalt (Institute for Graphic Instruction and Experimentation), Vienna. **1915–16** Student at the k.u.k. Kunstgewerbeschule (Royal and Imperial School for Applied Art), Vienna. **1916–19** Student at Johannes Itten's private school in Vienna. **1919–23** Student at the Weimar Bauhaus. **1920–24** Designs costumes and sets for theatres in Berlin and Dresden in collaboration with Franz Singer. **1923** Founds the 'Werkstätten Bildender Kunst GmbH' (Workshops for the Arts, Inc.), Berlin, with Franz Singer. **1924** The Werkstätten Bildender Kunst receive an honours certificate at the second German lace fair. **1925** Opens a studio for the design and manufacture of textiles and leather goods in Vienna; merges studio with Franz Singer's. **1926–31** Werkstätten Bildender Kunst closes; Dicker founds Studio Singer-Dicker in Vienna (architecture and interior design). **1931** Singer-Dicker Studio closes; Dicker opens independent design studio. **1932–48** Moves to Hronov, Bohemia; works as free-lance textile designer and drawing instructor. **1934** Is arrested and emigrates to Czechoslovakia. **1934–38** Resides in Prague; continues work as interior designer; joins German and Austrian émigrés in political activities. **1936** Receives Czech citizenship through marriage to Pavel Brandeis. **1938** Refuses opportunity to emigrate to Palestine. **1940** Exhibition at the Royal Arcade Gallery in London. **1942–44** Deportation to Theresienstadt; illegally organizes drawing and art classes for camp children.

Marli Ehrman (née Marie Helene Heimann)
1904 b. Berlin; **1982** d. Santa Barbara, California, USA.
1912–21 Attends Westend School for Girls, Berlin. **1921** Student at Territet Boarding School, Switzerland. **1923** Student at the Kunstgewerbeschule (School of Applied Art), Berlin. **1923–26** Student at the Bauhaus Weaving Workshop. **1926–27** Independent weaver in the Experimental Workshop. **1927** Passes journeyman's examination in Glauchau; receives Bauhaus diploma signed by Walter Gropius. **1931** Student at the University of Jena/Weimar; passes teacher's examination in Hamburg. **1932–33** Teaches in Selent, Holstein. **1934–37** Teaches at the Herzl School, Berlin. **1938** Emigrates to the United States. **1939–47** Head of the Textile Department of the School of Design, Chicago; teaches evening classes at Hull House, Chicago. **1947–56** Works as free-lance designer and consultant to industry; exhibits nationwide; receives numerous awards and prizes; designs the curtains for Mies van der Rohe's Lake Shore Drive Apartments, Chicago. **1956** Opens Elm Shop, Oak Park, Illinois.

Martha Erps (married name, Breuer)
1902 b.; **1977** d. São Paulo?
1920–23 Student in the Bauhaus Weaving Workshop. **1923** Exhibits a large carpet in the living room of the Haus am Horn. **1927** Marries Marcel Breuer; they divorce soon after. **?** Emigrates to Brazil; works as a laboratory technician at the University of São Paulo; discovers a new fly species; findings published in *Papeis Avulsos de Zoologia*, Vol. 20 (11 July 1967), and *Aquivos de Zoologia*, Vol. 17 (23 May 1969).

Hermann Fischer (Gustav Max Fischer)
1898 b. Hamburg, Germany; **1974** d. Harderwijk, the Netherlands.
1919–28 Works in business. **1928–32** Student at the Bauhaus. **1931** Marries Greten Kähler. **1932** Designs and makes an eight-harness loom; receives Bauhaus diploma No. 98; employed at the Rasch wallpaper company; moves to Nunspeet, the Netherlands, collaborates with Greten Kähler and Kitty van der Mijll Dekker in establishing a handweaving studio. **1934–50** Divorce from Greten Kähler who leaves the studio; Fischer carries on the studio work by himself while van der Mijll Dekker teaches at the Academy of Applied Art in Amsterdam and designs for industry; experiences economic difficulties, especially during the War. **1950** Marries Kitty van der Mijll Dekker. **1960s** Closes the studio.

Gertrud Grunow
1870 b. Berlin; **1944** d. Leverkusen, Germany.
1919 Lectures at the Lessing Museum, Berlin, on the interrelationship between colour and sound and its effect on the human psyche; meets Johannes Itten. **1919–25** Teaches synaesthesia (one sense reacts when another is stimulated) at the Weimar Bauhaus; coaches students in theories of harmonization. **1926–34** Teaches at the University of Hamburg. Although she influenced not only Johannes Itten but also Walter Gropius, no specific documentation of her teaching activity survives.

Trude Guermonprez (née Jalowetz)
1910 b. Danzig, West Prussia; **1976** d. San Francisco, California.
1930–31 Student at School of Art, Cologne. **1931–33** Student at the Municipal School for Arts and Crafts, Burg Giebichenstein, Halle (Diploma of Fine Arts). **1933** Student at the Textile Engineering School, Berlin. **1934–39** Head designer for Het Paapje Company, the Netherlands; establishes production workshop, handwoven fabrics and rugs. **1937** Studies Scandinavian weaving techniques in Finland. **1939–45** Free-lance designer for industry. **1944–46** Instructor at Volkshogeschool, the adult education programme of the Netherlands; board member of the Dutch Federation of Arts (textile branch). **1945–47** Artistic advisor in textile design for the de Ploeg Company, the Netherlands. **1946** Studies Swedish weaving institutions in Sweden. **1947–49** Teaches at Black Mountain College, North Carolina. **1949–52** Teaches at Pond Farm Workshops, Guerneville, California. **1950–51** Teaches at San Francisco Art Institute (California School of Fine Arts). **1952–54** Teaches summer sessions at California College of Arts and Crafts, Oakland, California. **1954–76** Teaches full-time at California College. **1960–71** Head of the Department of Crafts. **1960–76** Head of the Department of Weaving. Also works as free-lance weaver; has solo and group exhibitions; receives major commissions, fellowships and awards; is represented in permanent collections of major museums; gives lectures, workshops, conferences and seminars; is included in books and articles on weaving.

Dörte Helm
1898 b. Berlin; **1941** d. Hamburg, Germany.
1913–15 Studies at the Kunstgewerbeschule (School of Applied Art) in Rostock and the Kunstakademie (Academy of Art) in Kassel. **1918–19** Studies under Walter Klemm at the Kunstakademie zu Weimar (Weimar Academy of Art). **1919–20** Studies mural painting at the Bauhaus under Lyonel Feininger and Johannes Itten; enrols in courses of Kandinsky, Klee and Gropius. **1920** Solo exhibition in Rostock. **1921** Collaborates on the interior of Walter Gropius's Sommerfeld House. **1922** Passes journeyman's examination as decorative painter before the painters' and lacquerers' guild in Weimar; collaborates on interior paintings of Walter Gropius's Otte House in Berlin; joins the Weaving Workshop as a student. **1923** Member of the planning committee for the Bauhaus Exhibition; independent studies in portraits and woodcuts; free-lance illustrator of children's books. **1924** Returns to Rostock; works as an interior designer and free-lance writer. **1930** Marries the journalist Heinrich Heise. **1932** Moves to Hamburg; the Reichskulturkammer (Reichs Chamber for Culture) prohibits professional activity of any kind.

Florence Henri (married name, Koster)
1893 b. New York; **1982** d. Laboissière-en-Thelle (Oise), France.
1895–1908 Travels with her widowed father throughout Europe; residence on the Isle of Wight until her father's death in 1908. **1909–11** Lives in Rome; studies music at the Accademia di Santa Cecilia; meets avant-garde musicians, writers and painters, among them Umberto Boccioni and Ferruccio Busoni. **1912–13** Returns to England, then moves to Berlin, where she studies music with Egon Petri. **1914–18** Studies painting at the Kunstakademie (Academy of Art), Berlin. **1922–23** Private art studies, befriends the circle of avant-garde artists at Herwarth Walden's Der Sturm gallery. **1924** Marries Karl Anton Koster in Switzerland. **1925** Studies at the Académie Moderne under Fernand Léger and Amédée Ozenfant; exhibits in the Salon d'Automne. **1926** Meets Margarete Willers, a Bauhaus

student. **1927** Exhibits in the 'Exposition de l'Académie Moderne'; travels to Dessau; enrols in Bauhaus summer sessions and studies with László Moholy-Nagy, Wassily Kandinsky and Paul Klee; befriends Lucia Moholy; joins other Bauhäusler in exploring photography; returns to Paris. **1928** Decides to take up photography as a profession; produces first photographs using mirrors. **1929** Exhibits in 'Fotografie der Gegenwart' (Contemporary Photography) at the Folkwang Museum, Essen; is singled out by critics for her modern approach. **1930–39** Embarks on a brilliant career as photographer; travels and exhibits internationally until the Nazi occupation, under which photography is prohibited. **1940–45** Lives in Paris during the War. **1946–82** Resumes photography and painting, exhibits in European and American galleries.

Lily Uhlmann Hildebrandt
1887 b. Fürth, Germany; **1974** d. Stuttgart, Germany.
Studies with Adolf Hölzel in Dachau. **1911–13** Studies with Hölzel at the Stuttgart Academy. Marries art historian Hans Hildebrandt. **1919–22** Relationship with Walter Gropius. Specializes in glass painting, murals and textile designs. **1933** Denounced as 'degenerate artist' and forbidden to work and to exhibit. **1945** Resumes activity in the German art world.

Ruth Hollós (married name, Consemüller)
1904 b. Lissa, Poland.
Studies graphic design at a school of applied arts. **1924–28** Student at the Bauhaus Weaving Workshop. **1927** Passes journeyman's examination in Glauchau. **1928** Receives Bauhaus certificate signed by Walter Gropius. **1930** Receives Bauhaus diploma signed by Hannes Meyer and Gunta Stölzl. Becomes director of a handweaving studio for ethnic crafts in Königsberg, East Prussia. Marries Bauhäusler Erich Consemüller. **Since 1930** Works as a free-lance weaver.

Hedwig Jungnik (married name, Edvige Dostert)
1897 b. Nowy Tomysl, Poland.
1918–20 Student at the Kunstakademie (Academy of Art) in Breslau. **1920** Studies painting under Baron Leo von König in Berlin, and Professor Klemm in Weimar. **1921–23** Student at the Bauhaus Weaving Workshop. **1923–24** Designer at Villeroy and Boch, Saarbrücken. **After 1924** Works as a free-lance painter; marries, emigrates to France.

Ida Kerkovius
1879 b. Riga, Latvia; **1970** d. Stuttgart, Germany.
1899 Studies painting in Riga. **1903** Studies painting under Adolf Hölzel. **1908** Studies painting under Adolf Mayer in Berlin; advances to master pupil and receives independent studio space. **1911** Works as a free-lance artist; teaches at the Stuttgart Academy as Hölzel's assistant. **1920–23** Student in the Bauhaus Weaving Workshop. **1924–34** Works as a free-lance artist in Stuttgart; denounced as 'degenerate artist' and forbidden to work or exhibit. **1944** Loses most of her work through bombardment of her studio. **1950** Member of the Deutscher Künstlerbund (German Artists' Association). **1950–70** Works as a free-lance painter and weaver; has frequent exhibitions; travels abroad. **1954** Honoured by the State of Baden-Württemberg; receives the Distinguished Service Medal First Class of the Federal Republic of Germany. **1958** Awarded title of full professor. **1962** Given honorary membership of the State Academy of the Arts, Stuttgart. **1963** Becomes honorary board member of the Deutscher Künstlerbund.

Claire Kosterlitz (née Edeltraut Wagner)
1903 b. Oppeln, Silesia.
Educated in Oppeln and Breslau. **1921–22** Studies decorative painting at the Staatliche Akademie für Kunstgewerbe (State Academy for the Applied Arts), Dresden. **1922–23** Student at the Prussian Institute for Textile Industry, Sorau. **1925–26** Student at the Bauhaus Weaving Workshop. **1926** Marries Hans Kosterlitz, a doctor. **1938** Emigrates to the United States. **Since 1938** Works in her husband's medical practice; enrols in the New York Art Students' League; studies painting with Julian Levy; works as a free-lance artist; has numerous exhibitions in New York and New Jersey galleries; becomes a member of the Morris County Art Association.

Boris Kroll
1913 b. Buffalo, New York; **1991** d. New York.
1929 Works in family furniture business; interest in textiles for modern furniture leads to the study and mastery of handweaving, especially Jacquard weaving. **1938** Begins designing and producing handwoven upholstery and drapery fabrics; extensive use of Jacquard power loom; deeply influenced by Bauhaus philosophy. **1946** Establishes Boris Kroll Fabrics Incorporated. **1954** Establishes Boris Kroll Jacquard Looms in Paterson, New Jersey; further expansion includes research and testing facilities, dye plant, weaving mill and print plant. **1971** Receives honorary doctorate of Textiles from Philadelphia College of Textiles and Science.

Jack Lenor Larsen
1927 b. Seattle, Washington, USA.
1945–71 Studies architecture at the University of Washington; continues studies in furniture design and weaving. **1951** Receives Master of Fine Arts, Cranbrook Academy of Art, Michigan; opens New York studio. **1952** First major commission (Lever House, New York). **1953** Establishes Jack Lenor Larsen Incorporated. **1958** Establishes Larsen Design Studio. **1959** Collaborates with architect Edward L. Barnes in designing campus for Haystack Mountain School of Crafts, Deer Isle, Maine. **Since 1961** Designs and produces first stretch upholstery fabric; expands design activities to include all interior fabrics and furnishings; receives major commissions for industry, museums and public buildings.

Margaret Leischner
1907 b. Bischofswerda, Germany; **1970** d. Maplehurst, England.
Studies at the School of Applied Art in Dresden. **1927–30** Student in the Bauhaus Weaving Workshop. **1930** Passes journeyman's examination in Glauchau. **1930–31** Appointed Head of Dye Workshop. Assistant to Gunta Stölzl. **1931** Receives Bauhaus diploma No. 37, signed by Mies van der Rohe and Gunta Stölzl. **1931–37** Works as a free-lance designer. **1932–36** Director of the Weaving Workshop at the Textil- und Modeschule (Textile and Fashion Institute), Berlin. **1936** Passes Master's examination in Berlin. **1938** Emigrates to England. **1938–42** Designs for the Team Valley Weaving Industries in Gateshead. **1944–50** Designs novelty yarns for R. Greg & Co., Stockport; active in the Colour, Design and Style Centre of the Cotton Board. **1948–63** Senior lecturer and head of the Weaving Department at the Royal College of Art, London; Fellow of the Society of Industrial Artists. After her retirement, remains active as consultant and free-lance designer for industry.

Dorothy Liebes
1899 b. Santa Rosa, California; **1972** d. New York.
1919 Receives Bachelor of Science degree, San Jose State Teachers College, California. **1923** Receives Bachelor of Arts degree (applied design), University of California, Berkeley. **1928** Receives Master of Arts degree in Art Education, Columbia University, New York. **1929** Internship at French textile firm, Rodier. **1930** Opens first studio in San Francisco. **1937–39** Planner and director of Decorative Arts Exhibit for the 1939 Golden Gate Exposition (World's Fair), San Francisco. **1940–46** Designs textiles for industry. **1948** Moves studio from California to New York. **1948–70** Designs for industry; develops novelty yarns, Lurex and synthetics; works as consultant for E.I. Dupont & De Nemours & Co.; does industrial consulting and designing for mass production; receives awards and honours; her work is included in public collections.

Lore Kadden Lindenfeld
1921 b. Wuppertal, Germany.
1945–48 Studies textile design at Black Mountain College, North Carolina, under Anni Albers and Trude Guermonprez; studies art under Josef Albers; examined by Marli Ehrman as outside examiner. **1948–58** Works as a textile designer in industry (Herbert Meyer, Inc., John Walther Fabrics, Kanmak Textiles and Forstmann Woolen). **1970** Teaches at Haystack Mountain School of Crafts, Deer Isle, Maine. **1982** Lectures at International Art Institute, Kyoto, Seian College for Women, Kyoto, and Kyoto City University of Arts, Japan; receives Master's Degree in Creative Arts Education from Rutgers University, New Jersey. **1968–86** Teaches in the Visual Arts Department of Middlesex County College, Edison, New Jersey; works as a free-lance artist and weaver; has solo and group exhibitions; receives awards; is included in publications on art and weaving.

Julia McVicker
1906 b. Memphis, Tennessee, USA; **1990** d. Naperville, Illinois, USA.

1941—43 Studies weaving at the Institute of Design, Chicago, under Marli Ehrman. **1945—80** Co-founds, with Else Regensteiner, Reg/Wick Handwoven Originals, Hyde Park, Illinois; produces custom-designed handwoven fabrics for architects and designers; designs for industry; receives awards and honours; work shown in permanent collections; is a founding member of the Midwest Designer Craftsmen.

Else Mögelin
1887 b. Berlin; **1982** d. Kiel, Germany.
1906—19 Passes art teacher's examination in Berlin; studies at the Charlottenburg Kunstgewerbeschule (School of Applied Arts); paints; exhibits in the Berlin Secession. **1919—21** Studies under Gerhard Marcks in the Bauhaus Pottery Workshop in Dornburg. **1921—23** Student in the Bauhaus Weaving Workshop; visiting student in the Metal Workshop. **1923—27** Runs independent textile studio. **1927—45** Director of textile instruction at the Kunstgewerbeschule, Stettin. **1930** Passes journeyman's examination in Berlin. **1931** Passes master's examination in Berlin; receives commissions for public buildings as well as from private patrons. **1933** Curtailment of professional activity; denounced as 'degenerate artist'; confiscation of watercolours. **1945—52** Appointed as instructor and director of Weaving at the Hamburg Hochschule für Bildende Künste (Institute of Art); does free-lance work for public and private patrons. **1952** Retires from teaching; continues to work as a free-lance painter and weaver.

Alen Müller-Hellwig
1902 b. Lauenburg, Germany.
1920—23 Studies at the Kunstgewerbeschule (School of Applied Arts), Hamburg; passes journeyman's examination. **1923—24** Studies at the Kunstgewerbeschule, Munich. **1925** Passes her master's examination as an embroiderer. **1926** Runs independent studio in Lübeck. **1928** Passes her master's examination as a weaver. **1931** Receives honour's citations from the cities of Berlin and Barcelona. **1934—39** Runs Independent studio. **1937** Marries violin-builder G. Hellwig; awarded gold medal at the Paris World's Fair. **1940** Wins top honours at the Milan Triennale. **1951** Wins medal at the Milan Triennale. **1954** Wins Art Award of Schleswig-Holstein. **1966** Wins award from the Kunstgewerbeverein (Union of Applied Arts), Hamburg; receives honours citation from the City of Lübeck.

Greten Neter-Kähler
1906 b. Schleswig, Germany; **1986** d. Amsterdam.
1924—25 Apprenticeship in a Munich handweaving studio. **1926—27** Studies at the School of Applied Arts, Flensburg. **1928** Works in a Hamburg fashion house. **1929** Marries Hermann Fischer. **1929—32** Student at the Bauhaus Weaving Workshop. **1931** Passes journeyman's examination. **1932** Receives Bauhaus diploma No. 70, signed by Mies van der Rohe and Lilly Reich; moves to the Netherlands; collaborates with Kitty van der Mijll Dekker and Hermann

Fischer in establishing a handweaving studio. **1934** Divorce from Hermann Fischer; leaves the studio; marries the architect Bob Neter; specializes in silk and linen fabrics; designs and executes liturgical textiles. **1935—37** Director of the Weaving Studio 'De Kerkuil', Amsterdam. **1945—82** Director of the textile department of the School of Applied Art, Amsterdam; works as a free-lance weaver and designer.

Helene Nonné-Schmidt
1891 b. Magdeburg, Germany; **1976** d. Darmstadt, Germany.
1913 Enters the Königliche Kunstgewerbeschule in Berlin (Royal School of Applied Art); trains as a drawing teacher. **1924—30** Student at the Bauhaus Weaving Workshop; independent painting class under Paul Klee; receives Bauhaus diploma signed by Gunta Stölzl and Paul Klee. **1925** Marries Bauhäusler Joost Schmidt. **1930—33** Further studies in art instruction. **1933** Moves to Berlin; denounced as 'degenerate artist'; works clandestinely; bombardment and destruction of studio. **1945—48** Joint efforts with Joost Schmidt to revive the Bauhaus idea. **1948** Death of Joost Schmidt. **1953—54** Appointed by Max Bill to teach colour courses at the Hochschule für Gestaltung, Ulm. **1961** Moves to Darmstadt; begins documentation (left unfinished) of Joost Schmidt's career.

Lisbeth Oestreicher (married name, Birman)
1902 b. Karlsbad, Bohemia; **1989** d. the Netherlands.
Studies at schools of applied art in Vienna, Munich and Berlin. **1926—30** Student at the Bauhaus Weaving Workshop; designs prototypes for Polytex and Pausa companies; active in the Theatre Department under Oskar Schlemmer; takes dye course at IG Farben Hoechst, Frankfurt; directs the Bauhaus Dye Workshop; on three occasions in charge of Bauhaus sales at the Leipzig fair; designs dress patterns for the Ullstein and Bayer publishing companies; passes journeyman's examination in Glauchau; Bauhaus diploma signed by Mies van der Rohe and Gunta Stölzl. **1930** Moves to the Netherlands; designs for industry; runs an independent studio and works as a free-lance designer. **1935—42** Runs an independent studio in Amsterdam. **1942—45** Internment in concentration camp Westerbork. **1945** Liberation by Canadian troops; marries Otto Birman; becomes a free-lance designer.

Benita Otte (married name, Koch)
1892 b. Stuttgart, Germany; **1976** d. Bethel, Germany.
1911—13 Studies drawing in Düsseldorf; receives teacher's certificate. **1914** Obtains State teacher's certificate in physical education. **1920** Teaches drawing in Uerdingen, near Düsseldorf. **1920—25** Student in the Bauhaus Weaving Workshop. **1923** Participates in the Bauhaus Exhibition by designing, with Ernst Gebhardt, the kitchen for Georg Muche's Haus am Horn, as well as rendering the elevation and isometric drawings. **1925—33** Works as head of the Weaving Workshop at the Municipal School for Arts and Crafts,

Burg Giebichenstein, Halle; dismissed by Nazis. **1929** Marries Heinrich Koch, interior designer and photographer, director of the photography department at Burg Giebichenstein. **1933—34** Works as a free-lance designer in Prague. **1934** Heinrich Koch dies in an accident. **1934—57** Directs the Weaving Workshop at the von Bodelschwinghschen-Anstalten (therapeutic institute), Bethel; develops a colour curriculum based on Paul Klee's colour theory. **1957** Retires, continues her involvement with the institute and works as free-lance designer.

Gertrud Preiswerk (married name, Dirks)
1902 b. Basle, Switzerland.
Studies at a vocational school in Basle. **1926—30** Student at the Bauhaus Weaving Workshop; passes journeyman's examination in Glauchau; Bauhaus diploma signed by Mies van der Rohe and Gunta Stölzl. **1929** Summer course at the Johanna-Brunssons Weaving School, Stockholm. **1931** Studies the operation of silk power looms at the Vereinigte Seiden Webereien (United Silk Mills), Krefeld. **1931—33** In partnership with Gunta Stölzl and Heinrich-Otto Hürlimann founds S-P-H Stoffe, independent weaving studio, in Zurich.

Else Regensteiner
1906 b. Munich, Germany.
Studies at the Deutsche Frauenschule, Munich. **1925** Obtains teacher's certificate. **1936** Emigrates to the United States. **1939—42** Studies textiles at the Institute of Design, Chicago, under Marli Ehrman; takes courses in weaving and design at Black Mountain College under Anni and Josef Albers. **1941—45** teaches at Hull House, Chicago. **1942—45** Teaches at Institute of Design, Chicago. **1945** Co-founds, with Julia McVicker, Reg/Wick Handwoven Originals, Hyde Park, Illinois. **1945—57** Teaches at the School of the Art Institute of Chicago. **1957—71** Professor and head of Weaving Department, School of the Art Institute, Chicago; professor emeritus. **1972—78** Consultant, American Farm School, Thessaloniki, Greece. Works as free-lance weaver; has solo and group exhibitions, receives awards and honours; work shown in permanent collections; writes several books on weaving and design.

Lilly Reich
1885 b. Berlin; **1947** d. Berlin.
Studies embroidery. **1908—11** Works at the Wiener Werkstätte with Josef Hoffmann. **1911** Returns to Berlin; befriends Anna and Hermann Muthesius; collaborates with Else Oppler. **1912** Becomes a member of the Deutscher Werkbund. **1920** Elected first female board member of the Werkbund. **1920—24** Has an independent studio for interior design and fashion in Berlin. **1924—26** Has an independent studio for exhibition design and fashion in Frankfurt; works as exhibition designer for the Werkbund Commission at the office of the Frankfurt Fair; acquaintance with and start of collaboration with Mies van der Rohe. **1927** Runs an independent studio, Berlin. **1932** Appointed by Mies van der Rohe as director of the Bauhaus Weaving Workshop

(January); dismissed by the Berlin Magistrate (December). **1939** Travels to Chicago. **1943** Bombardment and destruction of her Berlin studio. **1945—47** Runs an independent studio for architecture, design, textiles and fashion in Berlin; teaches at the Hochschule für Bildende Künste (Institute for Plastic and Graphic Arts), Berlin.

Grete (Margarete) Reichardt (married name, Wagner)
1907 b. Erfurt, Germany; **1984** d. Erfurt, Germany.
1921—26 Student at the Federal-Municipal School of Applied Arts, Erfurt. **1926—30** Student at the Bauhaus Weaving Workshop; additional studies in the Carpentry Workshop and in dance under Oskar Schlemmer; independent painting classes under Paul Klee; journeyman's examination in Glauchau. **1930—31** Independent weaver in the Weaving Workshop; Bauhaus diploma signed by Hannes Meyer. **1931—33** Further studies and independent studio in the Netherlands. **1934** Establishes independent studio in Erfurt. **1939** Wins gold medal at the Milan Triennale. **1942—84** Passes master's examination; runs independent design and teaching studio; member of the German Union of Fine Artists; exhibitions throughout Eastern Germany; receives citations and honours from the East German government and cultural institutions.

Agnes Roghé
1901 b. Berlin; **1927** d.
1920 Takes a sculpture course at the Kunstgewerbemuseum (Museum of Applied Arts), Berlin. **1921—24** Student in the Bauhaus Weaving Workshop. **1923** Exhibits a carpet for the lady's bedroom in the Haus am Horn Bauhaus Exhibition. **1925—27** Student at a textile school in Berlin; teaches drawing and crafts at a private girls' school in Kassel. **1927** Dies as the result of an accident.

Margot Rolf
1940 b. Amsterdam.
1962 Apprenticeship in weaving at the de Uil Studio, Amsterdam. **1962—67** Works as an independent weaver. **1967—70** Student of Kitty van der Mijll Dekker and Greten Neter-Kähler at the Gerrit Rietveld Academy, Amsterdam. **Since 1974** Works as an instructor at the Gerrit Rietveld Academy, and as a free-lance weaver; works shown in numerous international exhibitions; receives several awards. **1975** Teaches at Haystack Mountain School of Crafts, Deer Isle, Maine.

Katja Rose (née Käthe Schmidt)
1905 b. Bromberg, Germany.
1925—26 Student at the Staatliche Schule für Frauenberufe (State School for Women's Occupations); takes book-keeping and typing courses at the Gronesche Trade School, Hamburg, and evening courses in drawing at the School of Applied Art, Hamburg. **1929—30** Works as a volunteer at the Dürer-Haus, Hamburg; volunteers and studies handweaving at the Handweaving Studio Klappholttal. **1931—33** Student at the Bauhaus Weaving Workshop. **1933—34** Student at the

Höhere Fachschule für Textilindustrie (Institute for Textile Industry); passes journeyman's examination in Berlin. **1934—36** Independent studio in Bromberg. **1936** Marries Hajo Rose. **1936—41** Teaches weaving at the Nieuwe Kunstschool (New Art School), Amsterdam. **1941** Returns to Germany; works at the Handweaving Studio von Weech in Bavaria. **1955—56** Director of weaving instruction at the Walter Kircher Company, Marburg. **1956—75** Teaches weaving privately and at institutions in Munich.

Kay Sekimachi
1926 b. San Francisco.
1946—49 Student at California College of Arts and Crafts, Oakland. **1954—55** Additional studies at California College of Arts and Crafts, Oakland. **1956** Student at Haystack Mountain School of Crafts, Deer Isle, Maine. **Since 1950** Breaks new ground in the fiber arts by employing unconventional material and exploring three-dimensional space; teaches at major universities, craft schools and art institutions; receives major grants and awards; works shown at major solo and group exhibitions; represented internationally in public collections; included in literature on weaving and fiber art.

Ré Soupault (née Erna Niemeyer)
1901 b.
Student at Johannes Itten's school in Vienna; follows Itten to the Bauhaus. **1921—25** Student at the Bauhaus Weaving Workshop. **1923—25** Collaborates with Viking Eggeling on his first abstract film, *Diagonal-Symphonie* which premieres in Berlin on 3 May 1925; oversees all technical aspects of Eggeling's film work. **1924—34** Works for the Scherl Publishing House in Berlin under the assumed name of Renate Green. **1927—29** Marries Hans Richter, Dadaist and abstract film-maker. **1937** Marries French Surrealist writer Philippe Soupault. **1938** Travels to Tunisia; receives special permission to photograph the *Quartier Reservé*; moves to Paris. **Since 1938** Works as translator (Lautréamont, Romain Rolland, André Breton, etc); writes articles for art magazines; makes television documentaries on Wassily Kandinsky and Mies van der Rohe. **1988** Publication of photo essay, *Eine Frau Allein Gehört Allen*, with Wunderhorn Verlag.

Gunta Stölzl (married names, Sharon, Stadler)
1897 b. Munich, Germany; **1983** d. Zurich, Switzerland.
1914—16 Studies decorative painting under Professor R. Engels and glass painting and ceramics under Professor Blaim at the Kunstgewerbeschule (School of Applied Arts), Munich. **1916—18** Works as a Red Cross Nurse behind the front lines. **1919** Continues studies at the Kunstgewerbeschule in Munich, participates in curriculum reform, encounters the Bauhaus manifesto. **1919—25** Studies at the Bauhaus; takes courses with Johannes Itten and Paul Klee, as well as two courses in dyeing and weaving technology in Krefeld. **1922** Passes journeyman's examination; continues to work in the Weaving Work-

shop. **1924** Assists Johannes Itten, who has left the Bauhaus, in establishing his Ontos Weaving Workshops in Herrliberg near Zurich. **1925** Assumes position of technical director at Dessau Weaving Workshop. **1927** Appointed as *Jungmeister* (junior master) with responsibility for the entire Weaving Workshop. **1929** Marries the Palestinian architect Arieh Sharon; loses German citizenship; birth of daughter, Yael. **1931** Forced to resign as director of the Weaving Workshop; forms a private handweaving business in Zurich, S-P-H Stoffe (S-P-H Fabrics), with fellow Bauhäusler Gertrud Preiswerk and Heinrich-Otto Hürlimann. **1932** Becomes a member of the Swiss Werkbund. **1933** S-P-H Stoffe dissolves due to financial difficulties. **1934** Receives commission for curtains for the Cinema Urban, Zurich; *Das Werk*, the Swiss Werkbund magazine, profiles her career. **1935** Partnership with Hürlimann results in S+H Stoffe. **1936** Stölzl and Sharon divorce; article on Stölzl in *Das Werk*. **1937** Becomes sole owner of Handweberei Flora (handweaving studio Flora); joins the Gesellschaft Schweizer Malerinnen, Bildhauerinnen und Kunstgewerblerinnen (Society of Swiss women painters, sculptors and craftswomen). **1941** Participates in the interior of the Swiss pavilion, Lyon. **1942** Marries Willy Stadler; becomes Swiss citizen. **1943** Birth of daughter, Monika, in Zurich. **1949—63** Busch-Reisinger Museum, Cambridge, Massachusetts, and the Museum of Modern Art, New York, acquire works by Stölzl. **1967—69** Dissolves her handweaving business; devotes herself to weaving tapestries only; Victoria and Albert Museum, London, acquires designs and fabric samples; represented in major national and international public and private collections.

Marianne Strengell
1909 b. Helsinki, Finland.
1929 Graduates from Helsinki Atheneum. **1930—36** Works for Swedish Society of Industrial Design in Stockholm; returns to Helsinki; appointed art director of an exclusive Finnish design firm; at the same time is co-owner of a design studio for interiors, furniture and textiles. **1937** Becomes instructor of weaving, costume and textile design at Cranbrook Academy of Art, Bloomfield Hills, Michigan. **1942** Becomes head of the department. **1942 until retirement** Designs for industry; works shown in national and international exhibitions; receives awards and honours; acts as consultant to foreign governments and International Labour Office of the United Nations.

Lenore Tawney
1907 b. Lorain, Ohio, USA.
1927—42 Works as proof-reader; attends evening classes at the School of the Art Institute of Chicago. **1941** Marries George Tawney. **1943** Death of George Tawney. **1943—45** Studies art at the University of Illinois. **1946—47** Studies at the Institute of Design, Chicago; studies sculpture under Alexander Archipenko, drawing and watercolour under Emerson Woelffer, weaving under Marli Ehrman. **1947—48** Continues her studies in Archipenko's studio in Woodstock, New York.

1949–51 Resides in Paris; travels in Europe and North Africa. 1954 Returns to the United States; studies tapestry weaving under Martta Taipale at the Penland School of Crafts, North Carolina. 1955 Experiments with open-warp weavings. 1956 Travels through Greece, the Near East, Lebanon, Jordan and Egypt. 1957 Returns to the United States; Marshall Field commissions a tapestry for the North Shore Shopping Center, Chicago; moves to New York. 1960–64 Interchurch Center, New York, commissions tapestry; studies gauze weaves under Lili Blumenau; develops open reed weaving and creates woven forms; Congregation Solel, Highland Park, Illinois, commissions ark veil; travels to Peru and Bolivia; the Museum of Modern Art acquires *Dark River*; First World Congress of Craftsmen is held in New York; studies Jacquard mechanism at Textile Institute, Philadelphia; executes line drawings of Jacquard cords on graph paper. 1964–76 Begins work in collage and assemblage; travels throughout the Far East, extended stay in India; integrates weaving and paper collage; elected Fellow of American Craftsmen's Council; gives up work on the loom. 1976–77 Travels to India. Since 1978 Creates Cloud Series installations; artist-in-residence at the University of Notre Dame, Indiana, and at the Fabric Workshop, Philadelphia; receives major commissions; exhibits nationally and internationally; receives citations and honours, including the gold medal of the American Crafts Council.

Angelo Testa
1921 b. Springfield, Massachusetts, USA; 1984 d. Springfield, Massachusetts, USA.
1938 Studies at New York School of Fine and Applied Art. 1939 Studies at the University of Chicago. 1940–45 Studies at the Institute of Design, Chicago. 1945–84 Designs woven and printed fabrics at Angelo Testa Designs, Chicago; designs first mass-produced collection of abstract, non-objective fabrics in the United States; receives awards and honours; work exhibited in private and public collections; featured in numerous design magazines; designs furniture and lamps; works as muralist and graphic designer.

Ruth Vallentin (married names, Citroen, Cidor)
1906 b. Hedingen, Germany.
1920–25 Student at the Bauhaus Weaving Workshop. 1925 Marries Hans Citroen. 1933 Emigrates to Paris; designs children's books for Flammarion. 1940 Flees to Switzerland. 1942 Works as a free-lance weaver in Geneva. 1952 Moves to Jerusalem; name changes to Cidor.

Kitty van der Mijll Dekker (married name, Fischer)
1908 b. Djokdjakarta, Java.
1917–25 Educated in The Hague, the Netherlands. 1925–27 Travels to Switzerland, the United States and England; studies at the Hornsey School of Art, London. 1927–28 Private studies in interior architecture. 1929–32 Student at the Bauhaus Weaving Workshop. 1931 Passes journeyman's examination. 1932 Receives Bauhaus diploma No. 66 signed by Mies van der Rohe; moves to Nunspeet, the Netherlands; establishes a handweaving studio; forms partnership with former Bauhäusler Greten Kähler and her husband Hermann Fischer. 1933 Receives silver medal for two Cellophane fabrics at the Milan Triennale. 1933–34 Designs for Dutch textile industry; receives commissions for public buildings and museums. 1934–79 Teaches at the School of Applied Art (since 1967 the Gerrit Rietveld Academy), Amsterdam. 1935 Receives gold medal for a fabric from the Dutch pavilion at the Brussels World's Fair. 1937 Receives Diplome d'honneur at the Paris World's Fair. Since 1938 Receives commissions for ceremonial fabrics from the Dutch Royal House; designs for Dutch textile industry; participates in major exhibitions. 1950 Marries Hermann Fischer.

Jutta von Schlieffen (née von Zitzewitz)
1903 b. Zitzewitz, Germany; 1982 d. Göttingen, Germany.
1922–24 Student at the Bauhaus Weaving Workshop. 1932–33 Assistant to Lilly Reich.

Marguerite Wildenhain (née Friedlaender)
1896 b. Lyon, France; 1985 d. Guerneville, California.
1919 Studies drawing and sculpture at the School of Fine and Applied Arts in Berlin; apprentice in a wood sculpture studio; designs for a Thuringian porcelain factory. 1919–26 Studies as an apprentice and journeyman in the Bauhaus Pottery Workshop under Max Krehan and Gerhard Marcks. 1926 Certified as a pottery master. 1926–33 Head of the Pottery Department at the Municipal School for Arts and Crafts, Burg Giebichenstein, Halle; makes an extensive collection of models for mass-produced items for the porcelain manufacturer Royal Berlin; dismissed by Nazis. 1933 Establishes pottery studio with husband Frans Wildenhain in Putten, the Netherlands; creates models for the Regout Porcelain Factory, Maastrict. 1940 Emigrates to the United States; works as an independent potter at Pond Farm, Guerneville, California. 1940–42 Teaches at the College of Arts and Crafts, Oakland, California. 1942 Appointed director of the pottery division of the Appalachian Institute of Arts and Crafts, Banner Elk, North Carolina; returns to California and works as independent potter at Pond Farm. 1942–43 Listed in *Who's Who* in California. 1949 Establishment of Pond Farm community; acts as potter-in-residence and teacher. 1952 Pond Farm community closes; Wildenhain remains; gives annual summer workshops; lectures; teaches; travels; attends national conferences; pottery included in exhibitions and museum collections throughout the United States and Europe.

Margarete Willers
1883 b. Oldenburg, Germany; 1977 d. Essen, Germany.
Attends private girls' schools. 1905 onward Studies painting and drawing in Düsseldorf and Munich; studies in Paris under Maurice Denis. 1921–22 Student in the Bauhaus Weaving Workshop. 1926 Meets Florence Henri in Paris. 1927–28 Operates independent weaving studio at the Dessau Bauhaus; works in the Experimental Workshop; studies with Klee and Kandinsky. 1928–43 Director of the Handweaving and Embroidery Studio at the Folkwangschule, Essen; maintains independent textile studio. 1943–55 Teaches at the Handweaving Studio in Bückeburg. 1955–60 Runs independent studio. 1960 Retires due to ill health.

index